THE CALL OF THE UPANISHADS

Other Books by the Author

Yoga—The Art of Integration

The Nameless Experience

From Mind to Super-Mind

The Intuitive Philosophy

The Play of the Infinite

The Dialogue with Death

The Miracle of Descent

The Being and the Becoming

The Eternal Light

The Creative Silence

Seek Out the Way

Can Fate be Changed

Evolution or the Law of Becoming

Journey with Death

Fullness of the Void

The Science of Meditation

J. Krishnamurti and the Nameless Experience

THE CALL OF THE UPANISHADS

ROHIT MEHTA

MOTILAL BANARSIDASS PUBLISHERS
PRIVATE LIMITED • DELHI

7th Reprint: Delhi, **2017**
First Edition: Delhi, 1970

ISBN: 978-81-208-0747-2 (Cloth)
ISBN: 978-81-208-0749-9 (Paper)

Also available at:

MOTILAL BANARSIDASS

41 U.A. Bungalow Road, Jawahar Nagar, Delhi 110 007
8 Mahalaxmi Chamber, 22 Bhulabhai Desai Road, Mumbai 400 026
203 Royapettah High Road, Mylapore, Chennai 600 004
236, 9th Main III Block, Jayanagar, Bengaluru 560 011
8 Camac Street, Kolkata 700 017
Ashok Rajpath, Patna 800 004
Chowk, Varanasi 221 001

Publisher's Cataloging-in-Publication:

The Call of the Upanishads
by Rohit Mehta
Includes index.
ISBN: 978-81-208-0747-2 (Cloth)
ISBN: 978-81-208-0749-9 (Paper)
I. Hinduism II. Upanishads
II. Mehta, Rohit

Printed in India

by RP Jain at NAB Printing Unit,
A-44, Naraina Industrial Area, Phase I, New Delhi–110028
and published by JP Jain for Motilal Banarsidass Publishers (P) Ltd,
41 U.A. Bungalow Road, Jawahar Nagar, Delhi-110007

CONTENTS

Chapter		Page
	Introduction	1
I.	The Golden Veil	10
II.	The Silent Night	30
III.	The Great Beyond	50
IV.	The Fire of Creation	87
V.	Existence Without Identity	116
VI.	The Nameless Being	144
VII.	The Bliss Eternal	175
VIII.	The Descent of the Spirit	204
IX.	The Fullness of the Void	221
X.	The Flame Without a Flicker	254
XI.	The One — And the Only One	291
	Acknowledgements	315
	Index	317

INTRODUCTION

The cultural and spiritual heritage of India is both vast as well as rich. But there is nothing sectarian or regional about it. It is so universal in its appeal and so catholic in its approach that it belongs to the whole world. Its setting is no doubt Indian, but its content is such as to cover all aspects of human life, irrespective of geographical units and historical expressions. It is both universal and timeless and, as such, applies to peoples of all ages and of all countries. It may be asked what indeed is the source from where such vast and rich heritage has come into existence—a heritage that has remained fresh and vital even though many centuries have rolled by since it made its first appearance in the dim dawn of time? One can say without the slightest hesitation that the source of this heritage lies in the Great Upanishads. The seers and sages of Ancient India, sitting under a tree, in a far-off forest, revealed fundamental principles of perennial philosophy to students who had gone to them with questions of deep and serious inquiry into the very nature of life itself. The Upanishads contain the essential principles of this Perennial—this Ageless-philosophy. The Upanishads can by no means be described as religious in character—if with religion we associate dogmas and creeds, priest-craft and authority, rewards and punishments. One has only to turn to the Muṇḍaka Upanishad to realise this in ample measure, for, here even the knowledge of the Vedas has been declared as mere lower knowledge. While dissociating itself from all narrow and sectarian expressions of religion, the Upanishadic teaching has laid clear and unmistakable emphasis on the spiritual perspectives of life. The Upanishads have made a clear distinction between knowledge and wisdom. While the seers and sages of those great days of the Upanishads imparted instruction to their pupils in all branches of human knowledge, they indicated to them that mere knowledge would be of no avail and that they should be inspired by Wisdom. These teachers saw to it that the flame of knowledge was kept alive so that the learning of the pupils would never come to an end—and yet they showed to their pupils that the light of Knowledge was meant only to make "darkness visible". With this awareness of "darkness made visible", through the processes of knowledge, these pupils were inspired to undertake the adventurous journey into the land of the Unknown where alone Wisdom can be discovered. This journey has to be unaided, for no teacher can lead a pupil into the realms of the Unknown. The journey to the Unknown is a flight of the alone to the Alone.

It is true that the entire teaching of the Upanishad centres round a teacher or a guru. But the role of the guru as revealed in the Upanishad is something most revolutionary. In the Bṛhadāraṇyaka Upanishad, we find Yājñavalkya , the most brilliant of the Upanishadic teachers, giving instruction to the great King Janaka. When the latter was pleased with the instruction of the guru, he offered rich gifts to him. But Yājñavalkya *spurned* them aside saying that a teacher cannot accept any gift from the pupil unless he has taught the pupil everything that he knew. This was the Upanishadic tradition of the guru. According to this the role of the guru was to make the pupil stand on his own feet, to make him completely independent so that he did not lean over the guru, making him into a psychological or a spiritual crutch. The role of the guru was to make himself superfluous—such was the great vision of the teacher as revealed in the magnificent teachings of the Upanishads.

The period of the Upanishads must have been a period of free inquiry. Between the teacher and the student there existed a relationship of complete understanding and cordiality. In these esoteric, or mystery schools of the Upanishads there was perfect freedom of thought and expression. As one reads the dialogues between the teacher and the pupil and as one enters into the spirit of the discussions and questions and answers with which the Upanishads are replete, one feels as if one is breathing the fresh air of the mountains. The teacher and the pupil had great respect for each other and yet there was an intimate nearness between them. We see here a beautiful combination of Freedom and Discipline, of Reverence and Cordiality.

The subject matter of almost all the Upanishads is Brahman, the Ultimate Reality, and Ātman, the Individual Self. But it is intensely fascinating to see how the same subject is dealt with in each Upanishad in such a manner that the feeling of "sameness" never arises. There is a freshness and a newness in each Upanishad because of which one never feels that it is the same subject of Brahman and Ātman that is being discussed. In the Upanishads one sees the truth of the statement that it is not the conclusion that matters— what matters is the process by which the conclusion is arrived at. The Upanishads are not concerned with the conclusions of thought—they are concerned with the process of thinking. The teachers of the Upanishads have never deviated from the strict rules of logic —but with logical clarity they have shown how logic is limited in its scope. While they have pointed to the realms beyond the mind, they have not even once derided the role of logic and reason. To utilize reason in order to show the inadequacy of reason—this is a difficult undertaking, but the teachers of the Upanishads have displayed a remarkable mastery over this technique of transcending the mind with the help of the mind.

Although the Upanishads have spoken about Brahman and Ātman, they have not dealt with these subjects as if they were remote and far-away from the daily avocations of man. To these abstruse subjects they have brought a touch of intimacy. This is because the teachers of the Upanishads were not dry, uninterested people. They were full of life, showing forth a living interest in men and things. They possessed minds that were perfectly open and therefore ready to respond even to the slightest whisper of life. When one sees the range of subjects with which the ancient Gurukulas were concerned, one realizes that there was no subject under the sun which was left outside their purview of study and discussion. One sees in these Upanishadic teachers and in their approach to life a brilliance of intellect existing side by side with an intensity of deep emotion. And so we see in these gurukulas an atmosphere where the unrelenting discipline of the mind co-exists with the friendly informality of the heart. Here no artificial effort had to be made to link up sciences with humanities—they were naturally linked up because the whole approach to life was integral.

It may be argued by the modern man that it is too late in the day to talk of the practical efficacy of the Upanishadic teaching in an age of science and technology where we are concerned with hard facts of life and not with such remote and obscure subjects as Brahman and Ātman. He may say, "Of what practical use is this discussion on Brahman and Ātman? Can it help us to resolve the confusions and the perplexities in which the present day civilisation seems to have got itself entangled?" We of this age seem to be thinking that science and technology alone are practical—and that philosophy is something impractical—it may be a good intellectual exercise to be indulged in during moments of leisure as a change, when other amusements have failed, but surely it can have no place in the hard and practical avocations of man's existence, so speaks the modern man of science and technology. But the above description goes ill with the Philosophy of the Upanishads. The Upanishadic philosophy is not dry-as-dust, it is not concerned with metaphysical speculations or with hair-splitting subtleties. It is not with something remote and abstract that the Philosophy of the Upanishads is concerned—its chief interest is in that which is intensely practical. Its concern with the practical aspects of life can be seen in the very theme of Brahman and Ātman which forms the substratum of its whole philosophical approach. Brahman and Ātman are not remote and obscure subjects. In the book entitled *A Source Book in Indian Philosophy*—edited by S. Radhakrishnan and C. A. Moore, it is said :

> The real which is at the heart of the universe is reflected in the infinite depths of the self. Brahman—the Ultimate as discovered objectively, is Ātman, the Ultimate as discovered introspectively.

Thus Brahman and Ātman deal with the Objective and Subjective aspects of life. Now the objective and the subjective are so inter-related that the one cannot be understood without understanding the other. Is not physical science itself confronted with this problem of the subjective projecting itself in the objective? As one moves from physical to biological and from biological to psychological sciences one realizes how the subjective is constantly impinging upon the objective so that an objective study of man and the universe is being constantly interfered with due to the ceaseless projection of the subjective. The Upanishadic philosophy took this factor into consideration and evolved an approach which undertook a search into realms both objective as well as subjective. And out of their Wisdom, the great teachers of the Upanishads declared that the nature of Brahman resides in the Ātman—that without knowing the subjective, the knowledge of the objective is incomplete and inadequate. The mystery of the objective world can be unravelled only by comprehending the secret that lies hidden in the subjective.

Many a student of the Upanishads has said that the Upanishads contain only stray and scattered thoughts—some of these thoughts are brilliant and almost dazzling, but there does not seem to be any homogeneous, integral philosophy. Some commentators, too, have expressed this idea and treated the Upanishadic teaching in terms of scattered ideas. These commentators have failed to see any cohesion behind these scattered concepts and ideations of life. In many of the commentaries one sees explanations of different verses and passages in a manner that presumes that there is no connection between them. They have dealt with the Upanishads not as a harmonious whole—but as different pieces strung together without any cohesion or unity between them. To say that the Upanishads do not contain a harmonious philosophy is to miss the very essense of the Upanishadic approach. It is true that the Upanishads contain enormous jumps from idea to idea, from concept to concept, from experience to experience. But that is how all great geniuses of mankind have presented their sublime discoveries of truth. The Upanishadic teachers were not placing before their pupils cut-and-dried systems of thought. They were not giving to their students a systematised statement of life's philosophy which they could memorize. They were not dictating to them full notes by the use of which they could pass their examinations and go out as full-fledged graduates. The Upanishadic teachers flew from summit to summit—and invited others to scale the heights they had climbed. In the Upanishads we see a record of these sublime flights of the mind and the soul—the flights are stupendous and dazzle a person who witnesses them. These teachers have moved from one idea to another, leaving the intervening steps to be worked out by students themselves. This was the dynamic nature of the Upanishadic teaching. The student had not merely to copy a perfect picture which the teacher may have drawn. The students were not expected to repeat what the teachers had said. They were not asked to remain merely awestruck by the great flights of the teachers. They had to cover, step by step, the ground that separated one flight from the other, one summit of thought from the other. The working out of the intervening steps had to be done by the pupil himself. This required a clear intellect, a bold imagination—but above all else an intuitive insight. The Upanishadic teaching must seem scattered and disjointed to one who looks only at the summits of thought. It is only by working out the intervening steps that one can discover the harmony, the wholeness in the sublime philosophy presented by the Upanishads. Unless one fills up the gaps, separating one summit from the other, one cannot see this wholeness. All seers and sages, prophets and mystics, have spoken the language of the summit—they have flown from height to height. But to many these teachings may seem elusive and impractical. This is so because those who listen to them do not care to work out the intervening steps. They feel inspired by the vision of the heights, but find it impossible to translate this vision into their daily lives. Very often people who listen to such mystics and seers say: "While we listen, it all seems so simple and practical—but once we are just by ourselves we feel that the vision has eluded us—we have been unable to grasp it." About the Upanishads, too, many have said the same thing. The teachings contained in them have seemed inspiring—but elusive, and so, impractical. Those who say this have not cared to work out the intervening steps. When this is done, the philosophy of the Upanishads does not seem scattered and disjointed—one discovers a wholeness in it—and so, that which had seemed impractical appears intensely practical. Speaking about the intervening steps, Sri Aurobindo in his book *The Foundations of Indian Culture* says something most significant. He tells us:

> (In the Upanishads) the largest metaphysical truths and the subtlest subtleties of psychological experience are taken up into the inspired movement and made at once precise to the seeing mind and loaded with unending suggestion to the discovering spirit. There are separate phrases, single couplets, brief passages which contain, each in itself, the substance of a vast philosophy and yet each is only thrown out as a side, an aspect, a portion of the infinite self-knowledge. All here is packed and pregnant and yet perfectly lucid and luminous brevity and an immesurable completeness. A thought of this kind cannot follow the tardy, careful and diffuse development of the logical intelligence. The passage, the sentence, the couplet, the line, even the halfline, follows the one that precedes, with a certain interval, full of an unexpressed thought, an echoing silence between them, a thought which is carried in the total suggestion and implied in the step itself, but which the mind is left to work out for its own profit. And these intervals of pregnant silence are large, the steps of this thought are like the paces of a Titan, striding from rock to distant rock, across infinite waters. There is a perfect totality, a comprehensive connection of harmonious parts in the structure of each Upanishad—but it is done in the way of a mind that sees masses of truth at a time and stops to bring only the needed word out of a filled silence.

In the Upanishads the flight from idea to idea resembles the paces of a Titan, striding from rock to distant rock across infinite waters. He who can work out the intervening steps of these Titanic paces can see the harmonious wholeness in the vast philosophy of the Upanishads. He who cannot, must regard the Upanishads as stray and scattered in their philosophic thought. These intervening steps have to be worked out by a keenness of intellect and a boldness of imagination—but these are not enough—for they need not be inspired by an intuitive insight. It has to be remembered that the intervening steps are implied in the Flight itself—they are not away from the paces of the Titan. There is a suggestiveness in the Flight—he who can intuit this suggestiveness can discover the intervening steps, and can say, as Sri Aurobindo has said, that "there is a perfect totality, a comprehensive connection of harmonious parts in the structure of each Upanishad".

The Upanishads contain a large number of inspiring and instructive passages and verses—it has not been possible to include all of them in this book. A certain amount of selection becomes inevitable when one has to deal with such enormous material as is contained in the Upanishads. For the purposes of this book we have taken those verses and passages that have a bearing on the mystical teaching of the Upanishads. It is mysticism which is the very core of the Upanishads—and so in understanding its mysticism one comes to the heart of its sublime and magnificent teaching.

It is significant to note that in spite of dark forebodings about the world and its future there is a silver lining which fills one with hope and cheer regarding the civilization of tomorrow. This silver lining is in the form of a new shift occurring in the religious and philosophical thought of the world. This shift is distinctly towards mysticism. The religious and philosophical thought of the world is seeking a new mystical base from where to act and to inspire the coming generation of man. In all ages, it is mysticism which has been the regenerating force of human civilization. It is this which gives depth to human understanding—and without it man would remain a mere plaything in the shallows and the superficialities of life.

Paul Tillich, an outstanding thinker and philosopher of our times says that modern man has lost one dimension of existence—and that is the dimension of Depth. He must regain that lost dimension if he is to know what real happiness is. It is with this dimension of depth that mysticism is primarily concerned. Alan Watts, another great thinker of our times, says:

> Modern man seeks depth by cutting into the surface. But the depth is known only when it reveals itself and ever withdraws from the probing mind.

Depth reveals itself—but only to a mind that has come to a stillness, having known its own limitations. It is with the revelation of depth that the great Upanishadic philosophy is fundamentally concerned. In this age, where science and technology are moving from victory to victory we need a restraining hand of philosophy—for without it science and technology may lead us into a world devoid of meaning and significance. They may lead us into vast extension of achievement—but extension without depth is like possessing a perfect technique of expression without anything to express. It is depth which gives a rich content to fill the form built with skill and labour, drawn from the techniques of modern science. Modern man needs today a meaningful philosophy if the achievements of science are not to lead him to greater and greater destruction—but to sublime and majestic heights of creative living. But from where shall he gather the necessary material for the formation of a right philosophy of life? The answer to that question lies in the Great Upanishads. It is in the Vision of Life given by the Upanishads that man can find the fundamental philosophy of Creative Living—a philosophy that can serve as a Beacon Light even in the midst of surrounding darkness, a philosophy that can lead him from the unreal to the Real, from darkness to Light, from death to Immortality.

ROHIT MEHTA

I

THE GOLDEN VEIL

The Invocation associated with the *Īśāvāsya Upanishad* is indeed most significant, for, it strikes the key-notes of the whole Upanishadic teaching. It contains the quintessence of the Vedāntic thought in all its purity and simplicity. The Invocation says:

> That is Whole; this is Whole. The Whole comes out of the Whole. Taking the Whole from the Whole, the Whole remains.

Looking superficially, the above statement seems utterly meaningless, for it violates all laws of mathematics. How can the Whole remain Whole when the Whole is taken out of it? It is quite obvious that from a quantitative standpoint the above statement is devoid of meaning. In terms of quantity, there can be no escape from the factors denoting "more" or "less". When something is taken out of something, the latter must register a quantitative loss. It cannot be the same when something is taken out of it. And yet the above Invocation speaks of the Whole remaining Whole when the Whole is taken out of it. What is the meaning of this statement?

The Invocation obviously speaks of the Quality of things. No quantitative process can cause any change in the quality of things. A gold bar may be broken up into tiny fragments—and yet each fragment contains the same quality of goldness as the entire bar. Qualitatively there is no difference between a grain of gold and a bar of gold. Quality is something indivisible. It is to this that the *Bhagavad Gītā* refers when it speaks of *Avibhaktaṃ vibhakteshu*—"Undivided even in the midst of division". The quality of things is independent of size or volume. Though expressed in Time and Space it remains unaffected by them. In order to comprehend the quality of a piece of music it is not necessary to examine its several parts as expressed in the extensions of time. The quality of a thing exists in its wholeness in the tiniest of its part. The Whole resides even in the part—that indeed is the very nature of quality. The Whole is not to be mistaken for Totality. When parts are put together we arrive at a totality—but the Whole is not made up of the parts. The Whole is greater than the sum of the parts. It is because of this that the quantitative increase or decrease of the parts does not affect the Whole.

The one central theme underlying all the Upanishads is that the Brahman and the Ātman are identical. The nature of the Brahman resides in the Atman. There can be no qualitative difference between the two. If they differ in quality then surely Ātman can never know the Brahman. Since the quality of things is indivisible, the quality of the Brahman must reside everywhere. Reality must be present in its qualitative aspect even in the lowliest of its expressions. Not to see the quality of things in all that is manifested is indeed to be caught in *MĀYĀ* or Illusion. To see quality in the midst of a quantitative variety is to see things as they are—for the quality of a thing is indeed the very nature of that thing.

In the background of this Invocation the first verse of the Īśāvāsya Upanishad assumes a new meaning. This verse which is very famous reads as follows:

> By Īśa (the Lord) enveloped must this all be—
> Whatever moving thing there is in the moving world.
> With this renounced, thou mayest enjoy.
> Covet not the wealth of another.

Here Isa or Lord is not to be understood in any anthropomorphic sense. Isa is really the Supreme. It is Brahman or Reality. The above verse says that Reality pervades everything. The World or *Saṃsāra* is in a state of constant flux; everything is moving away. But the opening verse of this Upanishad says that Reality abides even in this movement. How does Reality abide everywhere even in the moving objects? Is Reality also moving? If it moves, is it not circumscribed by the limitations of Time and Space? If that be the case, how can Reality be everywhere at the same time?

It is but obvious that that which is born in time, dies in time also. It is only the time-less that abides, for it is unaffected by the time-process. Reality must needs be time-less for it is only then that IT can be present at every moment of Time. It is only the Time-less that can be Omnipresent. Time implies succession in which things exist not all-at-once, but one after the other. Omnipresence and succession are contradiction in terms. Manifestation is obviously in time-succession where things happen one after the other. But in the Unmanifest all things exist together. Omnipresence is possible only when things exist simultaneously—and not one after the other. Simultaneous existence and successive existence are what the Time-less and the Time indicate. The simultaneous appears successive due to the refracting process of time. Time is indeed a refracting medium which breaks up the white light of Reality into the spectrum of variegated colours.

When the simultaneous existence of the Time-less is sought to be comprehended through the process of time-succession then the result is a paradox. The Upanishads abound in numerous paradoxes. In fact, the Paradoxes of the Upanishads would be a fascinating subject in the study of philosophy and mysticism. A paradox is the placing of two opposites in juxtaposition. There is no solution to a paradox, a paradox can only be resolved—or, more truly, dissolved. A paradox can be dissolved only when the opposites are seen as existing together—the two, not one after the other, but the two, existing at the same place and at the same time. Human mind cannot conceive of this. The two opposite things existing together would, according to mind's understanding, cancel each other—and therefore the result would be Nothingness. Many a Western scholar has stated that the Upanishads have pointed only to a Negative Way—that they do not give a positive philosophy of life. The Upanishads have spoken the language of paradox. The mind comes to its highest by grappling with the paradoxes. The mind first defines the opposites which are contained in a paradox. It then sees a conflict between these two clearly defined opposites. Torn and tormented by this conflict it attempts to reconcile them. In this effort it moves along the path of compromise and synthesis. Failing in these endeavours, it gets baffled because it finds that in bringing the opposites nearer, the opposites cancel each other leaving before it a field of nothingness. Unable to reconcile the opposites and afraid to enter the field of nothingness, the mind has nowhere to go. In this state of negativity, the intensely positive experience dawns upon the mind. Thus the Negative Way of the Upanishads is the most positive —for the positive can be born only in a field which is completely negative. The Emptiness itself is indeed the plenum.

The first verse of the Īśāvāsya Upanishad says that "whatever moving thing there is in the moving world" is enveloped by Īśa or Reality. The question that must arise is—what indeed is the nature of this Reality? If Reality is moving then surely IT cannot exist at the point from where IT has moved. How can Reality then pervade everything? Its all-pervasiveness naturally becomes restricted so that we cannot say that by "Isa is encompassed everything." The Upanishads tell us, including the Īśāvāsya Upanishad, that the Reality or the Brahman is both moving and unmoving—it remains unmoved even in the midst of movement. Once again it is a paradox which the human mind cannot resolve. The Brahman is verily the "Immutable centre of endless mobility." Poet Rabindranath Tagore gives expression to this idea in the following passage in his book entitled *Sadhana* :"

> The progress of our soul is like a perfect poem. It has an infinite idea which once realized makes all movements full of meaning and joy. But if we detach its movements from the ultimate idea, if we do not see the Infinite Rest and only see the Infinite Motion, then existence appears to us a monstrous evil, impetuously rushing towards an unending aimlessness.

To see the Infinite Rest and the Infinite Motion simultaneously is indeed to comprehend the nature of Reality. The Rest and Motion are not one after the other—but exist all at once. Rest is a condition of Fullness or Wholeness. A thing is in its Fullness in a state of Rest. In Motion this Wholeness is broken up into parts. In movement a thing is partially present—and yet if that movement is alive, and not dead, then it must be impregnated with the quality of the Whole. Rest and Motion are the Being and the Becoming of the Indian Philosophy. If the Becoming which is Motion is detached from the Being which is Rest then such Becoming is a "monstrous evil" rushing towards "an unending aimlessness". Now if the Movement is to be alive due to the presence of the Whole then surely Motion and Rest must exist simultaneously in it. Perfect Rest in the midst of dynamic motion—this verily is the phenomenon of Īśa or Brahman enveloping all—encompassing "whatever moving thing there is in the moving world". He who comprehends Infinite Rest in the midst of Infinite Motion, he verily knows the nature of the Brahman, he sees the whole in the Part, he perceives the Quality of things which retains its Wholeness even when the "Whole is taken away from the Whole".

But the question is: How to perceive the Quality of things, how to comprehend the Whole in the Part, how to see the simultaneous existence of Rest and Motion? This is indicated in the latter part of the opening verse of the Īsāvāsya Upanishad. It says *tena tyaktena bhuñjithā* —"with this renounced, thou mayest enjoy". What does this mean? Is there anything to be renounced in order to comprehend the nature of the Brahman? Very often it is said that by renouncing the world one can perceive the Reality and thereby come to the experience of joy indescribable. *Tena tyaktena* in the above verse is interpreted as renouncing the world. But the question is —why should the world be renounced if it is pervaded by Isa or Brahman? If everything is encompassed by Īśa, how can the necessity of renouncing anything arise? What is sought to be renounced is as much Īśa as that which is sought to be retained. And the Īśa at one place is not "less" than at any other place, for the Whole does not suffer any diminution even when broken up into tiny bits —"the Whole remains the Whole even when the Whole is taken out of it."

Then what does *tena tyaktena* mean? Its meaning becomes clear when we look at the last portion of the opening verse. It says: "Covet not the wealth of another". The wealth of another obviously means the wealth that is not given to you. And the Īśa Upanishad says—Do not covet something that is not given to you. To think of enjoyment in terms of somebody's wealth is entirely meaningless. And therefore the author of the Upanishad says—Enjoy that which is given to you. The Part that is assigned to one can alone be the source of one's joy—to covet the Part of another is to display ignorance of the fact that even the tiniest Part is impregnated with the Whole. The quality of the thing abides as much in the Part that is assigned to one as in any other Part. Why then must one seek the wealth of another? The Part that is assigned to one is as wealthy as the Part assigned to another. *Tyaktena* obviously means that which is assigned, given, set apart or left for oneself. An acceptance of what is assigned or given to one is indeed the surest basis of true enjoyment. To crave for what is not given is verily the path of frustration and sorrow. In the Third Discourse of the Bhagavad Gītā there is a verse which says:

> The righteous who eat the remains of sacrifice are freed from all sins, but the impious who prepare food for their own sake—verily they eat sin.

To eat the remains of sacrifice—this indeed is what is indicated in the phrase *tena tyaktena bhuñjīthā* —enjoy that which is assigned to you, that which has been set apart for you. Why does one covet another's wealth? It is because one has not discovered one's own treasures This discovery is possible only when one sees Infinite Rest in Infinite Motion—when Motion is detached from Rest—then such movement becomes monstrous evil, resulting in the frustrations of becoming.

To accept what is given is not a gospel of passivity. It is indeed the basis for true joy and a starting point for right action. In Acceptance one discovers the Infinite Rest. When Infinite Motion—which is the process of Becoming—is rooted in Infinite Rest then is all movement full of meaning and joy. In Infinite Rest one discovers the Quality of one's own Being—the Quality of the Ātman which is identical with the Quality of the Brahman.

The acceptance of that which has been assigned to one is not a gospel of postponement either. Many a time a person adopts an attitude whereby he says that he must accept his fate in the hope that the future will bring joyous tidings. This is no acceptance at all—it is submission—and, that, too, with an inner resentment. To accept what is given—what is set apart for oneself—is to engage in Right Perception. Very often man refuses to receive what is given because he does not see what it is. When one perceives rightly then one sees in the thing given the quality of Truth and Beauty and Joy—the quality of Brahman Itself. To accept what is given is to transform the thing into a window from which to look at the beauty of life itself. The experience of joy comes in the very perception itself. And so the action that emanates from that perception is rooted in joy. That is why the opening verse of the Īśa Upanishad says—Enjoy what is assigned to you—it does not say—Endure what is given to you. To accept what is given is to perceive the Quality of one's own Being. The process of Becoming which emerges out of this perception is naturally free from the elements of sorrow and frustration. And so the second verse of this Upanishad says:

> Working thus, a man may wish for a life of a hundred years.
> In this way—not otherwise thy actions shall not bind thee.

When actions arise from the source of joy arising out of right perception, man can easily expect to live upto a hundred years. The possibility of living upto hundred years indicates the utter absence of worry and anxiety. It is the frustrations of the mind that make a man look older than he is. It is worry that depletes his energies, leading him to premature death or old age. When man accepts what is given to him, perceiving in it the quality of his own Being, then he is freed from all factors that cause frustrations. In the perception of the Quality of his own Being, he discovers his own *Svadharma*—his own true Vocation. And does man ever get frustrated when he is engaged in his own Vocation? To covet the wealth of another is to forget one's own Vocation and get involved in the profession of another. This truly is *Paradharma*. The above verse of the Upanishad says that actions can never bind a man so long as they arise from the Ground of Acceptance. It is not Action but Reaction that binds a man—for reactions are a chain-phenomenon. They get entangled in an associative process where one reaction calls out another in a never-ending chain. Reactions arise from the background of covetousness—the desire to have what another has. When a man's vision is confused it is then that he covets another's wealth. A man who has discovered the Quality of his own Being is a Spiritual Aristocrat, acting on his own with grace and dignity. To discover the Quality of things is to accept what is given—for Quality resides everywhere, even in the tiniest and the lowliest. He who makes this acceptance as the basis of action is freed from all bondage here and now. Such a man can live as long as he likes for he has brought under control the very movement of Time itself. It is not the Mind, but the Spirit that moves him. And the Spirit verily is Timeless—Eternal and Unborn.

The Īśa Upanishad says—"Whoever neglects the Spirit goes to the regions of utter darkness." What indeed is meant by the neglect of the Spirit? The Spirit is obviously neglected when the process of Becoming loses the vital and living touch of the Being—where Quantitative riches are accumulated with a complete forgetting of the Quality of things. When this happens the process of Becoming naturally leads one to regions of utter darkness.

If, however, it is said that in Acceptance of what is given one discovers the Spirit—the Quality of Things—

then the question is what is Acceptance—how does one do it—and what is Spirit or the Quality of Things?

The Fourth and the Fifth verses of the Īśa Upanishad give a very vivid description of the Spirit, the neglect of which leads a man to regions of utter darkness. These verses say:

> The Spirit, without moving, is swifter than the Mind; the senses cannot reach IT; IT is ever beyond them. Standing still IT overtakes those who run. IT moves. IT moves not,
>
> IT is far and IT is near,
> IT is within all this,
> AND IT is outside of all this.

Here we come across the great paradoxes of the Upanishads. How can the Spirit be both moving and unmoving? If It stands still how can It overtake those who run? How can It be both far and near? If we add up all the above attributes of the Spirit, the result would be Nothing. With the opposites each cancelling the other, the Spirit indeed appears as Nothing and so the Quality verily is Nothing. And is this not true? We have stated above that the Quality is indivisible. Surely it is only Nothing that is indivisible—for something can be divided. Something is divisible and so must suffer diminution when anything is taken out of it. Something undergoes the fluctuations of "more" and "less"—but how can there be any fluctuation in Nothing? Nothing remains Nothing under all circumstances. And yet without the presence of Nothing, the entire manifestation must seem dead and devoid of purpose. Without this Nothing, the whole existence must appear a "monstrous evil, impetuously rushing towards an unending aimlessness." The Upanishads are verily concerned with the Mystery of Nothing. Does the Īśāvāsya Upanishad take us nearer to the unravelling of this Great Mystery?

Speaking about the Spirit, the Īśa Upanishad says that IT is incorporeal, IT is invulnerable, and IT is incorruptible. Incorporeal it certainly is, for IT is unborn and unmanifest.

Incorporeal IT must be for while IT contains all forms

—no form can contain IT—and so IT remains Formless in its true and intrinsic nature. While immanent in forms, IT remains supremely transcendent. But why does the Isa Upanishad describe IT as invulnerable? The invulnerable, surely, is something that cannot be assailed—something that defies all attacks, something that can never be wounded. Now what is unassailable? In order to assail something it is necessary to grasp it, to hold it. A thing can be assailed only when it is clearly defined—in other words, when it exists in Time and Space. Unless a thing is confined in a frame—whether a material or a mental frame—it eludes one's grasp. The Spirit or Reality is for ever elusive—for it is intangible, outside the grasp both of the senses and the mind. And the Intangible is always invulnerable, for it can never be possessed. IT is invulnerable not because IT is surrounded by strong walls of defence. The Intangible is not invisible, hidden behind subtle veils of manifestation. The Intangible is exposed and defenceless—and yet IT is invulnerable. The Intangible is fragile and yet strong—Its strength comes from the fact that It can never be possessed. And it is this which renders IT incorruptible. Needless to say, it is possession that corrupts—it corrupts both the possessor and that which is possessed. The possessor is corrupted because he grows insensitive by the very act of possession—but that which is possessed also becomes corrupt because possession is possible only by isolating a thing from its living context. And that which is torn away from its living context is bound to get corrupted for it is dead and therefore gets decomposed. Thus Reality or Brahman, or, the Quality of things, is for ever Intangible. Even when the Form is divided, it remains Whole. The Intangible is the intimation of the Formless in Form, of the Unmanifest in the Manifest, of the Transcendent in the Immanent. The eighth verse of the Īśa Upanishad says:

> The Spirit is incorporeal and invulnerable, pure and untouched by evil. It is wise, intelligent, encompassing and self-existent. It has appropriately distributed objects through the eternal years.

The last phrase in the above verse seems rather strange and mystifying. It says that the Spirit "has appropriately distributed objects through the eternal years". What does this mean? Obviously here the reference is to the Transcendent expressing Itself in the Immanent. And the verse says that in this process the Spirit has appropriately distributed objects. This indicates that each object is occupying its rightful place—in other words, each object is occupying its unique position in the entire sphere of immanence. Each object is so appropriately distributed that it can act with its own distinct and unique quality. It is needless to say that the Transcendent is the Whole, while the Immanent is made up of the Parts. When the Whole distributes the Parts, each Part occupies its rightful, appropriate place. The opening verse of the Īśa Upanishad says *tena tyaktena bhuñjithā* —it obviously means Enjoy the appropriate place that is given to you because it represents the distinct and unique quality of that unit of life. When the unit of life acts from its own appropriate place then there is no sorrow or frustration—in fact, that unit of life can hope to live a hundred years with no fear of getting involved in the bondage of action.

But we do not enjoy the appropriate place that is given to us—we covet the wealth of another. Why? This is because we do not see the appropriateness of the place that is assigned to us—we are not aware of the Quality of our Being. It is obvious that this appropriateness cannot be discovered by analysing and dissecting the Part—it can be discovered only when there is the Vision of the Whole. The Spirit is the Whole and so we must look at the Part with the eyes of the Spirit. It is to the eyes of the Spirit that the Parts seem occupying the appropriate places. It is only when we are able to see thus that it will be possible for us to enjoy that which is assigned to us without coveting the wealth of another. This is true *Aparigraha* or non-possession. But the question is: How to perceive with the eyes of the Spirit?

In the eighth verse of the Īśa Upanishad, quoted above, there is an indication as to how one can see with the eyes of the spirit. Such seeing is obviously not a conceptual approach. It is not arrived at by thinking or imagining. It is not a question of forming an idea as to how the Spirit looks at Its own creation. To know how to perceive with the eyes of the Spirit is to come to a communion with the Spirit. It is only in an act of communion that one can know how the Spirit looks at its own creation. How is one to come to this communion?

The eighth verse of the Īśa Upanishad says that the Spirit is *Svayambhū* — self-created. This shows that the Spirit is not the product of the opposites—but comes into existence by Itself. IT is thus Original—and not the resultant product of opposing forces. And so the Spirit or the Brahman can be known only in a state of originality. It cannot be found in the field of the opposites but only in a condition of originality. The original is Unique or Incomparable. The Brahman is often described as One without a Second. And so only in comprehending the unique and the incomparable that one comes to the experience of the Brahman. The Brahman resides in his Creation but only as the Unique, the Incomparable, the Original. But how can one see the Unique and the Original? It is here that the description of the Spirit or the Brahman given in the above verse proves of inestimable value. The verse describes the Spirit as *Kavi* or *Seer,* as *Manishi* or Thinker and as *Paribhū* or Pervader. In this description we are given an indication as to how one can come to the experience of the Svayambhū or the Original—how one can come to the communion with the Unique and the Incomparable.

The above verse says that the Spirit is *Paribhū* —meaning the Pervader or the Encompasser. Now what is the pre-condition for pervading or encompassing? Surely it is the Immensity of Space. The Original can be born only in a soil that is virgin. It is only in immense emptiness that the unique and the incomparable can be born. It is only in the consciousness which has infinite space that there can take place the birth of the Brahman, the *Svayambhū,* the Original. The unique and the original cannot be experienced by a consciousness that has no space. It is only the *Paribhū* that knows the arrival of the *Svayambhū* :

But what is meant by creating Space in consciousness? And how is this to be done? The space in consciousness is indeed the state of Love. And creation is possible only in a state of Love. But a state of Love is a condition of virginity of utter emptiness. Now a consciousness which is subject to modifications has no space in it. The modifications arise because of the play of the opposites. But how can there be Love where opposite or duality exist? And so *Paribhū* is a condition where the opposites have dropped away because of which there is clear, open space—space not broken up by objects, but space without any object. The pervading, the encompassing, is possible only in such space. But how can one come to this experience of immensity of space? Be it remembered that the virgin soil is not dead—it is tremendously alive, and yet possessing nothing. In the above verse while *Paribhū* indicates the Emptiness of the soil—the other two decriptions suggest to us the aliveness of the soil. The soil must be made alive, for without this, its emptiness is utterly barren. And how can the barren soil give birth to something that is Original and Unique? And so the consciousness, before it comes to the Immensity of Space, must be made alive. Alive and yet empty it is only such a consciousness that can know the Original and Unique—it alone can commune with Brahman, the *Svayambhū*

It needs to be remembered that the emptiness of space cannot be created. The space that is created is always a space with Object—the Space without an object comes into existence—it cannot be brought into existence. The question is—how does it come into existence? It is most interesting to observe that the soil that is alive is always empty, ready for new creation. What can a tired and exhausted soil produce? Nothing except weeds. But a soil that is living always produces something fresh and vital. Such is indeed the case with the soil of human consciousness. It must be kept alive, and this living quality itself will create immensity of space, a virginity of soil, in which the Original and the Unique can take birth. The question is—how is the human consciousness to be kept alive?

The verse of the Īśa Upanishad says that the Spirit or the Brahman is *Kavi* and *Manishi*—the seer and the thinker. We have seen that Brahman being *Svayambhū* is Original and Unique. And therefore in communing with the Unique man indeed comes to a communion with the Brahman. But such communion is possible only when there is immensity of space in human consciousness. Now it is only the consciousness that is alive, that can show forth this immensity of space. And the consciousness that is alive contains the factors indicated by *Kavi* and *Manishi*. The *Kavi* is indeed a Seer—but not a seer in the sense of just an observer. The *Kavi* sees with a sensitivity of perception—he sees with his entire being—there is a passion—an intensity of emotion in his perception. The *Kavi* sees many things which an ordinary observer is not able to do. The consciousness of the *Kavi* is one that is surcharged with emotion—it is one which vibrates and pulsates with emotion. Thus intensity of emotion—a quality of passion—is one of the essential factors that makes human consciousness alive. The *Kavi* is a Seer but not a disinterested seer—he is a seer whose very observation is surcharged with tremendous vitality born of an intensity of emotion. And yet the Spirit is also a Manīshī—a thinker with extraordinary brilliance and clarity. A clarity which can perceive the play of the opposite and in this very play see the cancellation of the opposites and therefore come to a perfect negativity of consciousness. An intellectual clarity must needs come to the point of perfect negativity. But this negativity is not to be mistaken for passivity. The negativity, is born out of the co-existence of an intensity of emotion and a clarity of thinking. It is true that the clarity of thinking brings the mind to an experience of utter negation—but this negation is vibrant with an intensity of emotion. There is the vitality of a Seer and the clarity of a Manīshī which render human consciousness alive and yet empty. The emptiness of such a consciousness is not to be mistaken for barrenness. Thus intensity of emotion, clarity of thinking and immensity of space constitute a state of human consciousness in which a communion with the Original, the Unique, the Incomparable is possible. The state of consciousness as indicated by the *Kavi*, the *Manishi* and the *Paribhū* is indeed that state where the *Svayambhū* is perceived. And to perceive the *Svayambhū* —the Unique and the Original—is to look at the world of Immanence with the eyes of the Spirit. And when this is done one understands the appropriateness of all things, one discovers the quality of Things, and in this discovery alone is it possible for one to come to the experience of *tena tyaktena bhuñjithā* .

The crux of the problem as posed by the Īśa Upanishad is to have Clarity in the midst of Intensity. One can have a clarity of thinking but such clarity is often dry-as-dust, showing forth disinterested impersonality. Similarly one can have an intensity of emotion but once again this is very often associated with a cloudy vision and a confused thinking. To have clarity and intensity at the same time—not one after the other—this indeed constitutes a state where human consciousness is alive and yet empty. A man must be a *Kavi* and a *Manishi*. at the same time, for thus alone his consciousness will have that virginity in which new and original creation is possible. It is only the Unique that can know the Unique—for it is only the Alone that can commune with the Alone. The Īśa Upanishad puts this same question in yet another form in the subsequent verses. It says:

> Into deep darkness fall those who follow action. Into deeper darkness fall those who follow knowledge.

In the normal experience of man Action and Knowledge are one after the other—not simultaneously. There is always a gap between the two. It is this gap which brings darkness and desolation in the life of the individual. Action which is not inspired by knowledge is mere activity. It is a mere *Upāsanā*—a meaningless practice. Similarly knowledge which is bereft of the vitalizing touch of action is dry-as-dust. The above verse says that mere activity leads a person to darkness, but mere ideation leads him to even greater darkness. An ideational knowledge as also repetitive activity are both meaningless. They lead a person to the realm of false values. It is the gap between the two which renders both of them ineffective. In the so-called spiritual life there is always an endeavour to bridge the gulf between Belief and Behaviour. But such endeavour exhausts the individual because the bridge is never completed and can never be completed. It has to be remembered that when a Belief is sought to be translated into Behaviour, the attempt is to construct a bridge between two points, one of which is fixed and the other is constantly moving. A Belief constitutes a fixed point but Behaviour which is related to life is subjected to constant flux—because life itself is in a state of flux. How can such a bridge be ever constructed? A Belief represents ideational knowledge; and Behaviour tends to become a repetitive activity. Neither of them can lead man to illumination. It is to this baffling problem that the Īśa Upanishad refers when it speaks of action leading to deep darkness and knowledge leading even to deeper darkness. What then is to be done? The Īśa Upanishad says:

> He who knows both knowledge and action, with action overcomes death and with knowledge reaches immortality.

Here the obvious reference is to the simultaneous existence of Knowledge and Action so that there is no question of bridging a gulf. In our normal experience we regard action as following thought. There is first the thought-pattern and then slowly, by toil and effort, we seek to create a behaviour-pattern in terms of that thought. We regard thought as always preceding action. But can this process be reversed? If it could be, then there would be action first and thought would be used only as a means to describe the action. The description by thought would emerge very naturally. When a person discovers something, out of that experience comes an expression which is natural and simultaneous. There is no gap between experience and expression while there is always a gap between belief and behaviour. A bridge can never be constructed between Thought and Action—but between Action and Thought, no bridge is necessary at all. If action could precede thought then the whole problem of frustrating struggle between Precept and Practice could be eliminated. It is to this that the above verse of the Īśa Upaniṣhad refers—for it says—"with action he overcomes death and with knowledge reaches immortality". It is a fact that man is afraid of death—and he wants to conquer death by acquiring a knowledge of immorality. An acquired knowledge is nothing but belief. With belief in immortality we wish to overcome death. But the attempt fails—the fear of death remains inspite of this belief. Immortality is an ideational concept—we are unable to translate it into that behaviour which is free from the fear of death. The gap for ever remains unbridged. Where thought precedes action there is bound to be a state of inner conflict—the conflict between a belief in immortality and the fear of death. But the Īśa Upanishad says—reverse this process so that action comes first and thought follows thereafter. It says—first DIE and then in that experience of death will come the knowledge of Immortality. The knowledge of Immortality is born naturally and spontaneously—it comes in the very wake of the experience of death.

It may be noted that precedence of Action over Thought is not an advocacy for thoughtless action. A thoughtless action is an impulsive action. It is an action born out of habit or instinct. It is obviously an action born out of inertia. But precedence of Action over Thought is a state in which action takes place when thought is not even born. The above verse of the Īśa Upanishad speaks of "overcoming death" by Action. It is needless to say that Death demands a total action for it does not leave anything behind. Such totality of action is possible only when action precedes thought. Where thought intervenes action is bound to be incomplete. Thought arises from the accumulated background of the mind. Its existence therefore depends upon keeping that background intact. A breaking up of this background would mean the end of thought itself. And so the intervention of thought in any action is for keeping up the continuity of the background. Thus thought restricts action and keeps it within the confines of continuity. How can an action functioning within the confines of continuity overcome death which is an experience of discontinuity? Death is a phenomenon of discontinuity. To overcome death therefore requires an action which is free from the restrictive influences of continuity. Such action is possible only when there is no intervention of thought. Where action precedes thought—there alone the experience of death comes. And from such experience emerges the realisation of immortality. The experience of death and the realisation of immortality are not separated by a time-leg —they are instantaneous. The action of overcoming death and the knowledge of immortality are simultaneous—not one after the other. This is the joint phenomena of the *Kavi* and the *Manīshī* . And out of such joint phenomena comes *Paribhū* —the virgin soil in which the Unique or the Original is born.

The Īśa Upanishad explains this idea further when it says:

> Immanence and Transcendence—
> He who this pair conjointly knows,
> With immanence overcomes death
> With transcendence reaches the immortal.

To know Immanence and Transcendence as a joint phenomena—that is what the Īśa Upanishad says. To know continuity and discontinuity simultaneously—this is what the above verse indicates. Continuity is represented by Immanence or the Manifest. Death is the cessation of the Manifest. Where the Manifest is totally negated—there comes the experience of death and so through the negation of the manifest man overcomes death. But the moment when the manifest is negated is also the moment when transcendence is experienced. It is like the opening of the window and the rushing in of the sunlight. There is no time-lag between the two. In the negation of continuity death is overcome and in entering the realm of discontinuity, Immortality is known or realized. Here we are not referring to a belief in immortality. A belief is a concept—and a concept functions within the confines of continuity. And therefore a concept of immortality indicates a state of ceaseless continuity. Immortality is not an endless continuity. A continuity is a time-process—even if it is endless, it is still a time-process. Now a time has a beginning and therefore an end. And so immortality when it is a product of thought is subject to the time-process. Such an immortality has an end—even though the end may be far away in terms of time. But an immortality that has an end is no immortality at all. To talk of an end with reference to immortality is to indulge in a contradiction. But such contradiction is inevitable so long as we think of immortality as an endless continuity. Immortality cannot be known by conceptual thinking. It is only when all concepts end that immortality can be known. And the ending of all concepts is death—the cessation of the immanent or the manifest. Immortality resides in the realm of Transcendence, the realm of the Unmanifest. Immortality is not of time—it is the experience of time-less-ness. The overcoming of death is in immanence, for it comes when the manifest is negated—but the knowledge of immortality is in transcendence, for, it comes when man steps out of time and enters the region of the Timeless. The experience of death and the knowledge of Immortality are simultaneous—for it is in death and there alone that man can know Immortality. The Īśa Upanishad says: let there be a complete negation of the manifest—the putting away of the veils of immanence—for when the veils of the manifest are rent asunder then there stands before man the Spirit in all Its glory.

The Īśa Upanishad almost concludes with that great and inspiring idea, for it says in its fifteenth verse:

> With a golden vessel
> The face of the Real is covered over,

That do thou, O **Pūshan,** uncover
That I, devoted to truth, may behold.

According to the above verse, the spiritual experience is a process of uncovering. Truth or Reality has been covered over. There are veils after veils of manifestation which have covered the Face of Truth. Brahman or Reality is in front of us—but we cannot see IT because a screen has been cast over IT. In the removing of the veil—which is a negative process—there comes the intensely—positive experience of directly perceiving the Face of Brahman. And strangely enough Reality is covered over with a golden veil. The veil being golden so fascinates and attracts us that we are unwilling to remove the veil. But who has put this golden veil over the Face of Truth? The veil is indeed cast by thought—and the thought has woven it out of the beautiful material supplied to it by its own accumulated background. Thought has naturally taken the finest material available to it—it has studded the veil with gold and silver, with all the jewels that it could find in its own treasure-house. But the veil of thought must needs be of the material drawn from the realm of continuity. It is this screen of continuity cast by thought which hides the face of the Real which for ever is Timeless and therefore outside the stream of mind's continuity. When the veil of mind's projections is removed then there stands in all its majesty the Supreme Spirit.

When the Spirit or the Brahman is seen, does not every object of the manifested world shine with a new light? When the Light of Reality shines then the Quality of each object is revealed. And when this happens man cries out with great jubilation and says to himself—*tena tyaktena bhuñjithā, mā gṛdhaḥ kasyasvid dhanam.* Enjoy what is given unto you, do not covet the wealth of another.

II

THE SILENT NIGHT

The Upanishads represent an inquiry—a deep inquiry—by the human mind into the fundamental problems of existence. They have followed the method of discourse and discussion in which the Teacher and the student have together explored the subjects of inquiry. Nowhere in the Upanishads has the Teacher spoken with an air of finality—he has encouraged his students to ask as many questions as possible, and when the answers have not been completely satisfactory, the students have not refrained from putting further questions so as to clarify the points of inquiry. Unless one understands this close relationship of the Teacher and the student, one may fail to enter into the spirit of the Upanishadic teaching. A state of inquiry constitutes a healthy condition of the human mind. But here one must make a distinction between inquiry and curiosity. Needless to say, curiosity arises from a shallow and a superficial mind. But inquiry, on the other hand, emerges from the depths of human consciousness. A deep inquiry is fundamentally concerned with three questions—the *How*, the *Why* and the *What*. All scientific inquiry, whether covering the physical or the occult sciences, relates itself to the question: *How*. Science is all the time concerned about finding out *how* things behave. Philosophy has its inquiry turned in a different direction—for it is interested to know *Why* things behave in a particular manner. But Mysticism, or religious experience is not satisfied with merely the *How* and the *Why*—it wants to find out *What* it is that is behind all patterns and motivations of behaviour. In the Kena Upanishad the main question under discussion is—What is it that impels and motivates the particular modes and patterns of action?

Who sends the mind to wander afar! Who first drives life to

impels us to utter these words. Who is
and the ear?

note that the very first ques-
:s to the impelling power of
els far and near. The ques-
Iow and *Why*—he wants to
ne eye to see and the ear to
he speech to speak and the
which the Teacher gives is
elling force he says:

e Eye of the eye, the Word of the
..., the Mind of the ... and the Life of the life.

The above statement seems rather strange. What does ear of the ear, eye of the eye and mind of the mind mean? The Teacher here is dealing with the question of the impelling force and he says that it is the ear of the ear which impels the ear to listen, it is the eye of the eye which impels the eye to see, and it is the mind of the mind which impels the mind to think. Obviously there is something more than merely the ear, the eye, the speech or the mind which impels these organs to engage in their respective functions. Evidently the Teacher seems to indicate that it is the Quality of hearing that impels the ear to hear, it is the Quality of seeing which impels the eye to perceive, it is the Quality of Speech that impels the speech to articulate, it is the Quality of thinking which impels the mind to think. Physical science has been trying to unravel the mystery of evolution by following a principle which it has propounded—namely: Organ precedes Function. But the Scientific understanding of evolution through the application of this principle has brought it into blind alleys. The Upanishad propounds a startling principle, given in the above verse, which says that it is Function which precedes Organ. It is the function which impels the organ. The function can and does bring into existence a variety of organs. The whole basis of structural evolution lies in the impelling power of the function. The function seeks to create finer and finer instruments of expression and it is this which lies at the root of the evolution of forms which science studies so diligently. Where does this function reside? It expresses through the organ and yet is beyond the organ. No scientist can find the Quality of hearing by dissecting the ear. The same is the case with regard to other organs. In the above verse the ear of the ear and the eye of the eye obviously mean the Quality of hearing and the Quality of seeing. Once again speech is not just the collection of words. If it were merely a collection of words—the speech would never become intelligible. There is a Quality which imparts a "livingness" to words—just as there is a Quality which gives to thoughts that factor which makes them alive. The above verse says that this impelling force is the Life of life. There is a difference between life and mere existence. That which transforms existence into life is the Quality of living. It is the presence of this Quality which makes everything alive. It is quite obvious that a study of grammar cannot supply meanings to be expressed in words. The study of grammar may enable a person to dissect and analyse a poem in terms of various grammatical terms—but a poem is not just grammar. The beauty of a poem lies in the living quality that has been imparted to words. This is the Quality of a poem. Thus it is the Quality of Things which constitutes the impelling force behind all that is manifested. The Upanishad describes this Quality as the Spirit. But the question is—how can this Spirit or the Quality of Things be known? The third verse of the Kena Upanishad says:

> There the eye goes not, nor words, nor mind. We know not, we cannot understand,—how can we then explain What IT is?

The Quality of hearing, seeing or thinking cannot be explained in terms of the ear, the eye and the mind, for the Quality is not to be found by dissecting the organ. The quality is not arrived at by separating the parts and examining each part minutely. While the parts become alive by the touch of the Quality, the latter cannot be grasped by the analysis of the former.

The Teacher of the Kena Upanishad says that this Spirit or the Quality is above the known and is also above the Unknown. The Teacher says that the Spirit is above the known. That which is known is the conceptual product of the mind. That which is known represents the thought of the mind. And a thought is the crystallization of thinking. Let us not forget that it is thinking which has a flowing and a living quality. A thought remains isolated from the living quality of thinking. And so while it is a structure—may be a beautiful structure—it has no quality of life in it. A thought obviously is something lifeless—how can the Spirit—the Quality of things—be ever known by something that is devoid of life? The Spirit cannot be known by thought. The known and the Unknown are only two aspects of thought. The mind which declares something as "Unknown" does so only through the instrument of thought. The known and the unknown are only the labels of thought. And so the Teacher of the Kena Upanishad says that the Spirit cannot be comprehended by thought—it matters not whether thought calls IT the known or the unknown. Thought cannot describe IT either in positive or non-positive terms. The Known and the Unknown are only the opposites of thought. The Spirit cannot be contained by the opposites, so long as mind recognises something as Unknown, so long the unknown is only another form of the known. Known and unknown are mere verbalizations of the mind. The Teacher of the Kena Upanishad says that the human consciousness, by its own effort, cannot know the Spirit. This limitation of human consciousness has been expresed most beautifully in the following verses of the Upanishad:

> What cannot be spoken with words, but whereby words are spoken, know that alone to be Brahman, the Spirit—and not what people here adore.
>
> What cannot be thought with the mind, but whereby the mind can think, know that alone to be Brahman, the Spirit—and not what people here adore.
>
> What cannot be seen with the eye, but whereby the eye can see, know that alone to be Brahman, the Spirit—and not what people here adore.
>
> What cannot be heard with the ear, but whereby the ear can hear, know that alone to be Brahman, the Spirit—and not what people here adore.

The above verses tell us that while the Spirit contains the ear, the eye, the speech and the mind—these latter cannot contain the Spirit. While the Spirit is immanent in the organ, IT is at the same time transcendent. If the Spirit were not immanent in the organ, the organ would be dead—it would cease to function. And yet the Spirit is transcendent—It is not exhausted by the organ—nay, it does not even suffer any diminution by being immanent in the organ!

The Sun sends out its millions of rays to illumine the dark corners of the entire Solar system—and yet it does not leave its place, nor does it become less by virtue of its sending out these rays. All things in the Solar system are sustained because of the immanence of the Sun—they would be dead if the Sun were to withdraw its immanence. And yet how can the blade of grass which exists because of the sun, know what the nature of that Sun is? Although by sun the blade of grass exists, it cannot comprehend the nature of THAT by which it exists. It is true that the organs function because of the Spirit—but how can the organs know that Spirit? After all, what is the instrument by which the organs know anything? Obviously by its own functional instrument. The ear can know by its function of hearing. No doubt this function can be refined and made sensitive. But after all what will this refined hearing do? It can make the ear aware of many octaves of sound—it can know the structure of sound in a variety of aspects. But the infinite extension of octaves cannot bring the ear nearer to comprehending the very Quality of hearing itself. It can refine its hearing, but it cannot know what hearing itself is. The mind can refine the structure of thought—but how can mind know what the essential quality of thinking is? The mind can know what thought is—but it cannot know what thinking is The quality of thinking cannot be caught in the thought-process by which mind functions. Thinking is a flux—how can it be caught in thought which is static? Thus the functioning faculty of the organ cannot give a comprehension of the Spirit—such is the teaching of the Kena Upanishad as indicated in the above verses. The question then is —Is the Spirit unknowable? It is true that Spirit is above the known and the unknown—but can IT be comprehended? Or does IT remain unknowable by man?

The above verses of the Upanishad say that to the functional faculties of the organ Brahman or the Spirit remains intangible. For, the verses say that Brahman or Spirit is not what the people here adore. What man adores is what he has caught in his functional faculties. He adores the Immanent but forgets that the Spirit cannot be contained in the framework of the Immanent. That which makes the Immanent alive is the Transcendent—but the Transcendent cannot be caught. IT eludes all forms—it slips out of the grasp of all functional faculties, be they of the body or of the mind. The Spirit remains supremely Intangible—but does this mean that IT is unknowable?

The second part of this Upanishad begins with this inquiry, for in its opening verse the Teacher says:

> If you think "I know Brahman well" then surely you know but little of ITS nature; you know ITS nature only as conditioned by man or by the gods. Therefore, Brahman, even now, is worthy of your inquiry.

The Kena Upanishad says that a man who says he knows Brahman well is a victim of mind's illusions. For, he who says that he knows Brahman well speaks only of the conceptual knowledge. It is a knowledge conditioned by the background of the mind. Even the knowledge of the gods is conditioned by the limitations of the instrument with which knowledge is gathered. Here by knowledge of the gods is to be understood as knowledge gathered through super-physical means. The Teacher says that whether the knowledge of Brahman is acquired through the normal processes of mentation or through super-physical means—all such knowledge is partial. It deals only with the expressions of Brahman—and not with Brahman Itself. Surely all speculation about the Whole, based on the knowledge of the Parts is misleading. The

Whole is not arrived at by just adding the Parts. The Whole is greater than the sum of the parts—and that "something" which renders the Whole greater is bound to be missed in all speculations, even though the speculation may be mathematically precise. It is that "something" which slips out of the mathematical calculations which is most germane to the understanding of the nature of Brahman. Here a question may arise: Is a knowledge of the Parts of any avail in comprehending the nature of Brahman? If it is, then what is its value? Does not man start by understanding the Parts? What he sees first is the Parts—the Whole is unknown to him. Has he not to come to the Unknown through the doorway of the known? If so, what must be the nature of this inquiry?

So far, in the Kena Upanishad we are witnessing a conversation between the Teacher and the disciple. The disciple has been pondering over the instructions of the Teacher, and out of his reflections he comes to a very significant truth which he utters in the following verse:

> I do not think I know Brahman well, nor do I think I do not know IT. He among us who knows not the meaning of "neither do I know, nor do I not know"—knows Brahman.

The Disciple says that he cannot declare that he does not know Brahman at all—and yet he cannot claim that he knows Brahman. He says he neither knows nor does he not know. To know and yet not to know—this alone is the state where Brahman can be known. What did the disciple know about Brahman? He knew the manifested aspect of Brahman—and manifestation consists of a totality made up of the parts. Having examined part by part, the disciple was able to say that although he did not know Brahman well—he knew something about IT—that aspect of Brahman as was revealed in manifestation. But such knowledge leaves more things un-explained than what it actually explains. The Manifest cannot explain itself save in the light of the Unmanifest. It is the Unmanifest which holds the key to the mystery of the Manifest. It is true that one can know about the behaviour of the Manifest—but this behaviour invariably shows certain tendencies for which there is no explanation in the realm of the Manifest. Does this not happen even in ordinary human relationships? We may have witnessed the behaviour of a friend whom we love for many years. On the strength of this behaviour we may say that we know our friend. And yet our friend very often displays such tendencies of behaviour as are completely outside the purview of predictability. On the basis of the knowledge of behaviour, spread over many years, we should be able to predict all aspects of our friend's conduct—and that too with certainty. But such is not the case. Inspite of all our knowledge, our friend remains unpredictable. Surely there is no explanation for this unpredictability in the sphere of knowledge that we have. Its explanation is somewhere else. And so we can say with regard to our friend that we know him and yet we do not know him. We can say with the disciple of the Kena Upanishad that "neither do I not know, nor do I know." To know what knowledge explains, and to know also what knowledge does not explain—this is the highest state knowledge to which mind can go. It shows the limitations of mind's positive knowledge. In the above verse the disciple says that he who knows the meaning of "neither do I not know nor do I know" comes to the comprehension of Brahman. To have in one's consciousness the co-existence of knowing and not-knowing is to bring that consciousness to the highest state of receptivity. The openness of mind consists in the simultaneous existence of knowing and not-knowing. When knowing and not-knowing exist instantaneously then there arrives spontaneously an interval between the Knower and the Known. Usually this interval is covered up by the mind with its projections. But where, having known, the mind declares that it does not know, then the interval remains uncovered—because the mind has nothing with which to cover it. It is in this interval between the Knower and the Known, where the process of knowing has ceased, that there takes place what one must describe only by the word—Miracle. So far the process of knowing had emanated from the Knower—but now in this interval it is the Known that communicates what IT is to the Knower. But this can happen only when the process of knowing as emanating from the knower ceases so that the interval is not covered by any projection of the knower. It is only when the knower is utterly negative, and yet aware that the known conveys Its secret to him. In the above verse, the Kena Upanishad refers to this interval—the space between knowing and not-knowing. The miracle happening in the interval has been stated beautifully in the following verse of the Kena Upanishad which says:

> He by whom Brahman is not known, knows IT; but by whom IT is known, knows IT not. IT is not known by those who know IT; IT is known by those who do not know IT.

It should be noted that the condition of not-knowing is not a state of inertia. The awareness of not-knowing comes in the wake of all the knowledge that the mind has acquired. The mind that knows what is explained but is not aware of that which has remained unexplained is an ignorant mind. In such a mind arises vanity of false knowledge. Since that which is explained can throw no light on that which has remained un-explained, the man of so-called knowledge is devoid of true knowledge. The above verse says—and rightly—that he who says he knows, does not know—while he who says he does not know, truly knows—for he knows the falseness of his own knowledge. Having examined what is explained and having become aware of what has remained un-explained, the inquirer declares that he does not know. When the un-explained cannot be predicated in terms of the explained then truly the inquirer, in all honesty, must state that he indeed does not know. The mind that can declare that it does not know is, by that very declaration, on the threshold of knowledge. Wisdom begins where the mind becomes aware of the falseness of the knowledge that it has acquired. The open mind is one which is conscious of what knowledge has explained and at the same time aware of what knowledge has not explained. This is a sensitive mind, ready to receive even the subtlest intimation of Brahman—this indeed is the mind that can respond to the Voice of the Silence. The Kena Upanishad says:

> Brahman is known in the ecstasy of an awakening which opens the door of life eternal. By Self we obtain power, and by wisdom we obtain Eternity.

The above verse describes the opening of the door of life eternal as an ecstasy of awakening. The Eternal is not ever-lasting—and so the Eternal is not of the sphere of continuity represented by the time-process. The time-process is the field of mind's operations. All the knowledge that mind gathers is circumscribed by this process. It knows the explanations given by the time-process regarding the phenomena of life. But there is much in life which remains unexplained in terms of the time-process. Its explanation cannot be found by extending the time-scale—for however much the time-scale is extended there is "that something" in life which remains unexplained. When human consciousness comes to that interval between knowing and not-knowing then there opens before it the door of life eternal. It has left behind the field of mind's continuity and it stands before the great Unknown of Discontinuity. It has left behind the continuing process of time and is face to face with the discontinuity of the Timeless. The door of life eternal has opened before him—but such opening has been possible because of the ecstasy of awakening. What is this ecstasy of awakening? The very word ecstasy means a state of being besides oneself. It is a state where man steps out of himself. It is a condition of freedom—freedom from the burden of mind's accumulations. In the interval between knowing and not-knowing the whole burden of mind's accumulations drops away and man is rendered simple and innocent. It is this simplicity and innocence which create a state of ecstasy—the man is beside himself because he has stepped out of his acquired nature, having regained his natural spiritual estate. By being beside himself, he has come into his own! And what greater power there can be for a man than to come into his own—having wandered into realms other than his own, he has come to his own estate where he instals himself as the Ruler of the Realm. But man comes to the rulership of his own realm only when he is divested of the trappings of his acquired nature. He becomes simple and it is only to the simple that the wisdom of life eternal is vouchsafed. The following verse of the Kena Upanishad presents this idea is a clear and a forceful manner:

> Brahman comes to the thought of those who know IT as beyond thought, not to those who imagine IT can be attained by thought. Brahman is unknown to the learned and known to the simple.

The above verse says that Brahman cannot be attained by the mind—IT comes to the mind. Brahman is not the product of thought—Brahman comes to the thought, but, only of those who have realized the limitations of thought. All attempts of the mind to understand Brahman by its own thought-process are fruitless. All the varied accumulations of the mind are of no avail in knowing Brahman. The verse of the Kena Upanishad says that Brahman is unknown to the learned. And who are the learned? They are those with many possessions. They are those who have many accumulations of the mind—those acquisitions of thoughts which they proudly display as their prized possessions. They cling fast to the tinsel which the mind has collected after much toil, and regard themselves as rich, forgetting that all that glitters is not gold! Brahman is indeed unknown to the learned—IT is known only to the simple. And the simple are those who are free from the burden of mind's accumulations. It is only the meek that shall inherit the kingdom of God.

Strangely enough at this stage in the Kena Upanishad, the Teacher interrupts the profound metaphysical discussion that has been going on so far in order to relate a story to his disciple. This evidently seems to be a digression—but it is not, for the story itself carries further the main topic under discussion. The Teacher tells his disciple the story about the war between the gods and the demons. In Hindu mythology there are any number of stories regarding the wars between gods and demons. It looks as if the gods and the demons were perpetually at war. This is not strange because they represent the two opposites of the mind. And a continual warfare between the two opposites is indeed the very life of the mind. The Teacher of the Kena Upanishad relates a story about one of these wars in which gods had triumphed over the demons. This victory had gone into the heads of the gods. They felt that they were all-powerful, for, had they not triumphed over the demons by their own prowess? However, the Supreme Spirit realised that this vanity on the part of the gods would be their undoing, and so decided to enlighten them on the real nature of things. The story says that the Supreme Spirit assumed a magnificent form and appeared before them. But the gods could not understand who the Supreme Being was. They therefore decided to find out who He was. For this purpose they deputed Agni, the God of Fire. When Agni approached the Supreme Being, the latter inquired who he was. Agni revealed his identity. The Spirit asked him what power he had by which he had become so well known—and Agni said he could burn anything and everything that may be placed before him. The Spirit put before him a dry blade of grass and asked him to burn it. Agni tried with all his might to burn the dry blade of grass—but he could not burn it. Crest-fallen, he had to return to the gods, declaring that he was unable to find out who the Supreme Being was.

Not daunted by this failure on the part of Agni, the gods asked Vāyu, the Lord of Air, to find out about the nature of this Great Being. When Vāyu revealed his identity and declared that he could sweep off anything on earth, the Great Being placed before him a dry blade of grass and asked him to blow it off. Vāyu rushed towards the blade of grass with all his ardour but could not even lift it from the ground. He too returned to the gods saying he was unable to find out who the Supreme Being was.

The gods then asked Indra saying "O Maghavan, find out who this great Being is". Indra hastened in the direction of the Supreme Being—but the Spirit completely disappeared before him, and in His place appeared an exquisitely beautiful Woman, highly adorned. She was Umā. Indra asked her who the Great Spirit was. And Umā replied—He was indeed Brahman, the Supreme Spirit, but for Whose help the gods would not have triumphed over the demons.

Why did the Teacher of the Kena Upanishad relate this story to his disciple who was well versed in deep philosophy? What is the meaning of this story? Be it remembered that before the story began we had come to that point in the Kena Upanishad where the disciple had declared that "Brahman comes to the thought of those who know it beyond thought, not to those who imagine It can be attained by thought." The above story conveys this very idea. One may ask: How? The story tells us that the gods wanted to know the nature of the Supreme Being. Let us not forget that the gods represent the mind—what religious books describe as the Higher Mind as against the Lower Mind represented by the demons. Even though the gods may be described as symbolizing the higher mind—still they are part and parcel of the mind with all its possibilities and also with all its limitations. The story says that the higher part of the mind wanted to find out the nature of the Brahman. How did the gods proceed with this inquiry? They sent first Agni, the Lord of Fire. But what is Agni? It is fire which releases the energy that is latent in all beings. The energy lying latent is a condition of inertia or *tamas*. Fire calls out this energy which has been lying latent. In other words, fire awakens the mind from its inertia. It releases the mind from the stupefying influence of *tamas*—one of the conditioning factors of the mind. And so the mind released from the deadening influence of *tamas* goes to find out the nature of the Brahman. But it returns crest-fallen, for how can the mind, still conditioned by other factors, come to the understanding of Brahman? And so Vāyu, the Lord of Air, goes in search of Brahman. Vāyu sweeps the sky with its power, for he is known as a traveller in space. What indeed is meant by traveller in space? He who travels in space moves swiftly and smoothly, for, he moves without any friction whatsoever. It is a movement without conflict. There is nothing to impede its movement and so its energy is not wasted in any frustrating struggle. One of the factors which conditions the mind is called *rajas* or activity. But why does activity condition the mind? Because it is motivated by conflict. The attribute of *rajas* denotes mind's process of becoming. But this process proves intensely frustrating because of pulls and distractions. The movement of becoming, motivated by mind's desires is beset with obstacles and impediments. Vāyu represents that movement of mind which is free from conflict and friction. This shows a condition in which mind is freed from the influences of *rajas*—the mind is active but its activity is devoid of conflict. And so when Vāyu goes in search of Brahman, it is the mind, freed from the conditioning factor of *rajas* that undertakes the journey. But here too the mind returns—for even though it is freed from *tamas* and *rajas*—inertia and conflict—it is still conditioned by *Sattva* It is true that *sattva* is the highest state of the mind; nevertheless, it is an attribute by which the mind is conditioned. It is a very subtle conditioning—so subtle that man does not even perceive its limiting influence.

In *tamas, rajas* and *sattva* we are concerned with the problems of unrighteousness, righteousness and self-righteousness respectively. *Tamas* is a condition where mind is too lazy to differentiate between the right and the wrong. There is nothing more unrighteous than a confused state of the mind. In *rajas* there is a struggle between the right and the wrong. It is a struggle of the mind to establish a supremacy of what it regards as the right. *Sattva* represents a temporary resolution of the conflict—and this results in self-righteousness. It gives to mind a sense of power, a sense of rulership, a sense in which it feels that it can keep the two opposites under control.

In the story which we are considering we saw that Agni and Vāyu, representing the mind freed from *tamas* and *rajas* failed to discover the nature of Brahman. And so the gods decided to request Indra himself to go and find out who the Supreme Being is. Indra is verily the god of the gods. He represents the highest that the mind can offer. Indra is the ruler of the gods and presides over his kingdom which is heaven. *Sattva* is indeed the heaven of the mind—it is a realm where harmony prevails. Heaven is that state where, for the time being, the conflict of the opposites has ceased—we deliberately say, for the time-being—because according to Hindu tradition man returns to earth after a temporary stay in heaven! Indra is the ruler of this heavenly state. The gods naturally depend upon Indra to bring them the news of the true nature of the Supreme Being. Mind has nothing further to offer—if Indra fails then surely the gods must reconcile themselves to the condition of not knowing the nature of the Supreme Being. Just as Agni symbolizes freedom from *tamas,* just as Vāyu represents freedom from *rajas,* so does Indra indicate that condition of the mind when it is freed from *sattva*. The limiting factor of *sattva* is self-righteousness; here mind clings to its virtues, its accomplishments. The mind that is ridden by *sattva* is afraid of soiling its so-called spiritual robes —and so while it gives, it does so with reservations. The mind limited by the attribute of *sattva* cannot abandon itself in giving what it has. But Indra symbolizes a state where there is generosity without any reserve. The name of Indra used in the Kena Upanishad is Maghavan. This very name shows generosity. Indra wields Vajra or thunderbolt as his weapon and it is with this that, out of the clash of the opposing clouds, he brings down rain on the parched earth to quench its thirst. And so Indra represents a mind that is freed from the limiting factor of *sattva*

But the question is: what does the mind, freed from *tamas, rajas* and *sattva* , see? Is Indra able to discover the nature of Brahman? Is the mind freed from all its three attributes able to comprehend the nature of the Supreme Spirit? Our story says that when Indra approached the Supreme Being, It disappeared from his gaze. There was Nothing, where, a while ago, the Supreme Being was seated. And soon into that Nothing came an exquisitely beautiful Woman, richly adorned, whose name was Umā. And it was she who communicated to Indra the nature of the Supreme Being. What does this signify? The mind that is freed from all its attributes must come face to face with Nothing—for all its projections have vanished. The whole creation of the mind is dissolved—the mind faces an Emptiness. If at this stage the mind calls it as emptiness, if it gives it a name, then in a subtle manner the mind gets entangled once again in its attributes. Indra saw Nothing, and then appeared Umā into that Nothingness. If mind had projected something into that emptiness then surely Umā would not have appeared. But when all the projections of the mind ceased, projections not only through *tamas* and *rajas* but through *sattva* as well, then into that Nothingness came from "somewhere" a Woman of un-surpassing beauty in the form of Umā .

But who is Umā and why does she appear? One of the meanings of the word Umā is Night. It also means tranquility. What can be more tranquil and silent than the night? The mind that is freed from its attributes is face to face with the Silent Night. The night represents a state of un-differentiation. It is during day that differentiations are seen. When the night comes there is a silent unity which pervades—in the darkness of the night all multiplicities have vanished. The mind freed from its attributes must needs face this Night of Emptiness. The mind liberated from even the attribute of *sattva* must stand in front of utter silence. Was Indra afraid of this Silent Emptiness? He was not, for he asked of Umā , the Night, about the nature of the Supreme Being.

It is interesting to note that in that Nothingness, caused by the disappearance of the form of the Supreme Being, there appears a woman of exquisite beauty. Why? It is to indicate that the mind freed from its attributes faces a Night—but it is not a fearsome night. The unknown is never fearsome. If human mind can really come face to face with the Unknown, it has no cause to be afraid. If the pulls of the known have completely dropped away then the Unknown comes in the form of Umā, the woman of exquisite beauty.

But even here the question may arise—Why Umā? It may be remembered that Umā is the consort of Śiva. The Hindu trinity consists of Brahmā, Vishṇu and Śiva. In this Trinity, Śiva is indeed a very interesting aspect. For while, Brahmā remains the Unmanifest—he is not worshipped as a deity, except very rarely— Vishṇu symbolizes the Manifest. Śiva is the presiding deity of what may be called an Interval between the Manifest and the Unmanifest. He is known as the Destroyer. He is known as the Lord of the Burning Ghat—one who lives in a Crematorium. He is where the continuity of the Manifest ends and the discontinuity of the Unmanifest begins. He is the One who has conquered Death. In the Hindu scriptures there is a *mantra* for the propitiation of the Lord of Death. But in this, the deity that is adored and worshipped is Śiva in His form known as *Tryambaka.* It is for Śiva to prolong the span of Continuity by pushing back the forces of Discontinuity —or vice versa, for he is the Guardian of the Interval between the Manifest and the Unmanifest.

The Kena Upanishad says that "Brahman comes to thought", It cannot be attained by thought. But when does It come? It comes only when the continuity of thought ceases—then from the realm of Discontinuity IT comes. It comes only in that Interval over which Śiva presides. As the Hindu Mythology says— Śiva is a wanderer at night. He can be contacted only in the darkness of the night. Thus it is at night, and there only, that Śiva conveys the intimations of the Unmanifest. The

Interval is where the Manifest is not and where the Unmanifest has not arrived. But the arrival of the Unmanifest is proclaimed by Śiva and that too in the darkness of the night. And so our story rightly says that it was Umā who appeared and conveyed to Indra the real nature of the Supreme Being. Man has to discover the nature of Brahman directly—and this can happen only when in the state of mind freed from all its attributes, the human consciousness stands unmoved in front of the dark and the silent night. Then the night conveys its gift to the aspirant. This gift comes anonymously, for the aspirant does not know who has given it—such is indeed the darkness of the night. And the gift comes suddenly, for the aspirant knows only when it arrives in his hands—for how can any movement be seen where the night is dark and silent? And so this fascinating story of Agni, Vāyu, Indra and Umā brings us to that great Upanishadic idea which says that Brahman cannot be attained by thought—It comes to the thought of those whose minds have been freed from its three attributes of *tamas*, *rajas* and *sattva*. "Brahman is unknown to the learned and known to the simple," the mind which is freed from its attributes is utterly simple—it is to such an unconditioned Mind that the Vision of Brahman comes.

The Kena Upanishad says that "Brahman is seen in Nature in the wonder of a flash of lightning—He comes to the soul in the wonder of a flash of vision."

The Kena Upanishad says that Brahman comes in Nature like a flash of lightning. Now the flash of lightning comes suddenly, instantaneously, out of the dark clouds which turn even day into night. Nobody knows from where the flash of lightning will come—nor does anyone know when it will come. Sometimes the sky remains overcast with dark clouds for a long period of time without any break causing the flash of lightning. But there are times when the break occurs all of a sudden. The flash of lightning vanishes as suddenly as it comes. It cannot be grasped, it cannot be put in the framework of time. The flash of lightning may be constant but it cannot be continuous. The lightning which is continuous is no lighting at all. It can only come in flashes—and each flash illumines the darkened path of man. Even though it lasts for a moment, that moment is so brilliant with light that the way is seen in all its vividness. The Teacher of the Kena Upanishad says that Brahman comes to man in the wonder of a flash of vision. Its appearance is so sudden that man is wonder-struck. And It comes like a flash in which is seen very clearly the path that lies before man. Brahman cannot be gradually perceived. It comes instantaneously and so he who is awake can see. To the awakened man, the flash is like a new Vision. This Vision pervades the entire being of man—he who has had a Vision of Brahman cannot be the same man again. The Kena Upanishad says that Brahman "is known when It is realized in every state of mind." What does every state of mind mean? Since mind is reflected in every pattern of one's being the Kena Upanishad says that when Brahman is known, every part of man's being is transformed. There is then no gap between perception and conduct. The very perception brings about a total revolution. It is not that one perceives Brahman and then starts practising what he has perceived.

The Kena Upanishad says that the arrival of Brahman is "like a wink of the eye". The revelation of Brahman is instantaneous—as sudden and quick as the wink of an eye. The experience of Brahman is momentary—but that moment has the richness of Eternity. Brahman or Reality can be experienced from moment to moment. Any desire to extend the moment would mean bringing the perception of Brahman in the time-process. But how can the Transcendent be ever perceived in the region of Time? It is only in the time-less moment that Brahman can be known. Does this mean that for the experience of Brahman one must discard living in the time-process? How can one discard the time-process? The day-to-day activities of man must needs be in the time-process. But he who has had the momentary glimpse of Brahman in the time-less moment returns to the time-process with a sense of ecstasy. He fills the time-process with that ecstasy. He is no longer the same person. He brings into the time-process a fragrance of the Time-less. Although Brahman comes like a flash of lightning, such is the brilliance of that flash that it illumines the entire being of man.

The Kena Upanishad says that Brahman is *Tadvanam* —meaning, the Beloved of all. And how does one adore the Beloved? Surely through Love. The Kena Upanishad says that it is only the adoration of Love which brings one to the experience of Brahman. It is only when human consciousness is filled with love that it experiences the arrival of Brahman. Reality comes not to a man of suppression and mortification. It comes suddenly when man is in a state of Love. Needless to say, love is not burdened with knowledge. Love is a state of utter simplicity. Love is not a product of mind's cultivation. Love arises in a mind which is freed from all its accumulations. Does love offer its accumulations to the Beloved? In approaching the Beloved, love puts away all its accumulations and offers itself to the Beloved. Bereft of all accumulations, when man stands alone in utter simplicity then, to such a man, Brahman comes in all its glory and majesty.

The Teacher of the Kena Upanishad instructs the disciple to worship Brahman as *Tadvanam*—for He is the Beloved of all—and, so, only along the Path of Love can He be found.

III

THE GREAT BEYOND

The Kaṭha Upanishad is the most widely known among all the Upanishads. Many Western scholars have described it as "one of the perfect specimens of the mystic philosophy and poetry of the ancient Hindus". The reason why this Upanishad has received such world-wide acclaim is not far to seek. It is the theme of Death discussed in the Kaṭha Upanishad which has evoked great respect for its teachings both in the East as well as in the West. From the earliest times death has been one of the most bafflling problems of man. It has been a never-ceasing challenge to the intellect of man. Modern man who has achieved so much in the field of science and technology stands utterly helpless in front of death. He may know how to conquer outer space—but in regard to conquest over death he is as ignorant as the primitive man. Unable to establish a mastery over death, man seeks with all his might to prolong earthly existence. If man could extend his span of life on earth then death would at least be postponed—for he knows that when the hour of death strikes, it would be powerless for him to do anything.

But death is such an unpredictable moment that even when the life span is extended, man is constantly in fear of being caught in the jaws of death. With this fear, dogging his steps, how can he be happy even when earthly existence is prolonged? Death is not only unpredictable, it is overpowering too, for when its call comes man feels utterly helpless. And furthermore death comes with a demand which is total—for it asks us to leave everything and follow it empty-handed. The demand of death seems merciless, for nothing whatever can be carried over its doorstep. And so the prolongation of earthly existence is hardly any consolation to man—for, he knows that the call of death may come any moment. In the midst of the joys of prolonged existence there is for ever the shadow of death cast over man. Of what use is the extended life-span if the shadow of death is always present? There is no escape from death, and so man must face it and demand from it the secret that it holds. For when the secret of death is known then can man say out of his own experience—"O, death where is thy sting? O grave where is thy victory"? It is neither the prolongation of earthly existence nor the knowledge about the after-death condition that can free man from the fear of death. Once again it is not a belief in re-incarnation or the immortality of the soul that can liberate man from the spectre of death. Man must know the Secret of Death—and this secret is known to none other than death itself. It is death and death alone that can communicate that secret —there is no other path but a direct communion with Death if man is to know this Secret of secrets without knowing which he must remain a stranger to the joys of life. But how can man extract this secret from death? It is this path which is indicated by Kaṭha Upanishad, where Yama, the Lord of Death, is the Teacher and Naciketā, the intrepid young inquirer, is the Disciple.

In the Upanishads we find an intimate relationship existing between the Teacher and the Disciple. It is a relationship in which the Teacher and the Disciple are in communion with each other. It is to indicate this relationship that this Upanishad begins with a very significant invocation. The Invocation says:

> May Brahman protect us both. May Brahman bestow upon us both the fruit of knowledge. May we both obtain the energy to acquire knowledge. May the study of us both reveal the Truth. May we cherish no ill-feeling towards each other.

As is evident, the above Invocation is recited by both the Teacher and the Disciple together. Both together ask for the obtaining of energy to acquire knowledge, for the seeking of knowledge requires much energy. Any wasting of energy would be detrimental to the pursuit of knowledge. In order that such wasting may not take place there has to be extraordinary clarity on the part both of the teacher and the disciple. The above Invocation says: "May the study of us both reveal the Truth". The Teacher and the Disciple are concerned with Truth—and Truth has to be discovered. The method of teaching contained in the Upanishads leads both the teacher and the disciple to discovery. The relationship between the teacher and the student is not static—it is intensely dynamic—it is a relationship in which the teacher and the student both learn together.

The last sentence of the Invocation says: "May we cherish no ill-feeling towards each other". A communion is possible when there is perfect understanding between the teacher and the student. When education becomes a journey together into the realms of Truth—then there comes into existence a relationship of respect and consideration between the two. In the Upanishads one sees this relationship of respect between the teacher and the student all throughout. There is a discipline, but it is one which is born out of freedom—for here it is not the one that teaches the other—it is both together learn from Truth itself.

The Kaṭha Upanishad is a beautiful example of this relationship of the teacher and the disciple. And the above Invocation is a fitting prelude to the great teaching on the subject of Death—a profound subject discussed in all seriousness by Yama, the Lord of Death and Naciketā, the young inquirer. But before we can enter into this discussion we must know the circumstances under which Naciketā went in search of the great Secret of Death.

It seems a rishi by the name Vājasravas was engaged in performing what is known as Viśvajit sacrifice with the sole purpose of getting heavenly rewards. The name Vājasravas means one who has become famous by distributing food. Now distribution of food is a symbol—it indicates performance of religious practices as ordained by the scriptures. And so Vājasravas represents traditional religion which requires the observance of certain outer practices with a view to get heavenly rewards. The traditional religion is one which is interested in rites and ceremonies, in the injunctions of the priest and the scripture, in the acceptance of creeds and dogmas and in the observance of certain patterns of behaviour and conduct. Vājasravas represents such conventional or traditional religion. He had a son called Naciketā. Now the word Naciketā signifies *Na-ciketā* which means something unperceived—something that is beyond the normal range of perception. And so Naciketā symbolises mysticism in religion—that aspect of religion which goes to the core of things and is not concerned merely with the outer behaviour or pattern of conduct. Naciketā is the son of Vājasravas—this itself is very significant. For, the history of religion tells us that when religion deteriorates into lifeless patterns of behaviour, there appear from time to time new expressions of mysticism which bring the human individual back to the fundamentals of spiritual life. And it is in the bosom of traditional religion that mysticism is born, raising a banner of revolt against the dead forms of conventional religious practices. It is with such revolt that Kaṭha Upanishad is concerned.

In the sacrifice which Vājasravas was performing, he was engaged in distributing goods and cattle in charity to the Brahmins. Naciketā watched this great act of charity —but he found that this pattern of charity was devoid of any spirit of charity. It was a charitable action but without any charitable content. For, he saw that his father was giving away in charity such cows as were utterly useless. And so he said to himself:

> By giving such cows that can calve no more and can give no more milk, and are even past drinking their water and are even past eating their grass, surely no man goes to heaven. He goes to no worlds of joy.

Here we find the mysticism of religion rising in revolt against the traditional religion. But what could the little boy say to the mighty father? And besides the father was well versed in the traditional forms of religion—he could easily silence the little boy by a show of learning. But Naciketā, too, was irrepressible—the flame of revolt had been lighted and could not be extinguished by mere head-learning in which his father was proficient. Naciketā asked his father who was giving away his cattle in charity: "Father, to whom will you give me?" The father pretended that he had not heard what the son had said. But Naciketā repeated the same question thrice. The father knew what the son was indicating by that question and so in great anger he replied saying: 'Unto death do I give you". Naciketā must have been taken aback by this reply of the father—but there was no going back for him. The father had given him in charity to Death—and so to Death he must go. The father was full of repentance and it was for Naciketā to console him. Naciketā thus addressed his father who was immersed in sorrow, realising that his son would soon proceed to the abode of Yama:

> Remember how the men of old passed away, and how those of days to come will also pass away; a mortal ripens like corn, and like corn is born again.

Naciketā tells his father that after all death is a normal affair—people died in the past and so will die in future too. Why should one be frightened of death, for, man ripens like corn and like corn is born again. From this it is clear that Naciketā was well aware of the idea of reincarnation. After all birth and death is an ever-recurring cycle—those who are born must die and those who die must be born again. Vājasravas who represented traditional religion should have been satisfied with this conventional explanation of the phenomenon of death given by his son.

And so Naciketā proceeds to the abode of Yama, the Lord of Death—but when he reaches his destination, he finds that Yama is away. Naciketā waits, for his mission to death would be incomplete without meeting the King of Death. For three nights he waited and the nights in the abode of death must have been fearsome. But after this long waiting he finds Yama returning to his palace. Yama is full of apologies to the young Brahmin whom he had kept waiting without any hospitality being offered to him. Why was Naciketā not offered any hospitality while Yama was away? The inmates of Yama's palace must have found it strange that a mortal should voluntarily go to the abode of death. They were accustomed to see people being brought to Yama—but Naciketā 's was the solitary instance where he had gone to death—he was not brought to death. The inmates of the palace of Yama must have felt utterly at a loss to know how to treat such a strange visitor who had gone knocking at the door of death—instead of death knocking at his door. And so Naciketā , fearless inquirer that he was, waited at the door of death even though no hospitality was given to him. Yama must have realized that here was a young man of strong determination and deep inquiry.

And so offering his apologies, Yama told Naciketā to ask for three boons as a recompense for the three nights during which he was kept waiting. Naciketā must have realized that he was in front of some one who had power and strength unsurpassed for he started asking for boons in a very cautious manner, lest the Lord of Death be annoyed with him. The first boon that Naciketā asked for was:

> O Lord of Death, may my father's anger be appeased and may he be happy and free from anxiety, and may he remember me and welcome me after my leaving you. This be my first boon.

Here Naciketā is concerned about the after-death condition. The traditional religion speaks of man entering the Kāma-loka —the astral world soon after his death. It is a state where emotional experiences preponderate. The sensorial experiences have been cast away with the shedding of the physical body. Naciketā wants to be sure that his passage through the emotional state would be free from pain and anguish. If Yama could assure him that his father would be happy and free from anxiety and would remember him with affection then he would naturally be greatly relieved. Yama readily grants this first boon of Naciketā.

The traditional religions, particularly Hinduism and

Buddhism, believe that during the after-death condition, man passes on from *Kāma-loka* or the Astral world to the *Svarga-loka* or the Heaven world where he lives for a considerable time, reaping the harvest of all the good deeds done during earthly existence. This is a period of uninterrupted pleasure. It is said that after man has done all the reaping of his good harvest, he returns to earth. Now Naciketā who seems to be moving cautiously before coming to the main theme of his inquiry, asks Yama to give him the second boon which he states thus:

> There is no fear in the regions of heaven; old age and death are not there. Having passed both they rejoice in heaven, beyond hunger and thirst and sorrow. Those in heaven enjoy long continuity. You know, O Death, that sacred fire which leads to heaven. Explain it to me—be this my second boon.

Naciketā asks Death to tell him about the sacred fire which leads to heaven. Most commentators have described the condition in the heaven world as denoting immortality. Surely there can be no immortality in the heaven world, for according to traditional religion the heaven world too ends. Needless to say immortality and end cannot be together—they are contradiction in terms. And so here, in this context, the word immortality has to be interpreted as "long continuity"—an almost endless continuity of time. It is interesting to note that Naciketā first wants to understand the problem of death in terms of continuity. And so in his second boon he asks Yama to tell him about the sacred fire that leads to heaven. Yama is naturally greatly pleased with this young man who seems to be asking "proper questions" and so gives to him most willingly the knowledge about the sacred fire. He imparts to him all the details regarding the lighting of this fire. Indeed, so pleased is Yama that he grants an additional unasked boon—and that is, that this sacred fire would in future be known as Naciketā Fire in honour of this brave and intrepid young inquirer. Yama says to Naciketā:

> This is the fire that leads to heaven which you chose as the second gift. Men will call it Naciketā's Fire-sacrifice. Choose now the third boon.

What was the third boon that Naciketā asked of Yama? Be it remembered that Naciketā had not gone all the way to the Lord of Death only to know about the after-death condition. He was not seeking a seemingly endless continuity of the heaven world—he knew that this continuity had an end. He was well aware of the fact that there was re-incarnation—the corn ripening and being born again. But after-death condition and re-incarnation seemed to him a never-ceasing chain devoid of meaning and purpose. Of what use was this chain of continuity with birth, death and rebirth appearing in ever-recurring cycle? Naciketā was seeking something more fundamental than merely the after-death condition. He formulates clearly his deep inquiry in asking for the third boon. Naciketā asks Yama the following fundamental question:

> When a man dies, this doubt arises: some say there is a "being" and some say there is "no-being". Teach me the truth and let this be my third boon.

Naciketā wants to know what happens in the actual moment of death—not what prevails in the after-death condition. His inquiry is—Is there a continuity of "being" in death—or is there no continuity of "being"? What is actually in the moment of death—Being or Non-being? In the hour of death, is there Existence or Non-existence? This is a profound metaphysical question which Naciketā has put to Yama. The traditional approaches to death are all concerned with finding out about the after-death condition. They are interested either in the prolongation of earthly existence or the continuity of after-death state. It is mysticism which is supremely concerned with the moment of dying—with death itself. It wants to know what happens in the actual moment of death—neither before nor after. In the above verse Naciketā asks the question about "*when* a man dies"—*not after* a man dies. He is not concerned as to whether there is existence or not after death—he wants to know whether there is existence or non-existence in the actual moment of death. In other words, Naciketā is not inquiring about survival after death—he wants to know what happens in the moment of death itself. By this question, Naciketā has put Yama in a very embarrassing position. And so Yama replies:

> This doubt arose even to the gods in times of old; for subtle and mysterious is the law of life and death. Ask for another boon. Release me from this.

So awkward is the condition of Yama that he asks Naciketā to release him from the granting of this boon. He says: "Ask another boon". But why? Yama says even the gods have not been able to find an answer to this question. But who are the gods? They are the beings with super-physical perception. He says even those with super-physical, or Occult powers have not been able to find an answer to this question because life and death are a mysterious phenomenon. It is not by journeying into invisible realms that man can unravel this great mystery. Yama says that the problem of life and death is so subtle that even men with higher faculties have not been able to understand it. And so he asks Naciketā to leave this subtle and mysterious question and ask for something else.

But Naciketā was not an ordinary inquirer—he knew what he was seeking. He tells Yama that if this is a very difficult question then where is he to go for an answer. He tells him that in all the worlds there is no other teacher who can explain the mystery of death as the Lord of Death himself. He makes it clear to Yama that there is no other boon greater than this—for he must know the mystery of death—and that too from the king of Death himself. But Yama again pleads with Naciketā and requests him to release him from the obligations of granting this boon. He says to him:

> Take horses and gold and cattle and elephants. Choose sons and grandsons that shall live a hundred years. Have vast expanses of land, and live as many years as you desire. Or choose another gift that you deem equal to this, and enjoy it with wealth and long life. Be a ruler of this vast earth. I will give you all you desire.
>
> Ask for any wishes in the world of mortals, however hard to obtain. To attend on you I will give you fair maidens with their chariots and their melodious music.
>
> But, O Naciketā do not ask me about the Secret of Death.

From the above verses it is quite evident that Yama has used all his persuasive powers to wean away Naciketā from the inquiry on which he was resolutely insistent. Yama has placed before him many temptations—such as would have broken the determination of anyone. All these temptations cover a wide variety of man's interests. Yama has given this variety in the hope that this young man may fall somewhere, and give up his inquiry. In fact, Yama is prepared to do anything, only if Naciketā would give up asking him about the Secret of Death. The Lord of Death seems to be approaching Naciketā almost with folded hands, telling him: "O, Naciketā do not ask me about the Secret of Death".

But Naciketā was above all temptations. He had entered the Palace of Death not for nothing. He was determined to stay on until he found the Secret of Death, and that too from Yama himself. And so to all the persuasive eloquence of Yama, Naciketā replies resolutely thus:

> All these pleasures pass away, O End of All; They destroy the life-giving power. And indeed how short is life. And so keep the horses and dancing and singing to yourself. Man cannot be satisfied with wealth. How can we even enjoy wealth with you in sight? Can we live whilst you are in power? No, I can only ask for the boon I have asked.

It is interesting to note that all that Yama has offered to Naciketā belong to the world of mortals. He was prepared to give him the utmost in the realm of the mortals. Yama said in so many words when he stated: "Ask for any wishes in the world of mortals, however hard to obtain". Wealth and long life, rulership of the vast earth and fair maidens with their chariots and singing, gold and cattle, sons and grandsons living upto a hundred years—all these belong to the mortal world. Yama has been careful not to mention anything whereby Naciketā would encroach upon the realm of immortality. He was ready to grant him long continuity in earthly life but he must keep away from the kingdom over which he presided. He could have the pleasures of continuity but not the secret of immortality. But Naciketā was brilliant in his intellect—he saw what was being offered by Yama. He rightly says: How can men live so long as death rules over them? In the above verse he calls Yama by the epithet—*Antaka*—meaning the End of All. He says how can man enjoy wealth when Yama is in sight? Yama may give to man with one hand but with the other he may take away all that he has given. When death knocks at the door, of what use are wealth and power and pomp? And so Naciketā says to Yama: "Keep the horses and dancing and singing to yourself for, I cannot be tempted by any of these". Inspite of all the persuasions of Yama, Naciketā declares in unmistakable terms thus to the Lord of Death:

> Solve then this doubt as to the meaning of the Great Beyond. Grant me the gift that pierces the veil of mystery. This is the only boon Naciketā can choose.

Yama had probably not come across any inquirer of such integrity as Naciketā. Finding that no temptation could distract Naciketā from his main subject of inquiry, Yama now prepares his young disciple to receive the Great Secret. In this work of preparation, Yama begins by telling Naciketā about the Two Paths. He says:

> The Good is one thing; the pleasant another. Both of these serving different ends are linked to man. It goes well with him who, of the two, takes the Good, but he who chooses the Pleasant misses the end.

Here Yama indicates the two paths—one denoting the Good and the other denoting the pleasant. But are the Good and the Pleasant opposed to each other? It is pleasure and pain which constitute the opposites. They, like all opposites, always go together. The opposites of the mind are such that one is contained in the other. Pain is contained in pleasure—it cannot be separated from it. He who seeks pleasure must be ready to receive pain also. To ask for pleasure and to demand that it should be free from pain is to ask for the impossible. In the very pursuit of pleasure, pain is always imperceptibly present. The cause of pain is in the pleasure itself—for pain is indeed the product of pleasure. Yama says he who moves along the path of pleasure misses the end, for he gets entangled in the never-ending play of the opposites.

In preparing Naciketā for the receiving of the great truth regarding Death, Yama indicates to him the Path of the Good that must be pursued. Now what is this Path of the Good—and how is it better than the Path of the pleasant? Surely the Good about which Yama speaks is not the opposite of Evil. If he talks of Good as opposed to the Evil then there is hardly any difference between the two paths. If they are opposites then each is contained in the other—and evil must be present where good is. The pairs of opposites, whatever they may be, work together—they are like the shadow and the substance. Of what use is the Path of Good if Evil is contained in it? Obviously Yama here speaks of Good as Absolute Good—not the good which is the product of mind's opposites. The play of the opposites is the sphere of mind's continuity. The two opposites are the frontiers of the Land of Continuity. Thought which is the instrument of the mind moves within these frontiers. Now if Good is not the product of the opposites then surely it must be outside the frontiers of the mind. Absolute Good is that which is not reached by the mind. It is outside the sphere of mind's continuity. And so in describing the Two Paths, Yama has indeed indicated the two distinct categories of experience—one which is within the confines of continuity, and the other which lies beyond. The path of pleasure lies within the frontiers of the mind but the Path of Good lies beyond those frontiers. Since Naciketā has asked about the meaning of the Great Beyond, Yama indicates to him at the very beginning that it is along the Path of the Good that the secret of the Great Beyond can be found.

Yama congratulates Naciketā for discarding the path of the pleasant and accepting the Path of the Good. Yama says to his young disciple:

> You have pondered, Naciketā, on pleasures and you have rejected them. You have not accepted that chain of possessions wherewith men bind themselves and beneath which they sink. There is the path of Wisdom and the path of unwisdom. They

> are far apart and lead to different ends. You are, Naciketā, follower of the path of wisdom—may pleasures move you not.

It should be clearly understood that Wisdom is not something opposed to ignorance. Wisdom has no opposite. It arises when both ignorance and knowledge are negated. In the above verse Yama says that men sink because they become heavy with the possessions which they have accumulated. Obviously the path of Wisdom is one where man becomes lighter having shed all his possessions—and is therefore able to swim easily in the current of life. The man of Wisdom is not one who sits idly on the shores, unconcerned about the current of life. He is in the current but does not sink, for bereft of all possessions, having nothing to guard or defend, he can abandon himself to the current of life. Such a person of abandonment cannot sink because the stream itself protects him. Yama says in the above verse that the man of unwisdom, "childish, careless and deluded by wealth", goes again and again to death. He remarks that they go to death again and again, but never actually die. He who knows how to die does not have to go to death again and again—it is death that comes to him, not as a Master wanting to carry away the slave, but as a friend and a companion, making life all the richer even as light and shade together give beauty to the landscape. By the phrase "going again and again to death" Yama obviously means to indicate that they come again and again under his sway. But the wise are not under the sway of death—they have conquered death and so move with death even while living. They who come again and again under the sway of Death are not even aware of the Great Beyond. Yama says:

> Not many are those who hear of It, and of those not many reach It. Wonderful is he who can teach about It, and wise is he who can be taught. Wonderful is he who knows It when taught by the wise.

It is obvious that he alone can teach about the Great Beyond who himself has known it. But this knowing is not by a process of thinking. How can the thought process take a man beyond the realm of thought? And the Great

Beyond is most assuredly outside the frontiers of thought. Yama says that "It is higher than the highest thought, and is above all thought". But then how can the Great Beyond be found? Yama says: "The way to It is the Teacher". It is not the teaching that can indicate the path—it is only the Teacher who can point the way. The Teacher is greater than the teaching. While the Teacher contains the teaching, the teaching can never contain the Teacher. The Teacher is always beyond the teaching; for he remains the unmanifest inspite of the teaching that he may have manifested. Wisdom arises only when the teacher and the taught are in a state of communion. Real communication is possible only where communion exists. As Yama remarks: "The sacred knowledge is not obtained through reasoning". The secret is communicated by the teacher to the pupil only in a state of communion. Naciketā has found a Teacher in the person of Yama. For Naciketā Death indeed is the Teacher. And Yama says that the Great Secret cannot be found by reasoning—but only by a communion with the Teacher. If Naciketā wants to know the meaning of the Great Beyond then he must be in communion with the Lord of Death who is the teacher. Yama says that the secret of death can be known only by communing with death—there is no other way.

Yama says to Naciketā, that he has indeed come to a state of communion where the Great Secret can be communicated. He describes this condition of communion beautifully when he says: " Naciketā is like a house open for the Lord". Naciketā has rendered his house open for the Lord to walk in. By rejecting the path of pleasure and possession he has made his house vacant for the Lord to reside. It is by the process of negation that Naciketā has created space—enormous space—in his house for the Lord to move. There can be no communion so long as the mind of man is engaged in positive action. By no positive effort can space be created in the mind of man. And it is only when there is space that the Teacher and the disciple can come together. A movement is possible only in space. But any movement by the disciple fills up the space and therefore renders it ineffective for communion. When all the activities of the disciple cease then in that House of Inaction, the Lord arrives. The mind of man cannot go to Truth—it is Truth that comes to the human mind—but it can come only when the mind is open, bereft of all possessions. Naciketā had come to such a state and therefore the Teacher says that ' Naciketā is like a house open for the Lord". Yama begins his instruction by telling Naciketā that:

> When the wise rest their minds on God that is beyond Time, hard to be seen, dwelling in the mystery of things, then he rises above joy and sorrow.

How can mind rest on God that is beyond Time? Mind can function only within the framework of Time—how can it dwell on something that is beyond Time? Here the resting of the mind signifies the mind that has come to rest. In such a mind there is no movement. There is a stillness, a deep silence. It is only here that man can come to the experience of God that is beyond Time, He who dwells in the mystery of things. It is in this experience that man rises beyond joy and sorrow, beyond pleasure and pain. It is in deep silence, and there alone, that man discovers the Good—for the Good is beyond the pairs of opposites. But here Naciketā asks a very pertinent question to Yama—his question is:

> Tell me what you see beyond right and wrong, beyond what is done and not done, beyond past and future.

This is the most difficult question which Naciketā has put—for how can any one say what is beyond right and wrong—or beyond what is done and not done? One can easily explain the opposites by contrasting one with the other. One opposite helps to explain the other—but where there is no opposite, with what can the explanation be given? In the language of the opposites there is no explanation for that which is beyond right and wrong—and outside the field of opposites there is no language with which to explain! Since language is the instrument of thought the boundaries of its field are naturally set by thought. And so Naciketā has put Yama in a very embarrassing position by asking this question for which there is no answer either in the field of thought or in the field of language. Naciketā asks Yama as to what is beyond Past and Future. Now past and future constitute the time-process. He wants to know what is beyond the time-process. Once again how can this be explained? Needless to say communication exists in the relative world—in the world of the Absolute no communication is necessary—for in a world of non-duality who is to communicate with whom? This communication or language is the instrument employed in the world of the relative. And the relative world exists in time-scale. It is utterly meaningless to make an attempt to explain the Timeless in the language of time. The instruments of the relative world are totally inadequate to give an understanding of the Absolute. Then what is the answer that Yama gives to this very difficult question which Naciketā has put to him?

> The Approach which all the Vedas declare, which all austerities indicate, and which men accept when they lead the life of continence, I will tell you briefly—it is OM.

Yama is careful to use the word *Padam*—an Approach while replying to this difficult question of his young disciple. An approach obviously indicates a direction. Yama says those who are intent on spiritual life pursue a particular direction. Vedas being knowledge also point to that direction. And it is only the direction that can be indicated. All scriptures, all gurus, all that is expressed by word or symbol or gesture—all these are but fingers pointing the way. They are like pointers indicating the path that may be traversed by the aspirant who wishes to come to the realization of spiritual verities. Yama too does not tell Naciketā in positive terms what lies beyond the Past and the Future or beyond right and wrong—he only indicates an approach, a direction. If Naciketā wants to know about the Beyond then he must traverse that path for himself. As a true Teacher, Yama is only pointing a finger in that direction. But we may ask what is the direction that Yama has indicated in reply to Naciketā's question concerning the Beyond? Yama says, this direction, this approach, this *Padam,* is the Sacred word—OM. What is this OM? Is it just a syllable of three letters which are A.U.M.? If so, how does this three-lettered syllable explain the great Beyond between the Past and the Future, between the right and the wrong? In the Hindu scriptures much instruction is given as to how this Sacred Word should be pronounced. OM is considered as the generalized symbol of all possible sounds. It is obvious that all articulate sounds are produced in the space between the root of the tongue and the lips. If properly pronounced OM represents the whole gamut of sound-production. One of the explanations given of the three letters A.U.M. is that they represent creation, preservation and destruction respectively. The sound *A* arises from the root of the tongue—where the tongue does not touch any part of the palate. And the sound *M* is the last sound terminating with the lips. In between is the sound *U* which represents the rolling forward of the impulse that begins at the root of the tongue and ends at the lips. And so all the articulate sounds lie between the letters *A* and *M*. But one may ask what has all this to do with the question about the Beyond which Nachiketa has raised?

Be it remembered that OM is not just a three-lettered syllable. By practice one can pronounce it correctly according to the rules of sound production. But the significance of OM lies in not what is uttered—but what remains un-uttered. It is not the articulate but the inarticulate sound which holds the key to the understanding of the Sacred Word. The articulate sound depends upon the inarticulate. Yama says, the mystery of the Beyond lies in the Great Word OM, but the mystery can be unravelled not in the articulate but in the inarticulate nature of the sound.

When Yama declares that the mystery of the Beyond lies in the Word, one is reminded of the famous sentence appearing in Christian scriptures, in the Gospel according to St. John, where it is stated that "In the beginning was the Word, and the Word was with God, and the Word was God". In the beginning was the Word—but can the Word be found by going to the beginning? To go to the beginning is to explore the Time-process. Can the Word be found in the stream of Time? No, for it is said that "the Word was with God". And so one must ask God to give us the meaning of the Word which contains the unravelling of the great mystery of the Beyond. But how to get that word from God? Will God tell us where He has placed that Word so that by travelling thither we may find it? But the above statement says that "the Word was God"—That the Word and God were not different. To say that Word was God is to speak of the co-existence of the Manifest and the Unmanifest. The Word was with God and yet the Word was God. He uttered the Word and yet kept the Word with Himself. And so if the Word contains the mystery then surely one must know God—God the manifest and God the unmanifest.

Yama tells Nachiketa that the mystery of the Beyond lies in OM. The question may arise: Is OM just the spoken Word—or is it something more? To use the phraseology of the Kena Upanishad one might say it is the Word of the Words: OM is that which enables all articulate words to come into existence. It covers the entire gamut of sound production and yet it is not the articulate sound. It is That which has remained inarticulate even after all the articulate sounds have been produced. This idea becomes clearer as one turns to the next verse of the Kaṭha Upanishad which says:

> This syllable OM is indeed Brahman. This syllable is the Highest. Whosoever knows this syllable obtains all that he desires.

Thus OM is equated here with Brahman. And Brahman is manifest even when It is unmanifest. The Word OM is the meeting place of both the Manifest and the Unmanifest—the articulate and the inarticulate—the sound that is uttered but at the same time the sound that has remained un-uttered. While in the former verse the Word was described as *Padam* in the second verse it is denoted by the term *Akshara*. Now *Akshara* means the Imperishable. OM is indeed *Akshara Brahma*—The Imperishable One. If it were only the articulate sound then it would be perishable—it is only the inarticulate that is Imperishable. But the Perishable draws its sustenance from the Imperishable. And so Yama says: "OM is the best support: It is the highest sustenance". But how to come to the knowledge of this Imperishable Word? Can one know It? If so, who is the Knower? Unless the Knower is known, how can the known be comprehended? And so in order to know the Great Beyond there has to be the knowledge of the knower. But who is the Knower? Yama gives an indication of this in the following verse:

> The Knower is not born; It does not die; It has not sprung from anything; nothing has sprung from It.

It is interesting to note that the word for the Knower that is used in this verse is *Vipaścit.* Its real meaning is one whose consciousness vibrates in harmony with. The question is—in harmony with what? Obviously in harmony with OM or Brahman. In other words, the Knower is the Pure Consciousness—a consciousness that is free from modifications. A consciousness that is subject to modifications cannot vibrate in harmony with Brahman. A modified consciousness has its own vibrations—and therefore it cannot be in tune with the vibrations of Brahman? Now a consciousness can be pure only if it is in its original state. The original is not the product of time—it is a citizen of the Timeless World, and the Timeless is neither born nor does it die. The original has not sprung from anything—and nothing has sprung from it. The original is not the product of the opposites—nor does it create any opposite. This pure or original consciousness is the Knower—for it is in complete unison with OM or Brahman. It is so completely tuned with Brahman that it vibrates with it in perfect harmony. Obviously this Pure Consciousness is the Ātman of the Upanishads. This Ātman is the Knower—and Yama tells Naciketā that if he wants to know the mystery of the Great Beyond then he must know the Sacred Word OM which is identical with Brahman. But Brahman can be known only by knowing the Knower —and the Knower is the Pure Consciousness or the Ātman.

Here the Kaṭha Upanishad has propounded one of the most fundamental doctrines of the entire Upanishadic teaching. It says that Brahman can be known only through the Ātman. This statement implies that the object can be known only by knowing the Subject. Yama tells Naciketā that it is only by knowing the Ātman that Brahman can be known. Naciketā has asked Yama to tell him about the Great Beyond. Yama indicates to him that the great secret of the Beyond lies in the Ātman—and nowhere else. The question is what is this Ātman and how is one to know it? Yama says:

> The Ātman, subtler than the subtle and greater than the great, is seated in the heart of each living being. He whose mind and the senses are composed beholds the majesty of the Ātman, and thus becomes free from sorrow.

It is obvious that that which is " subtler than the subtle and greater than the great" defies all quantitative measurements. The above phrase does not indicate that the Ātman is more subtle or more great—what it implies is that the Ātman is the subtle of the subtle and the great of the great—that which gives to the subtle the quality of subtleness, and to the great, the quality of greatness—that indeed is the Ātman. How can It be known? The above verse says that Its vision comes to one whose mind and the senses are utterly tranquil. What is meant by the tranquillity of the senses? Are the senses to be dull and unresponsive? Here in this verse, the word that is used is *Dhātu-prasāda*'—this would mean the good humouredness of the senses—the senses being in good disposition. Evidently it signifies a condition where the senses are not tense but completely relaxed. The senses do not experience any strain but are able to function with complete relaxation. But the above verse says that there has to be the tranquillity both of the mind and the senses. What is the tranquillity of the mind? The word used in this verse is *Akratu*—meaning, a mind that is completely free from all ideations—the mind in which all mentation has ceased, the mind which is free from all commitments whether of the good or of the bad. This is a supremely negative state of the mind— not a passive state, but a sensitive condition in which all positive ideations, both good and bad, have ceased. The above verse says that the Ātman reveals Itself in all Its majesty to one whose mind is utterly negative and whose senses are completely relaxed. The Ātman which is the subtle of the subtle and the great of the great can be known only to a consciousness that is sensitive—a consciousness that is completely relaxed because of the Ground of Negativity in which it exists. Yama tells Naciketā that it is only to the Pure and the Original consciousness that the nature of the Ātman is revealed in all Its glory and majesty. Yama further says that this Ātman:

> Though sitting still, It travels far, though lying down, It goes everywhere; It rejoices and yet does not rejoice—who else but the Pure Consciousness can know It?

The Ātman which shares the quality of Brahman appears to behave in a paradoxical manner. And all paradoxes have their resolution in the Interval that lies between the two apparently contradictory statements. The co-existence of the opposites is to be seen in the Interval which is outside the sway of Time. What is this Interval? Yama, in the above verse, indicates this Interval by saying that the Ātman rejoices and yet does not rejoice. To rejoice and not to rejoice are the two opposites. It is only the Interval that contains both at the same time. The seeming Emptiness of the Interval is the Plenum—the Fullness in which the rejoicing and the non-rejoicing co-exist—it is only of this Interval that one can say that in it the Ātman "though sitting still travels far, though lying down appears everywhere". Yama tells Naciketā about this Ātman which is most mystifying, for he says:

> This Ātman cannot be attained by the study of the Vedas nor by intellect, nor by much learning of sacred books. It is attained by him alone whom It chooses. To such a one Ātman reveals Its own nature.

Yama has already indicated to Naciketā that in order to know Brahman one has to know the Ātman. The Great Beyond, the Secret of Death, is to be found in the Ātman Itself. And so the endeavour of the spiritual aspirant must be to know the Ātman. But how can the Ātman be known? Here Yama says that Ātman cannot be known by any conscious effort. The mind through study and mentation cannot know it. But then what is to be done? Yama says that Ātman reveals Itself—It cannot be attained. But it reveals Itself only to those whom It chooses. What does this mean? Are we to remain at the whim and mercy of Ātman? What does the phrase "It chooses" mean? It obviously means that the Ātman cannot be sought by the human mind. It comes—one cannot go to It. When everything drops away, even the seeking of the Ātman then into that consciousness, pure and unsullied, that the Ātman reveals Its own nature. The choice is not with the consciousness—because the consciousness that makes choices is engaged in a thought process—it moves between the two points of duality. Such movement caused by choice brings into existence a diversity of modifications. How can the Ātman reveal Its nature to a consciousness that is agitated and ruffled by modifications? It is only when the choice of the mind ceases that the choice of the Ātman can appear. Surely the Ātman can reveal Its nature only to a consciousness that is responsive. The Ātman can walk only into a House that is empty. A house that is full has no room for the Ātman. But very often a house may be empty and yet utterly cold indicating by its coldness that none would be welcome in it. The house must needs be empty—and yet its emptiness must have an imperceptible warmth in it. Otherwise its empty space would be frightening. Though empty it will remain haunted and a haunted house is surely not an inviting place. What gives coldness to an empty house? It is the house that had to be discarded that is empty and yet cold. Those who had to discard the house are still present there imperceptibly. It is their imperceptible presence which makes the house unwelcome—it is this which renders its space haunted and therefore frightening. The house of human consciousness is rarely empty, and even when it is, its emptiness has the frightening look of coldness. Who would enter such a house? How can the Ātman reveal Itself in such a house? But what makes the house of human consciousness empty and yet cold? It is the conscious effort of making the house empty that imparts to it this coldness. A man who makes a conscious attempt at creating silence may achieve an emptiness but it is the emptiness that is contaminated by a coldness. That house has no warmth in it. It is an emptiness with a motive—and it is the presence of this motive which drives away every one even when the house is completely empty. It is the motive which continues to haunt the empty space. And so Yama says to Naciketā that the Ātman cannot be attained by any conscious effort on the part of man. It is attained by him alone whom the Ātman chooses—and the Ātman does not choose the mind that has been made empty—it chooses only the mind that has become empty. The mind that has been made silent is a haunted mind even though empty—but the mind that has become silent is a house where the Ātman is welcome, for it is warm even though empty. It is in such a house that the Ātman reveals its own nature.

Yama says to Naciketā that "when Ātman manifests Itself, man becomes free from the jaws of death." The secret of Death is communicated by the Ātman—but such communication requires a consciousness that is utterly pure, empty, and yet unhaunted by the imperceptible presence of the tenant It is only when the tenant leaves no mark of himself behind that the house of human consciousness can have emptiness with a warmth and a vitality in it. Into such a house the Ātman arrives—and where Immortality arrives, how can the fear of death remain? Yama says:

> The Ātman is beyond sound and form, without touch, and taste, and smell. It is eternal, unchangeable—and without beginning or end.

That which is without beginning or end is obviously Timeless and therefore Eternal. Immortality signifies eternity, not endless continuity. When the Ātman reveals its own nature then death is divested of all its fearsomeness—for here Śiva, the Destroyer becomes Śiva, the Naṭarāja—he who expresses himself in a Cosmic Dance of exquisite beauty.

Yama elaborates this theme of Ātman further and

says to Naciketā that the Ātman can be seen only by those who have "subtle and one pointed insight". He says that he who wants to see the Ātman must have a mind that is very sharp and alert—the mind capable of seeing the subtlest of things. A mind that is sharp and logical can see even the subtlest of thoughts, expressed on any subject. Such a sharp mind can immediately notice even subtle flaws in the logic of things. Nothing goes unnoticed by such a subtle mind. But Yama says that the mind has to be subtle but at the same time one-pointed. A sharp mind has a tendency to move fast and move endlessly. It has wide sweeps in which it seeks to cover a vast variety of subjects. It is a mind which has movement, but no pause. It knows Infinite Motion but does not know Infinite Rest. Yama says the mind which is sharp must also be at the same time one-pointed. Even in the midst of movement it must be able to rest. One-pointedness is a condition of rest. It is a condition where the mind can probe into the depths even as the sharp mind is able to encompass an ever-widening surface. The mind must have breadth as well as depth—it is such a subtle and one-pointed insight which alone can bring man to the perception of the Ātman.

Yama gives further instruction to Naciketā regarding the Ātman which, as he says, holds the key to the Secret of Death. Yama says that one's own life with its various avocations may be described as a Chariot. To this chariot are tied several horses—and these are the senses. The horses are strong and lively—they have to be kept in check. It is the mind which constitutes the reins controlling the horses. And the reins are held by Intelligence or Buddhi for that is the charioteer. And inside the chariot sits the Lord and Master of the chariot, the Ātman. It is obvious that the Master occupies his seat in the chariot only when the charioteer holds the reins. But very often our chariot is without a charioteer and so the horses are running away with the reins. In such a condition the chariot remains unoccupied, for how can the Master occupy it when there is none to hold the reins? Our chariot of life moves aimlessly, carried away by the horses. The mind too seems to be running away with the senses. Unless the charioteer is installed, unless Buddhi or Intelligence takes the reins in its hands, the chariot cannot move steadily, doing its appointed task. It is only the charioteer who will invite the Master to occupy his seat. It is only when Buddhi or Intelligence invites that the Ātman will come. It is said that Ātman is attained alone by him whom It chooses. Ātman chooses to enter the chariot where Buddhi or Intelligence controls the reins by which the chariot moves. In other words, Ātman enters the house where the mind is completely under the control of Buddhi. When the Buddhi holds the reins it is neither too tight nor is it too loose. If it is too tight, the horses would be suffocated in their movements—but if it is too loose the horses would start bolting, carrying away the reins and the chariot too.

In all religious and moral disciplines the most difficult question is the control of the mind. In matters of spiritual realization too it is mind which constitutes the biggest problem. It is the agitated mind which prevents the perception of the Ātman It is the veils projected by the mind which hide the Face of Ātman Yama gives to Naciketā intensely practical instruction about mind-control. He says:

> The wise should restrain speech in mind, and mind in the intelligence.

How can speech be controlled by speech and mind by mind? And yet this is exactly what man does through various moral and religious disciplines. When speech tries to control speech, there is frustration, or at best it results in some modification with reference to the pattern of speech. When speech tries to control speech then there may be alternating moments of speech and silence —but such silence only becomes an excuse for storing up calculated speech into which one bursts out when the so-called silence is over. Control of Speech by speech can result only in the modification of the patterns of speech; there can be no fundamental transformation. Such control only mounts up tension and ends up in frustration. Much more is this the case when mind is sought to be controlled by mind. How can mind control the mind? For such control man creates an artificial entity called the Higher Mind and through that he wishes to control what he calls the Lower Mind. After all mind is mind, whether you call it Higher or Lower. How can one part of the mind control the other part when mind does not lend itself to compartmentalization. A compartmentalized approach only seeks to keep the controller and the controlled in two distinct and water-tight compartments. But here the controller can do nothing else but keep a constant watch over the controlled lest it come out of its cage. All efforts to control the lower mind with the higher mind are frustrating and produce strains and tensions for the man who adopts such discipline. It is possible that sometimes the Higher and the Lower may come to a temporary truce where the lower agrees to change its behaviour pattern so as to appear more respectable. Such an adjustment may last for some time, it may become even a new habit of the lower mind. But a change by the adoption of new habit is no change at all—it is only a change of outer garment. Yama says, a wise man controls speech in mind and mind in the Intelligence. It is quite obvious that speech can be effectively controlled only when mind is silent. A chattering mind and a silence of words ill go together. If the mind is allowed to chatter then any effort that may be made for the control of speech would be fruitless. Similarly any effort to silence the mind with the effort of the mind is utterly frustrating. It can never be done. Control of mind, which means the cessation of the movement of the mind, can never come about by a conscious effort. An enforced silence makes the mind even more restless. The mind comes to silence and in that state quietly hands over the reins of control to the Intelligence or Buddhi. Just as effort to control speech by speech results in tension similarly control of mind with mind produces nothing but strain. When the efforts of the mind drop away then it is that Buddhi holds the reins —neither too tightly nor too loosely. Mind by itself is prone to go to extremes—these extremes are its opposites.

It moves from one opposite to another—from one extreme to the other. But the mind which has come under the influence of Buddhi moves, without any tension, along the Middle Way. When the mind moves along the Middle Way then the Charioteer has the reins in his hands, the reins by which he keeps the horses under check. When this happens, the Lord and Master of the Chariot, the Ātman, occupies his seat in the chariot. With the Ātman seated in the Chariot, there is a grace and dignity in its movement—for it glides through space unaware of any friction whatsoever. Yama says to Naciketā, the way to the Ātman is:

> ...a razor-edged path, hard to tread and difficult to cross.

The Middle Way is indeed the razor-edged path. To keep oneself on the thin edge of the razor is a hard accomplishment. Needless to say any wavering would throw the man on either side. Even a slight movement of the mind would carry the aspirant into the extremes either of the right or of the left. The mind cannot tread the Middle Way by its own efforts. Such a way would be only a compromise between the two opposites. But the Middle Way is not a compromise between two extremes—it is not a little of indulgence and a little of denial that makes the Middle Way. The Middle Way is that where indulgence and denial are not. It is in the complete negation both of indulgence and denial that the Middle Way is trodden. But the mind knows only indulgence and denial or a compromise between the two which it calls a synthesis between the two opposites. The mind cannot tread the middle way by its conscious efforts—it is only when the efforts of the mind cease and the reins are held by Intelligence or Buddhi that the Middle Way is trodden. It is razor-edged because it is very thin—it is like a mathematical line which has length but no breadth. It cannot be conceived of by the mind. The Ātman is to be found on the Middle Way—the Way not known to the mind, but the Way along which the mind moves when it is illumined and guided by Intelligence or Buddhi. Yama asks Naciketā to move along the Middle Way if he desires to know the Secret of Death, if he wants to commune with the Great Beyond.

The Secret of Death cannot be held by the Mind—for it is with the Ātman, and the Ātman is intangible. Yama says that those who are devoid of wisdom try to hold the Intangible as if it were tangible. What is held by the unwise is not the self—but the not-self. What the mind can hold is not the Ātman—it is the negation of the Ātman. The Secret of Death that is held by the mind is only an after-death condition—it is not the meaning of death. For the mind holds within its grasp only continuity and its modifications—that which is discontinuous ever escapes from the net of the mind. And the Secret of Death is in the discontinuous moment—not in the continuity of time. Yama says:

> Children pursue outer pleasures and fall into the net of widespread death; but calm souls, having known what is unshakable Immortality, do not covet any uncertain thing in the world.

Here Yama says clearly to Naciketā that those who seek security in the tangible things of life are for ever caught in the net of widespread death. To be caught in the net of death is to be inwardly destroyed. They enter the realm of utter insecurity. They come under the sway of death—they have no sway over it. They are crushed again and again for the net of death is widespread. He who is caught in it moves to frustrations caused by insecurity. But, Yama says, the wise one, having probed the depths of discontinuity, and known, in the moment of death the unshakable truth of Immortality, does not attempt to commune with the Intangible by grasping the tangible. He has found his true security in the realm of the Intangible—he is not caught in the insecurities of the tangible. The security of the Intangible is indeed the perception of the Ātman.

One may ask a question—and rightly—that Naciketā had asked Yama to grant the third boon. What has happened to this boon? Has Yama forgotten about it? Has he led Naciketā into disgressions so that the latter may forget about his boon? All the discussion with which

Yama was concerned so far was only to the end of bringing Naciketā to the point where his boon is granted. Yama asks Naciketā one pertinent question which is: "Is there anything that remains unknown to Ātman?" If there is nothing unknown to Ātman then surely the Secret of Death is also with the Ātman. If that be the case, Yama says to his disciple: "I grant your third boon and tell you to find the Ātman, for in finding the Ātman you will know the Secret of Death." Yama tells Naciketā:

> It is through Ātman that one perceives all objects in sleep or in waking state. Having realized the vast, all-pervading Ātman, the wise man feeleth no fear.

The waking and sleep conditions in the above verse refer to the physical and non-physical existences. Yama says all perception whether at the physical or at the non-physical level is due to Ātman. It is the omnipresence of Ātman that makes perception possible. The very perception of objects is possible because of the imperceptible presence of Ātman. If one knows the Intangible, ever present in the tangible then one is completely free from fear of death and consequent insecurity. It is because the Intangible is there that the tangible becomes perceivable. The very existence of the tangible is due to the Intangible. Yama says:

> What is here, the same is there—and what is there, the same is here. He goes from death to death who sees the separation between the two.

The Intangible is equally here as there. There is no difference between the "here" and the "there" so far as the Intangible is concerned. But he who sees the tangible here and the loss of the tangible there knows not what death is. Such a man goes from death to death for he has not known the meaning of death. He who sees only the tangible in the existing things is for ever caught under the sway of death. Even when alive he is under the sway of death. But he who has seen the Intangible even when alive sees the Intangible in death too, nay, he sees the Intangible in all its glory. The difference between "here" and "there" arises only when in the "here" the tangible is seen and in the "there" the absence of the tangible. But to see the Intangible here is to step out of the sphere of mind's continuity. He who can do this knows death in the midst of living. He who does not see the Intangible in the tangible goes again and again to the mansion of death —but returns empty handed, not having found the meaning of death. He seeks in vain for the tangible in the realm of death. But he who while alive knows the tangible and also communes with the Intangible—he knows both life and death. Even while alive he has found the meaning of death.

Yama tells Naciketā that the boon which he had asked is being given to him. In several verses of the Katha Upanishad, Yama declares: "This in truth is that", meaning thereby that the granting of the boon is done by indicating where the Secret of Death can be found. In verse after verse, he has stated that it is the Ātman that holds this secret, and so it is by communing with the Ātman that Naciketā can find the Great Beyond. Again Yama says:

> Like a Flame without smoke, the size of a thumb, is the Ātman —the Lord of the Past and the Future, the same both today and tomorrow.

Here the Ātman is described as Flame without smoke —what does this indicate? When does smoke arise in the flame? Obviously when there are impurities. So long as the impurities last so long there must remain smoke. But Ātman is utterly pure and incorruptible and so it signifies Flame without smoke. Yama says that the Ātman is the Lord of the Past and the Future—this is so because it transcends the time-process. It is immanent in time and yet is beyond time. Time symbolises change but Ātman remains changeless even in the midst of change. Yama declares this by saying that the Ātman is "the same both today and tomorrow." Because It is changeless, It is the initiator of all changes. Ātman is not static, It is indeed the immutable centre of endless mobility. Yama says no Naciketā — this indeed is the Secret which he had asked for in his third boon. To know the Ātman —the changeless in the midst of change—this alone is the discovery of that Secret, the knowledge of the Great Beyond.

In Naciketā, Yama has found a worthy disciple and so the Teacher explains to him the theme of the Ātman again and again showing him different facets of the same truth. He asks him:

> When the soul identified with the body and dwelling in it, is torn away from the body, is freed from it, what then remains? This verily is That.

When the life-giving force of the body withdraws, what is it that is left behind? Obviously that which remains is the dead body—the body devoid of life. But then where is Life? It has suddenly disappeared, beyond the grasp of man. This moment the body was pulsating with life, and the next moment it lies like a log of wood, unable to move or breathe. And yet that which gave movement and breath eludes the grasp of man. Yama says that this Intangible *something* which renders the body alive or dead is indeed that Ātman into whose keeping is the secret of life and death. There are no two secrets—one for life and the other for death. There is just one secret which explains the phenomenon both of life as well as death. It is the Intangible whose association or withdrawal determines life or death. Existence and non-existence both depend upon the Intangible. Naciketā had asked a question to Yama in the very beginning which said: "Please tell me what is in the moment of death: Is there existence or non-existence?" Why did not Yama immediately reply saying "yes" or "no"? How could Yama give any reply? For to say that there is existence would be wrong—but equally wrong would it be to say that there is non-existence. That which vitalizes the body, but that which is not caught when the body dies—it is this which verily holds the secret of life and death. Yama further explains this to Naciketā in the following verse:

> No moral ever lives by Prāṇa, which goes up, nor by apāna which goes down. Men live by something different on which both these depend.

Yama says that the life-giving force which vitalizes the body is not even Prāṇa—whether outgoing or incoming. He says that both these vital breaths depend for their movement on *something* else—and without this *something,* even breathing would not be possible. What causes the death of the body? Is it the withdrawal of Prāṇa? Yama says it is not so. For even the withdrawal of Prāṇa is dependent upon something—that something he describes as Ātman which vitalizes the body and yet is not in the body. If it were in the body, one would be able to find it when the body dies—and yet one cannot say that it is beyond the body, for, if It is, then how does the body get vitalized? In the body and yet not in it such is the paradox of the Ātman. He who can resolve it knows the secret of death and knows also the meaning of life. But the resolution of the paradox must occur in the split-second of the actual moment of death. The Ātman is realized only in a moment—for that which is Timeless cannot be known in the extension of time. It is the Timeless moment which indeed is the moment of death. It is here that the paradox of existence and non-existence is resolved. It is here that the Intangible which is the cause both of existence and non-existence is perceived. It is an experience which comes in the wink of an eye. It is sudden and instantaneous. It is in Sudden Awakening that man knows the secret of death and the meaning of life. But man does not for ever live in that moment; the moment must needs be momentary—but man returns to the field of Time. Out of non-existence comes a fresh existence. Out of the Timeless moment emerges a fresh journey into Time. But what is the nature of this journey? Yama says:

> Men may go again into the womb of the mother thus obtaining a fresh body—or he may go into the region of the Imperishable.

Yama says that ordinarily man returns to fresh birth after death. But there is also the possibility of man going to the region of the Imperishable and thus be free from the necessity of rebirth. Here in this verse the word *Sthāṇu* is used. And many commentators have interpreted this to mean that man may take birth as a plant or as the trunk of a tree. This seems meaningless. There was no reason for Yama to enumerate the details of re-birth—and if so, why should he mention only trees—there are so many other objects and categories of existences, that, a mere mention of plant seems completely out of place. But why should *sthāṇu* be interpreted as the trunk of a tree? *Sthāṇu* really means Firm or Motionless. Yama has been explaining to Naciketā the nature of the Ātman which is Changeless and Imperishable. Men who are rooted in the Changeless and the Imperishable are beyond the necessity of re-birth—they are free from the chain of birth and death. There are many who are governed by the necessities of re-birth—but there are some who have gone beyond this necessity. They may take birth but they are not under any compulsion or necessity. Yama here speaks of two categories of men who have come to death showing forth utterly different tendencies. All come to death but from death some return under the necessity of rebirth—while there are others who are free from such a necessity. They have conquered death and therefore have conquered life as well.

Yama anticipates the doubt that may have arisen in the mind of his disciple by this reply, and so like a true Teacher he formulates the doubt and gives a clarification of that doubt. Yama formulates the question of Naciketā, which is: "Why should there be this difference in those who emerge out of the moment of death, so that some are compelled to be reborn and others pass beyond the necessity of rebirth"? Yama here gives a very significant reply. For he says:

> He who knows not Ātman in this life, before the body passes away, must be born again in new worlds and new creations.

Why is there a necessity for rebirth for some and not for others? Yama says he who knows Ātman while living knows the meaning of the manifest and also the secret of the Unmanifest. Even while alive he knows what death implies. He who perceives the Intangible even in the tangible, he knows death in the midst of life. For such people physical death is only an incident among many incidents for they have known both death and renewal prior to the withering of the body. Without physical death they know how to be reborn. He who knows death and renewal from moment to moment, for him physical death has no lesson to teach. Such a person has gone beyond the sway of death. But those who have not known death while living have to return again and again from the doorstep of death. Even in physical death they are afraid to enter the mansion of Death. Even in physical death they cling to existence—and so to existence they are compelled to return. In such compulsion there is the fear of death and so there is no joy of living. They move between the frustration of living and the fear of death. Unable to leave their hold on the existence—they are afraid to enter the realm of non-existence. But without the experience of non-existence, existence itself becomes mere dust and ashes in the mouth of one who is compelled to live and therefore compelled to die. Such a man knows not freedom beyond compulsions of living. How can one live creatively under compulsions? How can the joys of life be experienced when one is under the compulsions of death?

If by knowing the Ātman while alive one conquers death, then how is this Ātman to be known? Naciketā asks a very pertinent question to Yama. He says:

> The wise say that the Ātman cannot even be indicated by saying It is this—then how am I to know It? Does It shine by Itself or does It shine by a reflected light?

If Ātman shines with a reflected light then surely It will be dependent upon something else. If It shines with Its own light then why can It not be pointed out? Surely that which shines with Its own light can easily be pointed out, for it has no moments of darkness in which It is not seen. Why is then the Ātman so intangible—so elusive that It cannot even be pointed out? Yama says:

> In the land of the Ātman, sun shines not, nor the moon, nor the stars, lightnings shine not there—much less the earthly fire. From Its light all these give light—and Its radiance illumines all creation.

Yama says the Ātman is self-luminous. Its light is not dependent upon anything or anyone. In fact it is the light of the Ātman that illumines everything—it is the light of the Ātman that makes all things visible. But if Ātman is self-luminous then why can it not be seen? Is there no means by which It can be perceived? Yama says:

> In a consciousness that is pure and clear, as in a mirror, can it be seen in this life; but in the regions of the departed only as a resemblance of dreams—or as a reflection in the trembling waters.

May we ask—what is this consciousness pure and clear like a mirror? A mirror clings to nothing and so is able to reflect everything—the purity of the mirror is gone when it attempts to possess any particular image. In fact, in such possession the mirror ceases to be a mirror. Similarly a consciousness which clings to nothing is pure and clear. In such consciousness is reflected the image of the Ātman without any distortion whatsoever. The face of the Ātman can be seen in the consciousness that is pure and clear. But what does the non-clinging on the part of consciousness mean? It is a consciousness which, while living, enters the House of Death. Before entering the house of death all metals and valuables, all possessions have to be discarded—for death demands that man must come alone, unarmed and undefended, into the mansion of Yama. But the question is: Does man leave the possessions behind or are they snatched away from him? Have they dropped away or have they been forcibly taken away? When possessions drop away just as reflections drop away from a mirror then is the consciousness rendered pure and clear. It is in this state of the dropping away of possessions that the consciousness, while alive, experiences the state of death. But in this state there is no disturbance, no hankering after what has gone. For the tangible does not cling to such a consciousness. This pure consciousness knows with clarity the tangible—and yet the tangible does not remain clung to it. The tangible comes and goes leaving the surface of consciousness pure and clear like a mirror. But normally man does not experience the dropping away of possessions—he knows only the snatching away of possessions. It is in this condition that he goes to the realm of death. He carries into this realm the remembrances of what has been snatched away—and so the reflection of the Ātman is like a reflection on trembling waters. It is not in the land of the departed that the secret of death is understood. It is only in the land of the living that one can know it. When the tangible comes and goes, but has no dwelling place in the consciousness of man, then in that pure and clear state, man sees the reflection of the Ātman. When no continuity to the tangible is given then in that consciousness the experience of discontinuity enters. The capacity of seeing the tangible and yet the wisdom of not holding on to it—this is what is meant as the experience of death even when alive. It is in this experience that man cries out that he knows—and all that one can say about the Ātman is—IT IS. No more can one say about it. Yama says:

> This steadiness of consciousness is called Yoga. One should be alert and vigilant—for Yoga comes and goes.

The steadiness of consciousness cannot be known in terms of continuity—it comes in a momentary flash. Yoga is not a continuity—it is essentially an experience of discontinuity. The above verse says—Yoga comes and goes—it cannot be fixed in a framework of continuity. But the momentary flashes of Yoga can be known by one who is vigilant. But vigilant of what? He has to be vigilant to see that nothing clings to consciousness—he has to see that the consciousness does not give any continuity to an experience. The continuity of experience is the possession of consciousness. When this happens, the mirror is no longer a mirror. The vision of the Ātman is gone—he may go to the realm of death but returns without knowing the secret of death.

Yama sums up the whole teaching of the Kaṭha Upanishad by saying:

> When all desires that cling to the heart disappear, then a mortal becomes immortal. This is the sacred teaching. When all ties that bind the heart are loosened, then a mortal becomes immortal. This is the sacred teaching.

Yama here shows the path of deathlessness to Naciketā and speaks to him of experience without accumulation. He does not ask him to kill all desires—he only says that the clinging of desires must go. The clinging is the giving of continuity. So long as there is no continuity given to desires, there is no clouding of vision. Let desires come and go—for that indeed is the state of living. But woe unto him who gives a dwelling place, a continuity, to this stream of desires. Once that is done, the consciousness serves no longer as a mirror. How can there be a perception of the Eternal and the Imperishable where the mind is closed due to the possessions to which it clings? A continuity to experience is given by thought —and so it is the mind free from all thoughts that alone knows what the Vision of the Ātman is. But a mind free from thoughts is a momentary experience—it is only in that moment that the Flash of the Eternal comes. Death is a momentary experience—but it is in that moment of death that Immortality resides. Yama asks Naciketā to be aware of that Moment of Death—then like a flash of lightning he will know the secret of death and the meaning of the Great Beyond.

Yama has granted the third boon of Naciketā —and Naciketā emerges from the Mansion of Death as a Great Conqueror—for he has conquered death—for even while alive he has entered the Palace of Death. When the tangible has dropped away he has seen the unsurpassing beauty of the Intangible—when the Manifest has voluntarily been left behind then the Vision of the Unmanifest has been vouchsafed to him in all its majesty. It is the man who knows how to die constantly, he alone knows the secret of Immortality—this is the life-giving message given by the Lord of Death to all inquirers who wish to know the meaning of death and thereby the significance of life itself.

IV

THE FIRE OF CREATION

Max Muller, the great European scholar has said about the Upanishads that they are "the sources of the Vedānta philosophy, a system in which human speculation seems to have reached its very acme. They are to me like the light of the morning, like the pure air of the mountains—so simple, so true, if once understood". Some of the modern thinkers of the West have said that Vedānta is the only scientific approach to religion which men and women of this civilization can accept. It may be asked: Does Vedānta display a scientific approach? What, after all, is a scientific approach? Its fundamental characteristic is—an objective perception of things. Science endeavours to look at all things from the standpoint of unbiassed objectivity. It has, however, to be understood that in all perceptions two agencies are involved—the senses and the mind. A mere sensorial impact is not perception. It is only when the mind puts its signature on sensorial impacts that the act of perception is completed. Now both these factors of perception have their limitations. These limitations arise out of their selectivity. In all acts of perception there is first the selectivity of the senses, and then the selectivity of the mind. It is quite obvious that a perfectly objective perception is not possible so long as these selective processes continue. Now science is concerned with the gathering of facts. Its propositions and hypotheses rest on the facts which it has been able to gather. But how can one be sure of the facts one has collected so long as the element of selection is there? It is quite possible that in the very process of gathering facts, the senses and the mind may be leaving out many things that may be of importance in arriving at right conclusions. Now we saw that science is concerned with unbiassed objective perception of things. In this task science endeavours to eliminate the selectivity of the senses by widening the range of sensorial response. Through telescopes and microscopes and many other devices, it breaks down the limitations of the senses. Through these instruments science is able to gather more facts than it would have been able to do if it had depended only on the information brought by the unaided senses. But this is only one part of the problem of objective perception. The second and the more difficult part is the mind and its selectivity. The selectivity of the mind functions through its process of interpretation. And the mind functions so fast that before we know the facts we are given an interpretation of those facts! Thus the mind by its selectivity gives a bias to our perception. And so unless the selectivity of the mind is effectively eliminated there can be no hope of achieving that objectivity of perception which is the aim of science. Now, the Upanishads are fundamentally concerned with the problem of eliminating the selective interpretation of the mind. Its main thesis is that for knowing the object, one must first know the subject. Unless the knower is known there can be no objective perception of the known. So long as the subject projects itself into the act of perception so long there cannot be an unbiassed perception of the object. Thus the Upanishads carry the scientific process futher. The Upanishadic philosophy is truly an objective philosophy, for, it enables us to see objects as they are without the interfering processes of the mind. When the interference of the subject is eliminated then the obiect can be seen as it is. The Upanishads have declared that the entire world is pervaded by Brahman or Reality—but we cannot see It because mind introduces a bias in our very act of perception.

This scientific approach of Vedānta is nowhere seen more clearly than in the Praśna Upanishad where the teacher and the students are engaged in a truly scientific inquiry into the nature of things. This Upanishad leads the inquirer from the known to the Unknown, from the manifest to the Unmanifest, from the grossly material to the supremely Spiritual.

It seems once upon a time six spiritual aspirants were desirous of knowing the true nature of things. They were in search of a teacher who would impart this teaching to them. They at last found one such teacher by the name Pippalāda. These six aspirants placed their problem before him seeking knowledge and understanding. But Pippalāda was no ordinary teacher. He said to them:

> Remain here for another year with Austerity, Purity and Faith. Ask then anything you desire, and, if I know I will tell you what you want to know.

Why did the teacher ask the aspirants to wait another year before putting their questions to him? He did not ask them to wait for one year in order to know the answers—he asked them to wait for the formulation of their questions. It is true that when a question is not properly formulated, its real answer cannot be found. In any serious inquiry, the formulation of a question is of utmost importance. The answer to a question depends upon how the question has been put. If the question is wrongly formulated then the answer, too, is bound to be wrong. Besides, a question that is superficially asked receives an answer which is equally superficial.

And so the Teacher tells these six aspirants to spend another year at the end of which they may ask whatever questions they wish to ask. But how will these students become more qualified to ask questions after spending one more year in the āśrama of the teacher? How will they be better prepared because of a passage of time? Let us remember that the teacher asked the students to wait for another year—but such waiting was not to be done in idleness. This waiting had to be by austerity, purity and faith. If a question is meant to be a serious inquiry then those who intend to embark upon that journey must have plenty of energy. Without such energy the arduous journey to the Land of Truth cannot be undertaken. Most people are unable to undertake such a journey because they have no energy—their energies are locked up in numerous things—in various pre-occupations. And so the teacher asked his students to prepare themselves for asking questions and thereby undertake a journey to Truth by *Tapa* or Austerity, by *Brahmacarya* or Purity and by Śraddhā or faith. The question may arise—will the students be able to undertake the spiritual journey with required energy by following the above practice of *Tapa*, *Brahmacarya* and *Śraddhā?*

Even the asking of a question needs a qualification is something strange which Pippalāda. has indicated here in the very beginning of the Praśna Upanishad. Very often our questions may be serious—but have they been asked with seriousness? Pippalāda. knew that the six aspirants would ask serious questions—that is, questions pertaining to serious topics—but he wanted the students to realize that it is not enough that the topics are serious—there must be a seriousness with which these questions should be asked. Not infrequently, we ask a question on a serious topic but then sit back comfortably to get an answer which is either accepted or rejected. To sit back for an answer is to display a superficial mind. And so very often a topic may be serious and yet the question based on that topic may come from a very superficial mind. To ask a serious question without any seriousness—this is what many so-called inquirers do. To bring home this fact to the six disciples, Pippalāda, says in the above verse that the aspirants may put their questions to him after one year—and that "if I know I will answer your questions." The teacher does not say that he will give answers—he only says that if he knows the answers to their questions then he will give, otherwise not. Here the teacher shows an intellectual honesty of the highest order. He does not pretend to know everything. But the above statement contains more than the intellectual honesty of the teacher. It indicates that there are no set answers to questions of deep spiritual inquiry. If there were set answers the teacher would have given them immediately instead of asking the students to wait for one year. If there are no set answers then from where are the answers found?

The answers to deep spiritual inquiry are to be found in the questions themselves. The solution of a problem is not away from the problem—it is in the problem itself. But to find an answer contained in the question, it is of the highest importance that the question be formulated aright. To find an answer, one has therefore to examine the whole process of questioning. If one knows how to put a question then one is sure to find an answer—and a right answer. To a mathematical problem there is a set answer which one can look up—but to a psychological question there is no set answer. In a psychological question the answer is in the question. And to find this answer the entire process of questioning needs to be examined. It is the need to explore the very process of questioning which is indicated in this verse of the Praśna Upanishad.

Pippalāda knew that his disciples would be able to put questions on serious subjects—but he was not sure whether they were capable of exploring the very process of questioning without which no deep understanding can ever come. That is why he suggested to the disciples that they should wait for a year and during that period prepare themselves by *Tapa* or austerity, *Brahmacarya* or purity and *Śraddhā* or faith. Now what is Tapa or Austerity? It is a process by which the energy of the mind is released from the entanglements of the non-essentials. For a serious inquiry man needs much energy—particularly the energy of the mind. Science tells us that energy is indestructible. This means that man does have energy but it is locked up somewhere, and that it can become available to him for his journey into the Land of the Real. And the release of energy is the first problem that man must face. The teacher of the Praśna Upanishad asks his pupils to free this energy from the non-essentials in which it is entangled. To do this is to engage oneself in *Tapa* or Austerity. *Tapa* is the process of sorting out the essentials and the non-essentials. It is a denial of the non-essentials. This denial brings about a release of energy. With the release of energy man faces a fresh problem and that is concerning the conservation of energy. He must see that the energy released by *Tapa* is not frittered away, but is conserved. Now *Brahmacarya* is indeed the conservation of energy. The energy released from the non-essentials may get involved in what the human mind regards as essential or good. After all man determines the essential and the non-essential only by the categorization of the mind. Surely mind must first be released from what it regards as non-essential, for, it gets involved in it by habit and tradition. But with the denial of the non-essentials, mind is sure to get entangled in the delights of the essential—what it regards as essential. And therefore the energy released by *tapa* has to be conserved by *Brahmacarya*. But what is the condition of the mind when the non-essentials are denied and when the essentials are not indulged in?

It is a condition where the mind stands still—for it has nowhere to go—when there is a denial of both good and bad, of both essential and non-essential, then it must come to rest. Its field of knowledge is the essential and the non-essential—when both are negated it stands face to face with the Unknown. And it is in the presence of the Unknown that real Faith or *Śraddhā* is born. A faith in the known is no faith at all—it is only loyalty. But loyalty and faith are poles asunder. One is moved by motive, the other is motiveless. It is only the man of faith who can undertake a journey into the Unknown. Truth cannot be sought. The mind that seeks Truth only moves in the realm of the familiar—and describes the familiar as Truth. When the land of the familiar is completely neglected then the Unfamiliar announces the arrival of Truth. The man of faith is not a sentimental being—on the contrary, he is one who has tremendous strength and courage. For what greater courage can there be than to stand in front of the Unknown?

The teacher of the Praśna Upanishad has indicated to the disciples a preparation by which, having negated the known through *tapa* and *brahmacarya*, they come face to face with the Unknown. When with Faith they stand before the Unknown then are they ready to ask questions—for then their questions themselves will contain the answers. It is when Faith is born that the teacher can help his pupils to examine the very process of questioning—for in that process lies the answers to all questions.

The Praśna Upanishad says that the students did as they were asked and so after the completion of the required period, one of the disciples, by the name Kabandhī Kātyāyana, approached the Master and said: "Master, whence came all created beings?" Here the disciple asks about the origin of creation—from where did creation originate. He inquires about the beginnings of the created world. The Teacher replies:

> In the beginning, Prajāpati, the Creator, longed for the joy of creation. He remained in meditation, and then came Rayi, matter, prāṇa, Life. "These two", thought He. "will produce beings for me."

The Prajāpati who is described as the Creator in the above verse is obviously the Cosmic Mind. The Teacher says that Prajāpati remainded in meditation and then came into existence matter and life. The whole creation obviously is described as the thought-projection of the Cosmic Mind. Sir James Jeans, the great scientific thinker, has described the Universe as a Great Thought. The above statement of the Upanishad speaks of the creation having come into existence through meditation. But the questioner wants to know how did the creation continue—how did the variety of beings come into existence? What was it that the Creator created by which a continuity of created things was maintained? The Teacher clearly states that Prajāpati created a duality—and the duality was the very source of continuity. Man too creates his world with Thought and maintains it with duality. Thought is intensely constructive when rightly used although thought cannot bring into existence anything new. Thought can bring into existence new patterns and structures—but it cannot put into them a new content. From where did Prajāpati bring the content with which to fill the structure of creation? We shall come to that question when we proceed with the discussion initiated in the Praśna Upanishad. With reference to the first question we are concerned only with the structure of things and the factors which give continuity to that structure. Pippalāda says that Prajāpati created a duality of Matter and Life, of *Rayi* and *Prāṇa*. The creation moves and maintains its continuity by an interaction of the two dual principles. The Teacher then enlarges upon the theme of duality by which the manifested world is maintained. He says:

> The sun is life and the moon is matter. All that has form, solid or subtle, is matter, therefore form is matter.

The Teacher makes this point of duality very clear lest his disciples carry away confusion of thinking on the subject. He speaks of duality present at every level in the manifested universe—for manifestation without duality is inconceivable. He says that sun is life and moon is matter. What is the significance of this? In this illustration he indicates that matter is dependent upon life even as moon is dependant upon the sun. The sun shines with its own light—but the moon receives its light from the sun. He says that matter derives its existence from life—a statement which physical science totally rejected in the 19th Century but the truth of which is being more and more recognised by progressive scientific thinkers of today. This subject of matter depending upon life for its existence is taken up for further scrutiny in the Second question of this Upanishad. There is, however, one statement in the above verse which needs to be seriously noted. The Teacher says that all forms, whether solid or subtle, constitute matter. Hindu religion and philosophy have talked of subtler planes of existence—they have gone upto the Buddhic and the Ātmic planes. The Teacher of this Upanishad says that the structure of even the subtlest plane is just matter. And so he indicates that matter may exist in various states—from the grossest to the subtlest. Just because a man travels into invisible planes thereby he does not transcend the realm of matter. The Praśna Upanishad not only says that matter can exist in different states—from the gross to the subtle. It says that Form itself is Matter. From this standpoint the form of thought or the form of sound is just matter—nothing more. A thought-form, however beautiful it may be, is just matter. A form, just because it is subtle, does not become Life—it remains matter. Such is the vast concept of matter which the Praśna Upanishad gives while describing the story of creation. There is a diversity of forms and there is a variety of states in which Matter is to be seen—but once again all matter is dependent upon life. It is through the interaction of Life and Matter that a continuity of manifestation is maintained.

Elaborating this theme of Life and Matter, the Teacher says that Creation is synonymous with time, for time is the field in which creation continues. It is Time which gives a continuity to creation. Time is obviously a movement in duality. Where there is no duality, there time too is not. A movement between the points of duality is indeed the stream of time. And so when the Creator created duality, He thereby brought into existence the movement of Time. The **Praśna** Upanishad says:

> The Lord of Creation is in truth the time of the year.

The Teacher takes the first measure of time as a year, the time taken by the earth to go round the Sun once. The mind which creates its own world also brings into existence a time-scale in which creation carries on its activities. But the teacher is concerned in the first question with the problem of Duality which is the very basis of Creation. And so he indicates the expression of duality everywhere. Explaining this he says that even the year, a measure of time, has two paths: The "Way of the South and the Way of the North." This is commonly understood as the Sun moving northwards and the Sun moving southwards. The characteristics of this movement are described by the Teacher in terms of duality—the one leading to good results and the other leading to evil conditions. To the inquiry of the disciple about the continuity of creation, the teacher has pointed to the principle of Duality existing at all levels of manifestation. He says that even if we take as a measure of time only a month, even then this principle of duality is perceived. For, there is the bright fortnight and the dark fortnight—one may be called Life and the other as Matter. The teacher says even if the measure of time is taken as a period of twenty-four hours, even then there is a duality of Day and Night. He says:

> Day is life and night is matter. Those who join in love by day waste life—but they follow the good path, those who join love by night.

Here the Teacher gives a very simple and yet profound explanation of the whole problem of Good and Evil, for, he says that an action performed at the appropriate time must be regarded as good. Needless to say, action has to be understood not merely in terms of pattern, but also in terms of motive or intention. There is a continual interaction between the two points of duality—but each interaction has its emanating point either in Life or in Matter.

It may not be out of place to mention here that the appropriate time in the above verse has not to be understood as the physical expression of time. In fact, the verses of the Praśna Upanishad speaking about Night and Day or about the Dark half and Bright half refer not to physical conditions but psychological states. The duality of manifestation is not physical dualities only—it indicates the principle of duality which is mental or psychological and of which the physical dualities are only gross expressions. The whole manifested world rests on duality, but physical dualities are only the visible aspects of that duality. The Teacher of the Praśna Upanishad has used physical expressions of duality only to illustrate the deeper and psychological manifestations of the dual principle. And so when the above verse says that "those who join in love by day waste life, but those who join love by night, follow the good path", it is to be understood in its psychological and not physical aspect. To join in love by day is a waste of life—why? Because day is a time of many pre-occupations—how can there be love when man is pre-occupied with many things? Love is a total action—the occupied mind knows not what love is. An occupied mind may show forth a pattern of love—but such a pattern has no content of love in it. To join in love by day is indeed a waste of life. Night is indeed the appropriate time for love, but night not in the physical sense. Psychologically night is a condition where mind is free from all its occupations. It is in a state of total surrender—and is that not the "appropriate time" to join in love? The teacher of the Praśna Upanishad rightly says that all actions performed at the "appropriate time" must be regarded as good. Bringing the discussion to a close on this first question, the Teacher tells the students that:

> Those who obey the law of the Lord of Creation, they in turn become creators and like him give birth to a pair.

Man indeed lives in the world of his own creation—he knows not the world of the Creator—for he has superimposed his own world upon the greater world of Prajāpati. And man creates his world by bringing into existence a pair or a duality. The movement between the poles of duality verily maintains this creation. Kabandhī Kātyāyana wanted to know "whence came all created beings". Pippalāda has very clearly indicated that duality is indeed the father-mother of all created things.

Then the second disciple, Bhārgava Vaidarbhī, approached the Teacher and asked him:

> Master, what are the elements that keep the union of being, how many keep burning the lamps of life, and which amongst them is supreme?

Dealing with the first question, the Teacher explained to the disciples the basis of creation—and brought the whole story of creation up to the emergence of the physical body—the body which derives its sustenance from food. In other words, he indicated the creation of the *Annamayakośa* —the physical body. Speaking about the creation of beings, he naturally ended with food—for, food is the basis of physical creation. Without food the duality at the physical level is powerless. Having heard this explanation, the second disciple wants to carry the discussion further. He asks about the forces that keep this physical being united and integrated. He has no doubt understood from the first question that it is duality that brings creation into existence and it is duality that gives it a continuity. But now the student desires to know—what is it that induces the movement of duality whereby creation is kept going? The teacher said that there are five elements—earth, water, fire, air and ether—which hold the body together. The keeping of the bodily organism together is surely due to these five elements—but the body kept together merely by the five elements would remain a house engulfed in darkness. It would be a house devoid of any activity. And so the disciple rightly asks—who keeps this body vibrant with activity?—who keeps burning the lamps of life in this bodily organism? Obviously that which keeps the body moving is the sense organism. It is the senses which keep the light burning. It is the senses that differentiate the living from the dead. The sentient and the insentient derive their distinction from the functioning of the senses. The lamps of bodily organism are kept burning by the senses. But the student has added one more question and that too a very difficult one by asking—who is supreme among these forces that keep the bodily organism united and functioning? Here the Upanishad gives an imaginary episode in which all the senses are pictured as placing their claim for supremacy. Each sense regards itself as supreme and all together declare that without them the body would disintegrate and the lamps would cease to burn. The senses thought, in their mistaken pride that they were supreme and kept the creation going by their unceasing movements. The Upanishad says that in order to remind the senses that they were wrong, Prāṇa or Vitality spoke out thus:

> Do not fall into delusion. It is I who, in my five-fold division keep the union of being: I am its foundation.

But how could the senses in their pride and arrogance accept this? They maintained that they alone were supreme—and not Prāṇa or Vitality as the latter had indicated. Our story says that Prāṇa did not utter a word but started withdrawing. Even a slight movement of withdrawal by Prāṇa was sufficient to make the senses restive. The Praśna Upanishad tells us:

> As when the queen-bee rises all the bees with her arise, and when she comes to rest again then all come again to rest, even so it happened to the senses. They realized that Prāṇa was supreme and made obeisance to it.

This verse gives an apt description of what happens when Prāṇa or Vitality begins to withdraw from the body. How can the senses function when the vitalizing element is not there? The body may remain as a structure with the five elements but its lamps would be extinguished. It is true that the senses keep the lamps burning, but how can the lamps burn if there is no oil? It is Prāṇa which supplies oil to the lamps which the senses keep burning. Just as the whole crowd of bees keep functioning so long as the Queen-bee is present—similarly the senses keep functioning as long as Prāṇa is present. With the withdrawal of Prāṇa the senses disintegrate—the lamps are there but the flame is gone for want of oil. Pippalāda says to his disciples:

> On Prāṇa all things rest as spokes in the centre of the wheel. Prāṇa is the chief bearer of gifts to the gods, the first offering made to the departed. Prāṇa is the poetry of the seers, the truth of the ancient sages.

Prāṇa is described here as a centre of the wheel—it is the axis round which the rim moves. It is Prāṇa that has enabled the seers and the sages to write what they have done to inspire peoples of all ages. But the above verse introduces a strange statement when it says that Prāṇa is "the first offering made to the departed". In this second question the Teacher is leading the students from the gross physical body, the *Annamaya- Kośa* —to the vital body—the *Prāṇamaya-kośa.* The religious tradition says that when the physical body dies the departing life-stream remains in the Vital Body. Thus it is that Prāṇa is the first offering to the departed. The above verse says that Prāṇa is the chief bearer of gifts to the gods. The word used for the gods is *Pitṛ*. It is through the Vital Body that the oblations to the ancestors are carried, for, the Vital Body is a link between the physical and the super-physical.

The Teacher says that the senses would be powerless without Prāṇa or the Vital Breath. He indicates that the following could well be the prayer of the Senses to the Prāṇa :

> Bestow upon us thy grace, O Prāṇa , with that invisible form of thine which is in speech, in the ear, in the eye and which is continuously existent in the mind. O Prāṇa, do not depart from us.

The form of Prāṇa is indeed invisible—the eye cannot see it but the eye cannot function without it, the ear cannot hear it, but the ear cannot hear without it. The above verse says that Prāṇa is continuously existent in the mind. Does mind contain Prāṇa? How does it live in the mind? It is this which forms the inquiry of the third question posed to the Teacher of the Praśna Upanishad. While the first question dealt with the creation of the gross physical body, the second question concerned itself with the Prāṇa which vitalizes the body and without which the body would disintegrate. But the discussion on Prāṇa has brought the pupils to that point where their interest is aroused to inquire as to where does this Prāṇa reside—and from where does it operate?

The third pupil, Kausalya, the son of Aśvala, put a very searching question to Pippalāda. His question was:

> O revered Sir, whence is this prāṇa born? How does it come into the body? How after diffusing itself does it abide here? How does it leave the body? How does it sustain the universe without and within?

The Teacher had to tell this pupil that he was asking an *Atipraśna* —meaning thereby a question that transcends comprehension by man's normal consciousness. The above question contains many points of deep importance. But realizing that the disciple was well qualified to ask such a question, the teacher takes up the inquiry and calls for a serious attention by the pupils. He says:

> Prāṇa is born from the Spirit. Even as a man casts a shadow, so does the Spirit cast its shadow and it is known as prāṇa. Prāṇa enters the body through the activities of the mind.

Surely everything is born of the Spirit, for nothing

could exist without It. But here the Teacher gives a simile of the substance and the shadow. The shadow is projected by the substance—so is the whole universe a projection of the Spirit. The shadow has no intrinsic existence—it enjoys only a projected existence. A shadow is elusive, for, it can never be caught. It escapes the grasp of man, for, it is intangible. This indicates that the Spirit is present in the universe only in an intangible manner. The intangible is the intimation of the Unmanifest in the manifest. The intangibility which resides in all objects is indeed a shadow cast by the Spirit—and like shadow it remains beyond the grasp of man. The Teacher says such is indeed the nature of Prāṇa.. It vitalizes the body but remains intangible. While closing the discussion on the second question, the Teacher said that Prāṇa has an invisible form informing the eye but not caught by the eye, informing the ear but not caught by the ear. This invisible form is the intangibility of Prāṇa—like a shadow cast by the Spirit. But the Teacher in the above verse introduces a new factor in the discussion, for, he says that "Prāṇa enters the body through the activities of the mind".

Thus the very existence of Prāṇa in the body is dependent upon the movement of the mind. The senses are vitalized by Prāṇa, but Prāṇa too in turn is impelled by the activities of the mind. It is an accepted postulate of all systems of Yoga that Prāṇa follows Thought. The movement of Prāṇa in the body can be controlled by thought. It is quite possible to focus the attention of Prāṇa on any centre of the body by a clearly defined thought-process. In fact, Prāṇa can be moved from centre to centre within the body by a concentration of thought. And so here the Teacher leads his pupils from the *Prāṇamaya-kośa.* —the Vital Body, to the *Manomaya Kośa* —the Body of the Mind. He has shown systematically how the physical depends upon the vital and now he shows how the vital too is dependent upon the mind. But before this subject of the mind can be further explored the Teacher turns to other parts of the question put to him by Kausalya. The Teacher has replied to his question dealing with the inquiry wherein the pupil had asked him: How does Prāṇa come into the body? But now the question posed by the student is: How does Prāṇa abide after diffusing itself in the body? Pippalāda. says:

> Just as an emperor commands his officials and appoints them to rule over portions of his realm in the name of the emperor, so does Prāṇa allocate the other vital breaths to their respective functions.

The Upanishad here describes the five-fold nature of Prāṇa. The Vital Breath or Prāṇa is but one; however, it is known by different names due to the different functions that they discharge. The Holy river, Ganges, flows from the Himalayas to the sea, but in its long journey it is assigned different names. Even though it is the same river it is known differently in different parts. Such is indeed the case of Prāṇa. It is the vitalizing force of the entire body —but in and through different centres of the body it discharges various functions. The five-fold nature of Prāṇa is only a functional division. This needs to be emphasised lest we begin to think that there are five different Vital Breaths vitalizing the body. The five-fold nature of Prāṇa is *Prāṇa*, *Apāna*, *Vyāna*, *Udāna* and *Samāna*. This five-fold division of the Vital Breath is, according to their location, the centre from where they function. Prāṇa is the vital breath located in the lungs. *Apāna* is located in the lower regions *Samāna* has its seat in the navel area, *Udāna* functions near the throat and *Vyāna* pervades the entire body. The proper functioning of all these Vital Breaths is essential for the health and the vitality of the body. The clogging of any vital breath affects the functioning of the body. Today, while the medical science knows much about the organic diseases of the body, it knows very little about the functional ailments of the body. This is because the functional ailments are rooted in the Vital Breaths. If they do not flow smoothly then surely the body must suffer in health. But why does the movement of the Vital Breath get clogged? And how can its movement be freed from obstacles which impede its smooth and even flow? It is not by drugs or by physical devices that the flow of the Vital

Breath can be resumed. Its movement, as was said in the earlier part of this discussion, depends upon thought. It is thought and thought alone that can direct the movement of Prāṇa. If the flow of Prāṇa is impeded, the cause is not in the body. No amount of physical treatment can bring about a resumption of the smooth flow of the Vital Breath. The cause is in the mind—and so it is in the mind that the correction has to be made. Modern medical science is beginning to realize the effect of mind upon the body. The functional diseases have their root in the mind, for, it is the defective functioning of the mind that has caused obstruction in the easy flow of Prāṇa through the different centres of the Body. Unless man knows how to deal with his mind he cannot regain his lost vitality—and without sufficient vitality the body must deteriorate causing a slowing down in its functioning mechanism. The Teacher in concluding his remarks on the third question says:

> He who knows the rising of Prāṇa, and how it comes to the body, how it abides there in its five-fold division enjoys long continuity.

The Teacher says that a man who knows the relationship of Prāṇa with the mind discovers an elixir of continued existence. Mind and body are inter-related but this inter-relationship is due to the functioning of Prāṇa. Prāṇa is indeed a bridge between the Body and the Mind. Prāṇa must be evenly distributed in the body so that it may discharge its proper functions. However it is not merely the location of Prāṇa in different centres of the body that matters—it is the functioning of Prāṇa that is of supreme importance if the body is to remain healthy and vital. But the functioning of Prāṇa depends upon the mind—and therefore to this mind must the pupils turn in their deep inquiry into the nature of things. And so Sauryāyaṇī Gārgya places before the Teacher the fourth question which is concerned with the functioning of human consciousness—or with the operations of the mind.

This question about consciousness is very graphically worded, for Gārgya,, the grandson of Sūrya, asks:

> Venerable sir, what are they that sleep in him? Who is it that beholds the wonder of dreams—and who is it that enjoys the

mystery of sleep with no dreams? Who is that in whom all these are established?

Obviously the above questions refer to the powers of consciousness. Human consciousness functions through the mind—by mind is not indicated just the thought mechanism but feeling and emotions too. The Hindu classification of the constitution of man speaks of *Manomaya Kośa* —the Body of the Mind—immediately after the *Prāṇamaya-kośa.* —the Body of Vital Breath. It does not speak of the Body of Emotions and then the Body of the Mind. This is indeed more scientific and true to psychological functioning than those classifications that speak of the Body of Emotions and the Body of Mind. In fact, the body itself is not a very happy term. A body denotes something static and fixed. When modern science has come to regard even physical matter as a mere "wave of probability" and not something solid, it is incorrect to speak of non-physical states of matter as something static. In fact, the non-physical states of matter must resemble more a wave than a substance—and a wave in a medium far more subtle than water or air. The word "*Kośa*" has a meaning which indicates a covering. It may be a covering like that of a thin cloud—or it may be a veil almost transparent. The different principles which we regard as the components of man are more in the nature of coverings than solid and static bodies. The manifest is like a veil—a golden veil—which hides the Face of the Unmanifest. Sometimes the veil is so thick that the Face is completely hidden—but when the veil is thin and iridescent then a glimpse of the Unmanifest comes through the manifest. This is the intangible intimating its presence through the tangible.

The Teacher of the Praśna Upanishad is now concerned with the Veil of the Mind—the *Manomaya Kośa*. There is another misconception against which a student of the deeper verities of life must be warned. And that is that the Body of the Mind and Mind are not identical. The Body is the abode but the abode is not identical with the functioning consciousness. Just as structure of thought and thinking are not identical, similarly the Body of the Mind and Mind are not the same. Mind is the faculty of consciousness that functions through the Body of the Mind. It is mind which vitalizes the abode in which it lives—but the house and the master of the house are not the same. Now this faculty of the mind is not just thought —it is a composite thing to be described as thought-emotion. Usually we separate thought and emotion and assign to each a different abode. But in the psyche of man thought-emotion is a composite process. We hardly know a thought completely free from emotion—and we hardly experience an emotion which is totally bereft of thought. The *Mano-maya Kośa* of Vedānta follows the scientific principle of regarding thought-emotion as a composite process, and not artificially separate one from the other.

In the above verse of the Praśna Upanishad, Gārgya inquires about the various layers of human consciousness —that which is awake, that which dreams and that which enjoys sleep undisturbed even by dreams. The Teacher replies to him thus:

> Like the rays of the rising and the setting Sun these powers of consciousness are centred in the mind.

When the sun sets, all the rays become one in the great disc of light, and again when the sun rises, these rays are spread far and wide, similarly mind functions in its field of consciousness in a variety of ways. The waking, the dream and the deep sleep are all modes of the mind —these modes bring about a modification in consciousness. It is the modifications which we term as deep sleep and dream and waking, but all the modifications have their root in the mind—that composite function which we have called Thought-emotion. The waking, the dream and the deep sleep conditions refer to the conscious, the sub-conscious and the unconscious layers of the mind. The mind is not what is seen at the conscious level only—it has a layer just below the surface of the conscious functioning —and it has also a depth which the conscious functioning cannot probe.

While dealing with this question of Gārgya, the

Teacher does not think it necessary to refer to the conscious layer of the mind. This part of mind's function has been already dealt with while speaking about the vitalization of the senses by Prāṇa and the Prāṇa moving at the behest of thought. So long as seeing, hearing, smelling, touching and tasting go on—that is so long as the senses, vitalized by Prāṇa, bring reports of the external world, so long mind is functioning at its conscious level. But then there is a sub-conscious level of the mind too—this reveals itself in the state of dream. The Teacher describes this condition very vividly in the following verse:

> And in dreams the mind beholds its own immensity. What has been seen is seen again, and what has been heard is heard again. What has been felt in different places or far away regions returns to the mind. Seen and unseen, heard and unheard, felt and not-felt, the mind sees all when dreaming.

Why does the mind see again in dream what it has already seen or what it has heard? This seeing and hearing again is the experience of unfulfilled desires in the condition of dream. During waking state we see and hear —but the experience remains incomplete. We would have liked to see and hear more—but could not because of various factors. Our seeing and hearing were interrupted by the "censor" who asked us to behave ourselves and not indulge in such activities as are not "respectable". Or during seeing and hearing, our attention was distracted and so the events and incidents moved on without our knowing them fully. There is also a third factor which contributes to the dream condition. While waking we saw and heard—but the imagination of man projects something more into the events and incidents of life. And so man feels that there is something more than what he sees or hears. That something is not there—but he wishes for that something to exist. This is the element of wishful-thinking. And so the material of dreams is drawn from suppressed-feelings, from distractions causing the experiences to remain incomplete and also from wishful-thinking due to which man desires to see more than what is. All these three factors constituting the dream state have been indicated in the above verse because it says "seen and unseen, heard and unheard, felt and not-felt—the mind sees all when dreaming." This is a condition where man is asleep—but his sleep is interrupted by dreams. And in dreams, while the conscious mind is inactive, it is the sub-conscious that springs into activity—for when the "censor" is asleep, the questions of respectability are thrown overboard. The Teacher has summed up the whole subject of dream in just a few lines, but his summing up gives a complete picture of the dream state. The above verse says that in dream, the mind sees its own immensity. The word used is *Mahimā* which would more appropriately be called Glory. In dream, the mind sees all its glories, for it has a vast sweep before it, and it can move unchecked by the interruptions of the censor. The mind can have a free play to its imaginations so that it can experience the seen and the unseen, the heard and the unheard and the felt and the unfelt.

But there is a state further than the dream—a state of sound sleep where there is no disturbance, not even of a dream. What is the experience of the sound sleep? How can any one say? It is a condition where the sleeper and the sleep have become one. The sleeper is not even aware that he is sleeping. It is this condition of sleep which has been described in the Praśna Upanishad. It is said that at the time of deep sleep....

> The person hears not, sees not, smells not, touches not; he speaks not, takes not, rejoices not, moves not—then they say "He sleeps".

There is a difference between sleep and death—for from sleep man awakens and resumes his normal activities in which the senses participate. Even during sleep the involuntary activities of the body continue—the heart beats and the digestive organs carry on their appointed tasks. As the Upanishad says: "In the city of the body the fires of life are burning; they sleep not." The vital breath functions but not the senses—for the conscious mind is not there to direct the movement of Prāṇa. It is true that Prāṇa vitalizes the senses, but if there is no mind to impel the

Vital Breath, the senses remain asleep.

But man rarely experiences sound sleep such as a child does. And even if man does go into sound sleep, he awakens from it not always refreshed, but heavy with inertia. Why is this so? Because while it has been a sound sleep it has not been a restful sleep. Even though the dreams of the subconscious have not disturbed him—there have been more powerful impacts of the unconscious—these impacts have dulled him. On waking he does not remember them and so concludes that he had a sound sleep—though seemingly undisturbed, it is a sleep which renders a man inwardly heavy, disinclined to do anything because of the inertia of sleep.

The question is: Must there always be a disturbance in sleep—either through the dreams of the subconscious or through the dulling impacts of the unconscious? If this be the case then man cannot be relaxed and refreshed. Has man to seek his relaxation elsewhere? Mind, so long as it functions by its own, must needs experience restlessness and therefore a tiredness which cannot be removed by sleep. The mind functioning on its own knows not what a restful sleep is, for, its sleep is always broken up by dreams or is rendered dull by the drugging effect of the unconscious. The Teacher of the Praśna Upanishad, however, says that—

> When the mind is overcome by its own radiance, then dreams are no longer seen; joy and peace come to the body.

What is meant by mind overcome by its own radiance? When the mind of man is rendered pure and innocent then it is bathed in the effulgent light of Intelligence. The mind overcome by its own radiance is a condition where Intellect is illumined by Intelligence. For such a mind there are no distractions of incomplete experiences and therefore no interruptions in sleep. For such a mind there is nothing that intervenes between the waking condition and the deep sleep condition. There is no passage through the state of dreams. As we saw, dreams arise due to suppressed feelings, mental distractions or wishful-thinking. When no such factor exists then man goes immediately from the waking state to the condition of deep sleep—and emerges from there completely refreshed and relaxed. Just as senses must be vitalized by Prāṇa, and Prāṇa by the mind, similarly mind too must be illumined by Intelligence if it is to discharge its functions well and wisely. It is to this condition of intellect illumined by intelligence that Pippalāda refers when he uses the word *Vijñāna-ātma,* the Intelligent being. So long as the mind sees, or hears, or smells, or tastes, or touches, so long must the residue of experience remain. And it is this residue which comes up again and again in dreams. To have experience without any residue whatsoever is to have the birth of Intelligence in the Intellect. Here the mind realizes that the seeing and hearing and touching and smelling and tasting is done not by the unaided powers of the mind—the mind does this because of the Intelligence that stands behind. When mind recognises the supremacy of Intelligence then is it that it is integrated. And it is only the integrated mind that knows what rest and relaxation are. The Teacher tells his disciples:

> He, verily is the seer, the toucher, the hearer, the smeller, the taster, the thinker, the knower, the doer—the person of the nature of Intelligence.

The Teacher has led his disciples from the Abode of the Mind to the Abode of Intelligence—from *Manomaya-Kośa* to *Vijñānamayakośa.* He has shown that the integration of mind depends upon Intelligence by which it must be illumined. The discussion of the Praśna Upanishad has come to the point of mind's illumination by Intelligence or Buddhi.

And so Satyakāma, the son of Śibi, the fifth disciple, asks the Teacher:

> Venerable sir, he who, verily, among men meditates till the end of his life on the sound OM—what world does he conquer thereby?

It is to the sublime subject of meditation that the pupils must now turn if they are to understand the state of mind illumined by Intelligence. It is meditation which enables the mind to open itself out to the influences of Buddhi or Intelligence. The disciple asks the Teacher that if a man meditated all his life on the sacred word, what would he achieve? The Teacher is however cautious and informs him that all depends upon what part of OM is being meditated upon. OM is a word of three letters. It covers a sound range starting from the root of the tongue to the closing of the lips. In this range, the three letters are uttered successively. But in this uttering of the word, the articulate sound is only between the first and the third—it is a range where the tongue moves between its root and the lips. Thus in the three letters of the word OM, A and M remain inarticulate—it is only the U which represents the articulate sound. But there is a difference between the inarticulate A and the inarticulate M. It is this difference that is indicated by the Teacher when he speaks about Meditation on the Sacred word. He says:

> He who rests on the first *mātrā* or measure is illumined thereby and after death returns speedily to earth.

The first *mātrā* or measure denotes a sound where the tongue does not even touch the palate. It indicates an innocence of sound—but this innocence is like that of a child. The child says more by the inarticulate sound than by the articulate. But his inarticulation is born of innocence—the innocence of ignorance. There is a purity in his sound but this purity belongs to a period where temptations have not yet arisen. The meditation on the first *mātrā* or measure is like the meditation of a child—a meditation in its elementary stage. The above verse says that illumination does come to one who meditates, but the meditation on the first *mātrā* is of such a nature that man soon returns to earth. The wings of the mind have no strength to soar higher. He attains to earthly greatness but cannot rise above the pulls of the earth. This is the path of Action where man achieves great success in his actions on earth. The Teacher then says:

> If he rests his mind in meditation on the first two *mātrās* or measures, he is led to the regions of the moon.

Now moon is an indicator of emotions. And therefore the meditation on two *mātrās* or measures symbolises

Bhakti—the path of Devotion. The verse of the Praśna Upanishad says that "after enjoying heavenly joys, he returns to earth". A devotee experiences heavenly joy—he knows the ecstasy of emotion. The emotional experiences of devotion come when the devotee sees the manifested form of the Deity. He feels that he has seen, heard and touched his Deity. The second *mātrā* or measure of the Sacred Word deals with the articulate sound—it deals with that which is manifested. The Devotee ever longs to see the Manifested form of the Deity. It is Brahman with attributes—the *Saguṇa* Brahma—which is indeed the subject of the devotee's meditation. And here in the second *mātrā* of the Sacred Word, the disciple sees the *Saguṇa* Brahman—the Reality with attributes. This is meditation with seed. This leads man to the regions of the moon. When man returns to earth, he does so with the joys of heavenly gifts. Meditation on OM has still another aspect—that aspect which is Meditation without seed, where man travels into the regions of the Unmanifest—he soars into the inarticulate sound, but the inarticulate sound of the disciple at this stage has innocence—not born out of ignorance, but innocence that arises out of knowledge. The Teacher says:

> He who meditates on OM with three *mātrās* or measures comes to the regions of the Sun and becomes one with its Light.

To meditate on the three *mātrās* is to come to the experience of the Un-manifest but after knowing the glories of the Manifest. These three stages of meditation indicate a movement signifying the journey of the soul from the innocence of childhood through the imperfections of man to the perfection of the super-man. When man learns to meditate on the three *mātrās* of OM then he knows both the Manifest and the Unmanifest nature of Reality. From Intellect he transcends to the land of Intelligence—the region of Buddhi. The Teacher says that the man who meditates on the three *mātrās* of OM is:

> Free from all corruption even as a snake sheds its old skin.

The snake slips out of the old skin—it has not to struggle in order to discard that skin. It drops away. Similarly all corruption of the mind drops away when man reaches the heights of the Unmanifest as he meditates on the three *mātrās* of OM.

The word, OM, used in these verses is only a symbol. The Teacher of the Praśna Upanishad himself says that:

> The word OM, O Satyakāma, is the immanent and transcendent Brahman.

And so the subject of meditation discussed in the fifth question refers to the Immanence and the Transcendence of Brahman. So long as man deals with the Immanent aspect of Brahman, so long is his meditation with seed—but when he soars into the meditation leading him into the regions of Transcendence then is he free from all seeds—his meditation is a state where the meditator and the object of meditation have become one. He is no longer in the realms of ideation—he has come to a different category of knowledge—it is knowledge by Being. The meditation on the first and the second *mātrās* dealt with Action and Devotion. The meditation on the three *mātrās* bring man to Knowledge—a direct Knowledge of Reality. The Teacher ends this discussion by saying that this meditation on three *mātrās* brings an aspirant to the knowledge of that Person who is *Ajara* and *Amara*—he who remains uncorrupted by time—he who is Immortal. These two words describe both the Immanent and the Transcendent Brahman. *Ajara* is in time, and yet not corrupted by time. Brahman is in Manifestation—and yet remains untouched by the stream of Time in which the manifest exists. Why is this so? Because Brahman is *Amara*—Immortal or Timeless. Because Brahman is Timeless, It does not get affected by the processes of Time even when It manifests Itself in time.

The Teacher has led the disciples from the *Manomaya Kośa*, the abode of the Mind, to the *Vijñāmaya Kośa*, the Abode of Intelligence. Intelligence or Buddhi is the charioteer, but only the Master of the Chariot can say where the chariot shall go. He knows the direction, for it is

Ātman that alone knows his *Svadharma*—the direction of his own Vocation. Where will intelligence direct the chariot without the intimation given by the Master of the Chariot? And so Intelligence for ever points to the Master who is seated in the Chariot. And where the Master is seated is indeed the *Ānandamaya Kośa* —the abode of Bliss Eternal.

The Praśna Upanishad says that Sukeśa Bhāradvāja put the last question to Pippalāda. His inquiry was: Where is the Person of sixteen forms? It seems once a Prince by the name Hiraṇyābha Kausalya asked Sukeśa whether he knew the Person of sixteen forms. Sukeśa said that he did not know. The Prince moved away in silence not having found an answer to his question. And so Sukeśa now turns to the Teacher saying: "Master, tell me where is that Person of sixteen forms?"

The Teacher says: "My beloved son, the Person of sixteen forms is here and now—it is not far from your body". Pippalāda tells the disciples that surely the Person of sixteen forms must have thought: "What shall constitute my manifested nature—and when will the manifest cease to be manifest?" Having thought thus He manifested himself in the numerous things that He created. And to each created thing he gave a Name. It is the Name which differentiates one object from the other. To the innumerable forms created by him He thus gave Names. The manifested world is a region of *Nāma* and *Rūpa* —of Name and Form. Each object is known by its Name, but man soon forgets the Real Name of objects. He gives to them his own name—the name given out of the background of his mind. The Person gave to each a Real Name—but man assigns to each a name born out of his likes and dislikes. So habituated he becomes to this name that he forgets the Real Name, nay, he forgets that the name is only a symbol, a token, and that behind the Name stands the Person himself. He clings to the Name, and since the Name is associated with a Form, he clings to the Form too. And when the forms die, and with that the name also, then the man is immersed in sorrow. But this is a man whose mind is unillumined by

Buddhi. He whose intellect is enlightened by Intelligence knows what the following verse of the Praśna Upanishad indicates:

> As the many flowing rivers tending towards the ocean, on reaching the ocean, disappear, their name and form are broken up, and one only speaks of the ocean; even so these sixteen forms disappear, their name and form are broken up, and one speaks only of the Person, one who is not made up of the parts, but is Formless and Immortal.

The Teacher has brought the pupils to that height of illumination where one sees the Many in the One and the One in the Many. The rivers are called rivers so long as they are in their courses—but they cease to be rivers when they merge into the ocean. There is the One but there is also the Many. The Many and the One do not contradict each other. He who sees the Many but also sees the One in the Many knows both the Manifest and the Unmanifest. He knows the sixteen forms but also knows the Person who creates and uncreates at his will these forms of great diversity. This person is none other than the Ātman, for the Teacher of the Praśna Upanishad says that the Person of sixteen forms is here and now present —in the very body of the inquirer.

Bringing the entire discussion, which began with the first question, to a close, the Great Teacher of the Praśna Upanishad says:

> These sixteen forms find rest in Him like spokes in the centre of a wheel. Know ye, the Person, the Ātman that should be known so that death may afflict you not.

So saying Pippalāda informed the pupils that that was all that he knew about the great problems of life.

The Teacher had communicated all that could be communicated. There is communication by words and there is a communication in silence. Words are used so long as mind speaks to mind. The whole of the Praśna Upanishad is mind speaking to mind. But when mind comes to the limits of its communication, it becomes silent. Pippalāda says: 'This is all I know, and this that I know, I have communicated to you'". That the teacher and the disciple were moving within the range of the mind is clear from the following words of the pupils. They addressed to Teacher saying:

> Thou indeed art our father who hath taken us to the other shore of nescience.

The other shore of nescience—that is what the Teacher has brought them to. Ignorance and knowledge are the two opposite shores. From question to question the Teacher has taken the pupils from the shore of ignorance to the shore of knowledge. They together have covered the two opposites of the mind. But while taking them to the shore of knowledge the teacher has indicated to the pupils the limitation of knowledge. He has told them that the Land Beyond still remains unexplored. He has told the disciples that there is nothing beyond in terms of the mind. The mind cannot go further. That which is unexplored cannot be measured by the scale of the mind.

The Teacher has brought the pupils to the doorstep of the Palace where Ātman, the King of Kings resides. Through the understanding of the senses and the Prāṇa, the mind, both conscious and unconscious, and the Intelligence directing the mind, the Teacher has indicated to the pupils the House of the Person who displays His sixteen forms and yet gathers them within Himself. To commune with the Person is what the pupils must do for themselves. All communication must lead to the point of communion—beyond that it cannot go. For, communion cannot be taught. It comes, but it comes only when man moves away from both the shores, the shore of ignorance as also the shore of knowledge, for then alone he enters the realm of Bliss. The work of the Teacher is over—for now, it is the flight of the alone to the Alone.

V

EXISTENCE WITHOUT IDENTITY

The Praśna and the Muṇḍaka Upanishads both belong to the Atharva Veda and so there is a great similarity between the two. In fact, the Muṇḍaka Upanishad takes up the teaching of the Praśna Upanishad and carries it further. To indicate this similarity between the two, we find that both the Upanishads have the same invocation. The Muṇḍaka Upanishad also begins with the listening and the seeing without which no integration of man is possible. To know how to listen and to know how to see—these are prerequisites for serious inquiry. Learning demands a total listening and a total seeing. To listen without any interpretation and to see without any evaluation—this alone is the background in which the discovery of Truth is possible.

It may be interesting to note that one of the meanings of Muṇḍaka is razor. This meaning is very apt in relation to the teachings of this Upanishad. The teachings of the Upanishad are sharp like a razor, clearing the forests of the mind, cutting down mercilessly all weeds and parasitic growth. This Upanishad is very uncompromising in its fundamental approach to life. Indeed it cuts through the confusion of thought with a sharp razor, cleansing the mind of all tendencies towards vacillation and compromise.

The Muṇḍaka Upanishad begins with a question put by *Śaunaka*, a householder, to *Aṅgiras*, a teacher of great repute and learning. The question is very simple. He asks:

> Master, what is that, which when known all is known?

The Teacher does not give a straight answer to this question—because no straight answer can be given. He, therefore, tells his pupil, *Śaunaka*, that there are two kinds of knowledge—*Parā* and *Aparā*—the Higher and the

Lower. Perhaps it may be well to describe the *Parā* and the *Aparā* as Wisdom and Knowledge. It is needless to point out that Wisdom and Knowledge are not identical. Wisdom is not arrived at by the extension of Knowledge. Not even an infinite extension of Knowledge can bring one nearer to wisdom. It needs to be remembered that Wisdom and Knowledge belong to two different dimensions. There is a qualitative gulf between the two. Knowledge is *Paroksha,* meaning thereby indirect; while Wisdom is *Pratyaksha* meaning direct or immediate. A quantitative increase of indirect knowledge does not lead us to direct knowledge. What then distinguishes the *Parā* from the *Aparā* —the Higher from the Lower? The Teacher says:

> The Lower knowledge is the knowledge of the Ṛg Veda, the Yajur Veda, the Sāma Veda, the Atharva Veda, and also the knowledge of Phonetics, Ritual, Grammar, Etymology, Metrics and Astronomy. And the Higher knowledge is that by which the Immutable is known.

The above description of the Lower or the *Aparā* knowledge is most shattering. To say that even the knowledge of the Vedas is a Lower knowledge is indeed very devastating. What can there be more sacred than the Vedas? If Vedas too constitute Lower knowledge, then what can be higher than these. Along with the Vedas the six limbs or the accessories to the study of these Sacred Books have been declared by the Teacher of the Muṇḍaka Upanishad as Lower or *Aparā*. This is indeed sharp as a razor, for it demolishes all our concepts of Higher knowledge. According to the above statement, all knowledge gathered through the external sources is Lower because it is indirect. The knowledge gathered from the sacred books does not become sacred or higher. It is not the sacredness of the book that matters—what matters is the sacred approach. The word "Sacred" means that which is Inviolate or Inviolable. And therefore that which is sacred is uncorrupt or incorruptible. Even the most sacred of the books may become corrupted if the approach to it is not sacred. Thus the sacredness lies not in the object—but in the approach made by the subject. If the approach of the subject is corrupt then anything would become corrupt, even the Vedas. Any book or subject can become profane when approached with a corrupt mind. Similarly anything can become sacred when the mind that inquires is not corrupt. If Vedas and their six limbs of study are lower knowledge, it does not mean that we must establish some other books in their place so as to come to Higher knowledge. It is not the substitution of books or subjects that transforms the profane into sacred. It is not by discarding the Vedas and their six limbs that one can come to Higher knowledge. Here there is no question of either acceptance or rejection of the Vedas and other limbs of learning. What matters is the profaneness or the sacredness of the mind that undertakes an inquiry. The above verse says that the "Higher knowledge is that by which the immutable is known". The question may arise—is there a book by studying which man can come to the understanding of the Immutable? Is there a particular branch of learning which gives this Higher knowledge—the knowledge of the *Akshara* or the Immutable?

The following verse of the Muṇḍaka Upanishad must set at rest all doubts of Śaunaka regarding the Higher Knowledge. The Teacher gives here the test of one who has come to Wisdom, for he says:

> By means of the Higher knowledge the wise behold everywhere Brahman, which otherwise cannot be seen or grasped, which has no root or attribute, no eyes or ears, no hands or feet, which is eternal and omnipresent, all-pervading and extremely subtle, which is imperishable and the source of all beings.

The above verse says that the Wise behold Brahman everywhere although otherwise Brahman cannot be seen. Obviously the wise must possess special sight with which to see That which otherwise is not seen. Is this an occult or super-physical sight? To this question, too, the Teacher gives an emphatic reply. To see Brahman who is otherwise unperceived does not require any clairvoyant sight. To the clairvoyant sight Brahman will remain as unperceived as it is to the normal sight. The Teacher says: "Brahman is Eternal and Omnipresent". Eternal is obviously time-less. And time-measurement is essential for any comprehension to which the mind comes. The mind must measure everything; and its measuring rod is time. Even when man brings super-physical sight into operation, the interpretation of what has been seen is done by the mind. Clairvoyance is only an extension of the normal sight. It is a recognised fact that it is not the eye that sees; it is the mind that sees. Even when the range of the eye is extended, the perception is still by the mind. But how can mind measure that which is Immeasurable? The Teacher, *Aṅgiras*, says that Brahman is Omnipresent. Now Omnipresence can never be understood in terms of space. That which is omnipresent is present everywhere. How can a thing be present everywhere? If it is present at one place then it cannot be present at another place—unless by omnipresence we mean present successively. A successive presence is no omnipresence at all. For successive presence, we need the framework of time. If we introduce the factor of time then we must admit that Brahman is omnipresent—but Its omnipresence is qualified by a condition, which is, that It is not present everywhere at the same time. It implies that there are certain moments when Brahman is not present at a particular place. Such a qualified omnipresence is no omnipresence at all. If at certain moment of time, Brahman is not present at any particular place, then obviously It cannot be called Omnipresent. If Brahman is Eternal and Omnipresent then surely It is beyond Time and Space. Time and Space go together—they are a pair which cannot be separated. In fact, time and space are not two different things. Two points separated in space need time to cover that distance—and two points separated in time require space for their very existence, for, what keeps the two points of time separate? Why do they not merge into one another? Surely it is space that keeps the two points of time away from each other. And so Brahman being Eternal and Omnipresent is Timeless and Spaceless. But time and space constitute the framework in which alone mind functions. And so Brahman, the Imperishable, cannot be known by any functioning processes of the mind. Wisdom or *Parā Vidyā* has a sight by which it beholds Brahman—but it is a sight not governed by the interpretations of the mind. Brahman can be seen not by clairvoyance nor by any other paranormal faculty. The wise behold Brahman everywhere which otherwise cannot be seen. The Muṇḍaka Upanishad is concerned with this seeing by the wise—and the Teacher leads, step by step, his pupil to that perception which is utterly free from the interpretation of the mind. Speaking about Brahman, the Teacher says:

> Even as a spider sends forth and draws in its thread, even as plants arise from the earth and hairs from the body of man, even so the whole creation arises from the Imperishable.

Here the Teacher gives illustrations from the vegetable, the animal and the human kingdoms. It is true that everything comes from Brahman or the Imperishable. But has Brahman to make an effort to create Its universe? The Teacher says the creation is absolutely effortless—as effortless as the hairs growing on the body of man. He says—look at the earth which is inert but it gives birth to plants which are rich in colour and variety. And see the spider—it weaves a thread from itself and when it withdraws the thread, the thread becomes once again a part of the spider. The spider creates and also uncreates by its own volition, needing no help from anywhere. Such is indeed the creation of Brahman. It is effortless, it contains rich variety and it is created out of Itself even as the spider weaves its own thread. But the creation of man needs exhausting effort. It is monotonous in nature, containing the marks of mind's continuity, but above all it is a creation which is dependent upon the material drawn from his environment. Where there is inner fullness, the outer creation is bound to be spontaneous, full of a variety and carrying the mark of the unique and the original. The Teacher says that "Brahman expands by *tapas*". Has Brahman to engage in austerity? And if creation is from austerity, then how can it be effortless and spontaneous? Here *Tapas* does not mean austerity. One of the meanings of *Tapas* is Warmth. Brahman creates out of warmth. It means that the creation of the universe is an act of love. And love is effortless and spontaneous. Effort comes only where there is a motive. If love has a motive then it is no love at all. Brahman creates the universe out of love, for, It is motiveless. There is no motive underlying the universe. In fact there is the warmth of Brahman present in all parts of the universe. It is this warmth which sustains it. And the warmth is everywhere. To feel this warmth in the creation is to experience the presence of Brahman—for, Brahman is omnipresent, but its Omnipresence reveals itself through warmth which nourishes the entire universe—from the subtlest to the greatest. The Teacher says that the knowledge of Brahman is the Higher knowledge, it is Wisdom or *Parā Vidyā*.

But a question may arise of what use is *Aparā Vidyā*: the Lower knowledge? Has man to give up Lower knowledge in order to pursue the Higher? The words Lower and Higher do not denote correctly what is meant by the *Aparā* and *Parā Vidyā* respectively. The *Aparā* or the Lower is the knowledge of the Immanent, while *Parā* or the Higher is the knowledge of the Transcendent. But what is man to do in order to come to this Transcendental knowledge? Is the way to it by rejecting the Immanent? The *Aparā* and the *Parā Vidyā* are the means to the attainment of the end which one pursues. It is the end which determines the means. And so the Lower and the Higher have reference to the end. It is in terms of the end that knowledge is called either Lower or Higher. A man may do whatever he likes, but his doing is influenced by the end he pursues. He may do seemingly great things, he may study the highest scriptures, he may retire into the forest—but the question is: To what end? The pattern of action by itself is neither good nor bad—it is the end which makes it so. The Teacher of the Muṇḍaka Upanishad impresses upon his pupil this very fact in the verses that follow. He says:

> This is the truth. The sacrificial works which were revealed to the rishis in the hymns have been described in many ways in the Three Vedas. Practise them, being desirous to attain their true results. This is your path leading to the fruits of your works.

This is a strange instruction given by the Teacher specially when in the very beginning of this Upanishad he declared that the Vedas and their six limbs are all the Lower or the *Aparā Vidyā*. How does the above verse harmonise with the earlier statement of the Teacher? The above verse speaks of hymns described in the three Vedas. Why three and not four? The three Vedas are the *Ṛg Veda*, the *Yajur Veda* and the *Sāma Veda*. These three Vedas contain hymns dealing with the performance of sacrifices. The *Atharva Veda* does not contain any injunctions regarding the performance of sacrifices—that is why it has been excluded from the above verse. The priests of the three Vedas are the *hotā*, the *udgātā* and the *adhvaryu*. They preside over the various sacrifices mentioned in the three Vedas. The participation of these priests is necessary in order to produce desired results. The ends for which the sacrifices are performed can be realized well and truly due to the participation of these priests. The Teacher of the Muṇḍaka Upanishad says: "Practise these sacrifices, desirous of attaining their true results". He further says:

> When the fire is well lighted and the flames flicker, let a man offer his oblations in the space between the two portions of melted butter.

Aṅgiras, the teacher, tells the pupil that these oblations should be offered with faith at the proper time. If the man has no faith in what he is doing then surely he cannot hope to get the reward for which he performs the sacrifice. Here faith obviously means conviction. An action done without conviction has no meaning. Now there is a difference between conviction and faith. A conviction is based on logic. It is the product of mathematical thinking. It arises from the examination of the "pros" and the "cons" of a situation—and the pros and the cons are the two opposites of mind. A conviction represents a positive knowledge of the mind. But mind can speak with positivity only with reference to that which is predictable or recurring. Its positive knowledge has validity where logic or mathematics is concerned. In those experiences which cannot come within the framework of logic or mathematics, the positive knowledge of the mind is of no avail. A mind can arrive at a conviction—but it cannot arrive at faith. Faith comes to the mind—but to a mind that knows the limitations of its positive knowledge. Since Lower knowledge or *Aparā Vidyā* belongs to the domain of the mind, to act effectively one must have conviction. He who acts without conviction in the realm of the Lower knowledge is bound to be ineffective in his actions. This is what the Teacher, *Aṅgiras*, says to his pupil with regard to the performance of sacrifices. He says—let these be performed with conviction. To perform any action with conviction is to understand the implication of such action. A conviction indicates a perception of the end or the goal with reference to the action performed. The Upanishad says:

> A man who performs sacrifices when the flames are shining, and offers oblations at the right time, is carried by these oblations on the rays of the sun to where dwells the sole sovereign of the gods.
>
> The luminous oblations say to the sacrificer: come hither, come hither, and lead him on the rays of the sun, worshipping him all the while and greeting him with the pleasant words: This is the holy heaven earned by your good deeds.

The sole sovereign of the gods is obviously Indra. The Muṇḍaka Upanishad says that those who perform sacrifices according to the scriptural instructions get heavenly rewards. Indra is supposed to be the ruler of heaven. Does heaven have a particular geographical location? Obviously not, what then is the meaning of obtaining heavenly rewards? Heaven is a state of mind. The mind projects its heaven as well as hell, and the heaven of the mind is just the opposite of earthly existence. The performance of sacrifices helps one to arrive at a particular mood of the mind. In this mood man feels happy and relaxed. These sacrifices also help him to contact super-physical entities who help man to attain a frame of mind which he regards as heavenly. It is a common experience of many that sound exercises a particular influence on the mind of man. When Sanskrit verses are recited with proper intonation, and, added to that, when there is the fragrance of incense and the energising effect of the fully lighted fire with its seven-fold flames—then there comes to man an exhilarating feeling of joy and happiness. This mood lasts while the sacrifices go on and while their after-effects remain—but soon man returns to his earthly existence. A happiness that is dependent upon external factors is bound to be short-lived. It is true that a performance of sacrifices does produce some results provided there is mental conviction in such performance. But the results are extremely temporary because they are within the confines of mind. Heaven is the opposite of earth—and those who reap heavenly rewards move only from one opposite of the mind to the other. Very soon from heaven man returns to earth —and from there once again strives to attain to another heaven. He moves from sacrifice to sacrifice, from oblation to oblation and from priest to priest as an escape from the problems of earthly existence into the respites of heaven, however temporary they may be.

And so the Teacher, *Aṅgiras*, says:

> Frail indeed are those rafts of sacrifices, conducted by eighteen persons, upon whom rests the inferior work; therefore they are destructible. Fools who rejoice in them as the Highest Good fall victims again and again to old age and death.

The mention of eighteen persons in the above verse refers to the sacrificer and his wife and sixteen priests who are considered necessary for the performance of sacrifices. But the Teacher says that the raft of sacrifice is very frail —it cannot take the man to the other shore. It may enable a man to cross over little streams but surely not the vast ocean of *saṃsāra* or the world. The performances of sacrifice may fulfil limited ends because they constitute "inferior work" and therefore produce inferior results. Very often a question is asked: Are rituals and ceremonies necessary? This question has no meaning as long as we have not inquired into another question, namely, necessary for what? In other words, unless one is clear as to the end which one seeks, a question like that cannot be satisfactorily answered. If one is seeking a little escape out of the worries and anxieties of life, then such rites and ceremonies may be useful. They may temporarily take a man out of the miseries of earthly existence into the delights of heaven. But he who seeks these temporary delights again and again finds himself in a more miserable state after his return to earth. These temporary delights serve as drugs—the more one takes them, the more is one addicted to them. The Muṇḍaka Upanishad says:

> Children, immersed in ignorance in various ways, flatter themselves saying: We have accomplished life's purpose. Because these performers of sacrifice do not know the Truth owing to their attachment, they fall from heaven, misery-stricken, when the fruit of their work is exhausted.

A performance of sacrifice is to be understood as referring to all observances of outer religious practices. For, such observances are indeed ceremonial in their nature. These practices break the otherwise monotonous routine of life and therefore serve as temporary escapes. But as the above verse says, such people fall from their heaven when the effect of the drug is over. They do not realize that the results that they achieve are transient—they pass away and create a further craving for a fresh intoxicant. The teachings of the Muṇḍaka Upanishad are indeed razor-like, for, they are ruthless in their nature, almost calling a spade a spade! The teacher describes these performers of sacrifices as children—meaning those lacking in maturity. They are immature people lost in the non-essentials, and, clinging to the non-essentials thinking that they are essentials. The teacher says that they "flatter themselves saying—we have accomplished life's purpose". These people strut about, looking down upon others, who fail to engage themselves in these rituals and ceremonies, who are not true to the observances of religious patterns.

These are the conformists of all creeds and religions—for them, he who does not conform to these practices is a renegade, almost a lost soul beyond any redemption! The Muṇḍaka Upanishad further says:

> Ignorant fools, regarding sacrifices and humanitarian works as the highest, do not know any higher good. Having enjoyed their reward on the heights of heaven, gained by good works, they enter again this world—or even a lower one.

Why have the humanitarian works been put along with the sacrifices? Is man not to engage himself in humanitarian works? Should man be so immersed in his own salvation that he forgets the miseries of others? What is the meaning of these two—the sacrifices and the humanitarian works—being bracketed together? Why does man perform sacrifices? He does so because there are scriptural injunctions. And sacrifices bear results only if they are performed in strict obedience to scriptural instructions—that is what the priest and the sacrificer believe. Thus it is not because of the joy of sacrifice but because of the reward that it may bring that a person engages himself in sacrificial performances. And since reward is more important than the performance of the sacrifice, the sacrificer is intent upon following the scriptural instructions. The following of instructions is more important than the joy of performing a sacrifice. A conformity to rules is more important than the doing of the things. Why? Because the interest is not in the doing but in the reward—whether material or so-called spiritual—that will be his because of the following of instructions. Now a mind that seeks reward, status, recognition is a corrupt mind. Most often our so-called humanitarian work is undertaken by such a corrupt mind. Needless to say such humanitarian work hardly differs from the performances of sacrifices in conformity with scriptural injunctions. The so-called humanitarian also becomes a conformist engaging himself in service bcause it is good to serve—for, service brings a heavenly reward in the shape of social or spiritual status! It has to be remembered that service which is not natural and spontaneous, a service that is cultivated, a service which has a motive—whether material or so-called spiritual

—is no service at all. A service to be true has to be anonymous, for it is only when the server is not present that true service comes into existence. How can a corrupt mind engage itself in humanitarian work? A corrupt mind may follow the injunctions of humanitarian work, may build up quantity after quantity of charitable work—but its work is no better than a sacrifice, a ceremonial performed with an eye to heavenly reward. A corrupt mind knows no compassion—and where compassion is not, how can charity exist? The Teacher of the Muṇḍaka Upanishad says, with utter ruthlessness, that the man of sacrifice and humanitarian works enters again and again this world—or "even a lower one". He is worse than even an ordinary person, for the latter does not pretend to be holy. One who pretends to be holy—or thinks he can become holy by the observances of outer practices, be they of a sacrificial nature or of a humanitarian nature, enters indeed a lower world—for it is a world of pretensions and make-believe.

The Teacher is expounding the idea of the Lower and the Higher knowledge. He has clearly indicated the path of Lower knowledge. He says to his pupil that let people perform sacrifices and engage themselves in humanitarian works, but let them know what they are pursuing. As was said earlier, the end determines the means—in fact, the end is in the means—and so a conformity to means or patterns does not lead man to heights of spiritual experiences. The problem is not the refinement of means—the problem lies in the formulation of the end. If the end is polluted, how can the refinement of means be of any help at all? If the end is corrupt its corruption will be present in the means too, even though the means may have been outwardly refined and polished. When the end is pure, the means will become pure naturally and almost effortlessly. How strange it is that in all our religious and spiritual disciplines we are concerned with the refinement of the means, the refinement of the instruments, rather than with the finding out of the end and its contents. The problem of spiritual life is not the refinement of the means so much as the purification of the end.

The Teacher in the following verse makes a very profound and significant statement regarding the end which man must pursue. He says: "Nothing that is Eternal can be produced by what is not eternal". The Eternal is free from the corruption of Time. There is no greater corrupting influence than time. How can the Eternal which is pure and uncorrupt be produced by the corrupting influences of time? And so the end which is produced by time must needs contain the corruption of time. If the end is to be pure then its birth must be not in time but in the time-less. Now time is the creation of the mind and time is also the field in which mind functions. And therefore any product of the mind must contain the corrupting influences of time. A man pursuing the end, created out of the projections of the mind, is following something perishable, something that will soon get corrupted. How can time which is perishable know that which is Imperishable? To go after the purposes and ends formulated by the mind is to pursue a mirage—it may seem attractive, but it can never quench the thirst of the spiritual aspirant.

Strangely enough the Teacher has brought the pupil to a point where he has impressed upon him the fact that in spiritual life, the fundamental problem is not—How—it is *Why*. How to lead a spiritual life is not so important as to find out why one wants to follow a spiritual path. The inquiry into the why is an inquiry into the end. The very inquiry into the contents of the end will indicate to the enquirer the means that may be employed to fulfil the end. In fact, the means will naturally emerge out of that very process of inquiring into the nature of the end. The *How* is contained in the *Why*—such is the mystery of spiritual life.

But how to find this mystery? To unravel this mystery is indeed to know *Parā Vidyā* —the Higher knowledge. But the question still remains: Where is one to go for the unravelling of this mystery? The Muṇḍaka Upanishad says:

In order that the spiritual aspirant may understand the Eternal, let him, fuel in hand, approach a guru who is well-versed in the Vedas and who is rooted in Brahman.

The verse says that the aspirant must approach a guru with fuel in hand. Why in this strange manner? In the āśrama of a guru, fire is the most sacred thing. And so the tending of the fire is one of the important aspects of the ashrama life. This tending of the fire symbolizes a condition of constant vigilance without which spiritual inquiry would be of no avail. Eternal vigilance is the price which Truth demands from those who want to understand its secrets. The pupil who goes to a guru must go with fuel in hand to indicate that he too will participate in this act of vigilance. The discovery of Truth is not something which the guru gives and the pupil takes. The discovery of Truth comes only in moments of vigilance—and in this supreme act of vigilance the guru and the pupil must be together. The fuel in hand indicates the desire of the pupil to participate in this act of vigilance. He who goes without fuel in hand does not possess the required qualification for a deep spiritual inquiry.

While the above verse describes the manner in which the pupil must go to the guru, it, at the same time, gives the true characteristics of a guru. It says, a guru must be "well-versed in the Vedas and rooted in Brahman".

Here the Muṇḍaka Upanishad speaks of the guru well versed in both the *Aparā* and the *Parā Vidyā* —the Lower and the Higher knowledge. A proficiency in the Vedas or the Lower knowledge is necessary, for, it sharpens the mind. The *Aparā Vidyā* is the realm of the mind. The mind has not to be neglected. The mind has to be both alert and negative. The alert mind is proficient in all aspects of the Lower knowledge. It is capable of exploring the whole field of *Aparā Vidyā*. But the alert mind also knows the limits and the boundaries of Lower knowledge. It is in this awareness of the limits of *Aparā Vidyā* that it becomes negative. Having known what the *Aparā Vidyā* can teach, such a mind also knows what the *Aparā Vidyā* cannot teach. But such awareness comes only to a mind that is vigilant. If the guru is not well-versed in the Vedas or the Lower knowledge then surely he does not possess an alert mind. How can he dissolve the doubts of his pupil? But if the guru is only well-versed in the Vedas, then how can he lead the pupil to the discovery of Truth which is Imperishable? And so the guru must be rooted in the Imperishable. This means that the guru must be able to soar into the realms of the Time-less even as he is able to move unimpeded in the kingdom over which Time presides. The inspiration of the Time-less and the technique of efficient movement in the sphere of Time—it is these which constitute the characteristics of a real guru. To such a guru the pupil must go with fuel in hand declaring his readiness to participate in the act of Eternal Vigilance so that both the teacher and the disciple may come to the discovery of Truth.

There seems to be a strange contradiction in the Upanishadic teachings, for, while on the one hand they emphasised complete freedom of thought and inquiry by the aspirant, they have at the same time stressed the need for a guru. In fact, the whole Upanishadic teaching centres round the guru. Is this contradiction real or only apparent? For this, one must clearly understand the role of the guru. Does man need a guru on the path of spiritual inquiry? Will not the presence of a guru restrict that freedom of inquiry on which the Upanishads lay such great stress? How can the need for a guru be reconciled with freedom which is the basis of true spiritual inquiry?

The guru as indicated in the Upanishads is not a mere instructor. As the above verse of the Muṇḍaka Upanishad says the guru must be a *Brahmanishṭha*, one who speaks not from head-learning, but soul-wisdom. He speaks not from the mind, but from the deep recesses of the heart, from the very centre of spiritual realization. It is because of this that the Upanishadic teacher never indulges in moralizings. He uses the instrument of logic, but with that very instrument he shows the limitations of logic. He logically indicates how logic is inadequate! He induces his students to ask questions, for, his main concern is to encourage clear and logical thinking on their part. The role of the guru in the Upanishads is to help his pupils to sharpen their minds. But that is not all. He shows to them that the sharpened mind cannot go beyond a particular point. By discussion and questioning, he brings his students to that point. By logic and clear thinking he enables his pupils to go to the other shore of the mind. But at that point he leaves them to work out the problems for themselves. He indicates to them that the guru cannot go further with them from that other shore of the mind. The guru of the Upanishads helps the students to see clearly the two opposites of the mind. In seeing the opposites the students themselves find out that the problem has remained unsolved. The work of the Upanishadic teacher is to bring his students to the realization that the fundamental problems of life cannot be solved by the mind. This he does not by declaring it as a conclusion—but by bringing the students to realize for themselves how mind is unable to go beyond the opposites—and how the opposites have no answer to the deep inquiry of the aspirant. Thus the Upanishadic guru plays a negative role. He does not allow the students to rest unless he has gone to the length of utter negativity with reference to the subject of his inquiry. From that point of negativity it is for the student to discover the content of Truth. No teacher can take a student further from that point of negativity. There the teacher declares: "My work is over. From here you must move alone—for it is only the alone that will find the Alone". And so the guru of the Upanishads does not take away the freedom of the enquirer—on the contrary, he helps him to deepen this freedom. He does not condition his mind with any positive statements regarding the ultimate Reality—he gives him a staff of Nothingness with which to undertake the steep climb, leading to the great summit of Truth.

The Muṇḍaka Upanishad provides one of the great examples showing the negative role of the teacher. The very word Muṇḍaka denotes a process of negation. And this is what the teacher, *Aṅgiras*, does. He has led his pupil, Śaunaka, to the utter negation of the *Aparā Vidyā* or Lower Knowledge. But what next? What lies beyond the negations of the mind? The *Aparā Vidyā* has been negated but where is the *Parā Vidyā* to be found? *Parā Vidyā* is indeed the knowledge of Brahman, the Causeless Cause of the entire creation. But even here the process of negation has not been completed—for one must negate the cause of creation before one can come to the comprehension of the Causeless cause. The Upanishads deal with two fundamental factors—Brahman with attributes and Brahman without attributes. The former is caused by the latter—but the latter is not caused by anything—It is a Causeless cause. The Teacher says:

> It is the self-luminous and formless Purusha, uncreated and existing both without and within. It is devoid of prāṇa, devoid of Mind, pure and higher than the supreme Imperishable.

The supreme imperishable in the above verse indicates the *Saguṇa* Brahman—the Brahman with attributes. The Teacher says that the ultimate Brahman is even higher than this—for it is without attributes. *Parā Vidyā* or the Higher knowledge concern itself with the comprehension of this ultimate reality—Brahman without attributes. But even here the Teacher has to use negative terms. In the above verse he says that the supreme Brahman is *Amūrta*, *Aprāṇa* and *Amana*. It is devoid of Form, devoid of *Prāṇa* and devoid of Mind. Though Formless, it gives birth to innumerable forms; though Mindless, it brings into existence mind with its manifold expressions. The entire creation is a projection of Brahman—it comes out of It just as the thread comes out of the spider. The thread has no independent existence apart from the spider. Similarly creation has no independent existence—it lives and moves and has its being in Brahman. The whole creation is devoid of instrinsic significance—it has a projected significance. It exists just as an image exists in the mirror—but the image in the mirror lasts so long as the person whose image is cast stands in front of the mirror. The entire creation is exactly of this nature. So long as man regards it as having a projected significance, so long is he free from *māyā* or illusion—but the moment he gives to projected significance an attribute of instrinsic significance then he is caught in the fabric of *māyā* —he is unable to see things as they are—but darkly, as through a glass.

But a question may arise: Are the projected and intrinsic significances completely separate from one another? Is there a gulf between the two? And if there is a gulf, is it unbridgeable? If not, with what can it be bridged? Creation is but the projection of the Creator. But then how does creation sustain itself? A thought-image is the projection of the human mind. But how does it sustain itself? The image lives so long as the mind holds it. When the mind ceases to dwell upon it, then it disintegrates, it withers away, its existence is no more. This entire creation is sustained so long as Brahman holds it in Its consciousness. And so Brahman must be imperceptibly present in Its creation—without that imperceptible presence the universe would wither away, would disintegrate, would cease to exist. When the human mind holds an image the presence of the thinker is imperceptibly there, for, without it the image would vanish in no time. The Creator is imperceptibly present in Its creation. This is the sublime truth to which the Teacher comes as he expounds this deep subject of Higher knowledge to his disciple, Śaunaka. The Teacher says:

> Brahman alone is verily the universe. He who knows this Brahman, the Supreme and the Immortal, hidden in the cave of the heart, cuts asunder even here the knot of ignorance.

To cut asunder the knot of ignorance is to come to the Higher knowledge—to arrive at *Parā Vidyā*. While seeing the image in a mirror, he who also sees the person who has cast that image—he knows the creation, but also the Creator as present in the creation. To see the Creator in the creation is indeed to come to Higher knowledge. He who sees only the creation is lost in the *Aparā Vidyā* —he will be baffled by the problems of creation. But he who sees the Creator in the creation is both *śrotriya* and *Brahmanishṭha*, to use the phraseology of the Muṇḍaka Upanishad employed in another context. He who knows only the creation is a *Śrotriya* —well-versed in the Vedas. But he who sees the Creator in the creation is rooted in the *Parā Vidyā* even while he is fully familiar with the approach of the *Aparā Vidyā*. The Creator can be found at every point of creation. To indicate this the Teacher says that It is "hidden in the cave of the heart". The word cave indicates that which is imperceptible. One needs extraordinary sensitivity to see the Creator in the creation, for while manifest It is hidden. The Muṇḍaka Upanishad describes It as "moving-in-secret".

The *Parā Vidyā* is indeed esoteric knowledge even as *Aparā Vidyā* is exoteric. But esoteric is not something kept secret by man. Paradoxically, the secret lies in the open, the esoteric is for ever exposed to the gaze of any one. It is there for one to see, but it is the blindness of man which prevents him from seeing that which is in front of him. This blindness is not due to any organic defect. It is said that there is none so blind as one who refuses to see! The blindness of man is of this nature. No man can hide the esoteric from the gaze of another. He who cannot see the esoteric has closed his own eyes, man turns his back on the light and cries out that it is dark! The exoteric knowledge is the knowledge of creation—but the esoteric is the knowledge of the Creator imperceptibly present in the creation. This is the meaning of Brahman "dwelling in the cave of the heart". To the superficial gaze, Brahman is unseen; but he who brings a dimension of depth in his perception, sees the Creator seated in the heart of its creation. The Teacher tells Śaunaka:

> That which is radiant, subtler than the subtle, that by which all the worlds and their inhabitants are supported—that verily is the indestructible Brahman. That alone is to be struck. Strike it, my good friend.

The Teacher asks the disciple to strike the Imperishable Brahman. What the Teacher indicates is about making Brahman the target, the end, the goal. In the earlier part of this discussion we were examining the question of the End and the Means. We saw that the problem of spiritual life is fundamentally that of End but the end which the mind projects contains all the corruption of the projector. It is contaminated by the motives and intentions of the mind. The mind may use beautiful words to denote and describe its End—but behind the word lies all the corruption of the mind. Here the Teacher says to his pupil: Make Brahman the target, the very end of your inquiry. But Brahman can become the target only when all the ideals and the goals of the mind cease. When the mind is completely freed from all its ideals then there can come before man the target of Brahman. The pursuit of ideals is the part of Lower knowledge—it matters not how beautifully and nobly the ideal may have been worded. To follow an ideal is to pursue the image of the mind. It is as fruitless as the performance of sacrifices or the doing of so-called humanitarian work. The ideal which is projected by the mind is as ugly as the mind itself. Angiras asks Śaunaka to make Brahman the target and strike It. But how to strike It? The Teacher instructs the pupil thus:

> Take the Upanishad as the bow, the great weapon, and place upon it the arrow sharpened by meditation. Then having drawn it back with a mind directed to the thought of Brahman, strike that mark.

Take Upanishad as the bow: What does this mean? What is Upanishad? It is the teaching—and teaching constitutes mind's knowledge. And therefore the Teacher says make your knowledge—what your mind has gathered—into a bow. A bow has two ends which are brought together—but not too close as otherwise the bow itself would break. The two ends of the bow are the two points of mind's knowledge—the two opposites which cover the range of mind's understanding. In the bow, the two ends are tied with a string—and the string so tied is tense—for unless the string is taut the bow cannot be effective. When the two opposites of the mind are brought closer then they are perceived together—it is not a co-existence of the opposites—but it is a condition where the opposites are brought as close together as possible. The closeness of opposites naturally creates a tension. They exercise a great pull over each other. It is the seeing of two opposites close to each other which makes the mind experience a tautness, a tension even as the string of the bow experiences it when the two ends are tied together. It is on this tense string of the bow that the arrow is to be placed. But the arrow must be sharp and not blunt if it is to hit the target. What is this sharp arrow? The above verse says that the arrow has to be sharpened by meditation. The word used is *Upāsana* which really means practice. The mind is obviously the arrow—but this arrow must be sharpened if it is to hit the target. It has to be sharpened by practice. It really means that it has to be made alert. It is only the alert mind that can serve as a sharpened arrow. But what is this alert mind? It is the mind which rests on the taut string of the bow—the bow which has brought the two opposites close to each other. The alert mind is one that sees clearly the two opposites—but to see the opposites is to know what they indicate and imply. The mind that knows the implications of the two opposites with reference to any situation is indeed alert and sharp. To see their implications is to see how and why they pull at each other—what lies behind these pulls—the pulls that make the string so taut, the pulls that make the consciousness so tense. The mind that sees the pulls and their implications is a sharp and an alert mind. It is an arrow which can accomplish its work. But how?

In order to release the arrow, the string on which the arrow rests must be drawn back a little. When the string is drawn back then its very tenseness flings the arrow far where the target lies. This drawing back, even when the string is taut, is the relaxation of the mind in the midst of its tenseness. This relaxation releases the energy that is stored in the tension. The arrow lying on the tense string is of no use. It becomes useful when the string is relaxed without breaking the tension. Relaxed in the midst of tension is a contradiction in terms—it is a paradox. And yet it is in that paradox that the solution lies. The tenseness of the mind is caused by the proximity of the opposites which intensify the pull of one over the other.

In this the thought-process of the mind is brought to a red-hot condition. Now a relaxation is possible only in this red-hot condition. The string that is not taut will sag when drawn back—but a string that is taut will not sag and yet show forth relaxation when drawn aback. This is exactly the condition of the tense mind experiencing relaxation. The mind is tense and yet not thinking—that is what the sharpened arrow resting on the taut string drawn back really signifies. The above verse says that when the string is drawn back then it is that the mind is directed to the thought of Brahman. But Brahman cannot be thought of —what then does this statement mean? It means a mind which has been rendered free from all thought-processes. But it is not a dull mind freed from its thought-processes. It is a sharpened mind, free from the movement of thought —the arrow resting on the taut string ready to fly off because of the drawing back of that string.

When the arrow is released, with the string relaxed and yet tense, then it reaches the target—it hits the mark. In the following verse the Teacher describes this condition very clearly, for he says:

> The arrow is to be struck by an undistracted mind, for then the arrow becomes one with the target.

How can the arrow fail to hit the mark when it has become one with it? The consciousness relaxed, in the midst of tension, is sharp as an arrow. It hits the mark, for in that condition it has become the mark itself—the two have become one—the mark and the arrow—the end and the means. When the Ātman discovers the nature of Brahman within itself, then where is the end and where is the beginning? The end is in the beginning. To know this is to come to *Parā Vidyā* —the Higher knowledge.

The Teacher tells the disciple:

> Know the non-dual Ātman alone, and give up all other talk. It is the bridge to Immortality.

Reading the above verse one is reminded of the words of Jesus Christ where He says: "Enter ye first the kingdom of God." The entry into the kingdom has to be first, not last. When one enters this kingdom then all the rest is added unto him. The Teacher of the Muṇḍaka Upanishad says the same thing, for he declares: "Give up all other talk and know the non-dual Ātman." Without knowing the Ātman all other talk is meaningless. To indulge in other talk is a sheer waste of time and energy. Without knowing the Ātman, all spiritual disciplines and all descriptions of Reality are devoid of any significance. The Teacher emphasises the word "non-dual" with reference to Ātman. Is there a second Ātman too that one must talk of the non-dual? What the teacher, Aṅgiras, indicates is that this Ātman to be known is not by the mind, for the mind knows everything in terms of duality. The Ātman of the mind is the opposite of the non-Ātman. It is needless to say that the Ātman that has an opposite is a dual Ātman. And so the Teacher says that the Ātman to be known is not of the mind—but that which is beyond the concept of the mind. The Ātman which is beyond the conceptual frame of mind is alone non-dual. It is this Ātman which is a bridge to Immortality. The Ātman which has an opposite may serve as a bridge to continuity, but it cannot lead one to the experience of Immortality. Continuity exists in the sphere of duality. A movement between the two points of duality is a movement in continuity. Immortality is experienced in the cessation of all movement, for, where movement is not, there is neither birth nor death. A movement begins somewhere and therefore ends somewhere. But where the mind has come to a cessation of all thought-movement there is no duality. The experience of the Ātman is this experience of the non-dual. When human consciousness comes to the experience of non-duality there it knows the Ātman—and since the nature of Ātman is identical with the nature of Brahman, the non-dual experience is indeed a bridge to Immortality. Brahman is Imperishable—if Ātman enables one to commune with Brahman then one communes with the Immortal and the Imperishable. To say that the Ātman is the bridge to Immortality is to indicate that in Ātman resides the nature of Brahman. To know the non-dual Ātman is indeed to know Brahman. The Teacher says that for such a man:

> The fetters of the heart are broken, all doubts are resolved, and all actions are free from the bondage of cause and effect, when Brahman is beheld both as immanent and transcendent.

The immanence of Brahman is the subject matter of study in the Vedas and the various limbs of the Vedas. It constitutes the field of Lower knowledge or *Aparā Vidyā* But the transcendence of Brahman is what is indicated in *Parā Vidyā* or the Higher knowledge. When both the Higher and the Lower are known then is man free from all fetters—even the fetters of cause and effect—the bondage of Karma.

But have immanence and transcendence to be known one after the other—or the experience of the two is simultaneous. If this experience is not simultaneous then there is a time-lag between the immanent and the transcendent. Such time-lag separates the two in space, so that Transcendence does not become the sub-stratum of Immanence. But how can the Immanent exist without the Transcendent? In terms of the above verse Brahman is beheld simultaneously as immanent and transcendent—for thus alone the fetters of the heart are broken and man is freed from the bondage of Karma. This simultaneous experience of the immanent and transcendent has been expressed very beautifully in the following verse of the Muṇḍaka Upanishad:

> Two birds, united always and known by the same name, closely cling to the same tree. One of them eats the sweet fruit, the other looks on.

The above description of the two birds indicates that even though seemingly two, they are one, for, they are united always and are known by the same name and they cling to the same tree. And so though two, they are one. It is the simultaneous existence of the two—the two existing together. No language can ever explain co-existence—but the above description is as close to it as one can express. For, here the description indicates as if the two birds are existing at the same spot and at the same time. The Teacher, however, says that of the two birds, one eats the sweet fruit of the tree and the other looks on. What does this mean? It indicates to us that while one bird partakes of the fruit, the other is only a witness to what is happening. In this co-existence there is a strange phenomenon—for there is taking place at the same time and on the same spot two utterly contradictory activities. There is a witnessing in the midst of participation. One bird eats and the other witnesses—but the witnessing is not after the bird has finished eating. The eating and the witnessing are simultaneous. Here we see the immanence and the transcendence existing together. In immanence there is a participation by Brahman in all that is manifested—but in transcendence, Brahman is a witness to Its own participation. Man would behold Brahman both as immanent and transcendent if he were to show forth in his consciousness this witnessing in the midst of participation. To be a participant in all works and activities and yet at the same time to be a witness of that very act of participation—this is the way that the Teacher of the Muṇḍaka Upanishad indicates for coming to the experience of non-dual Ātman which is a bridge to Brahman, the Imperishable. When one becomes a witness to one's own participation then one discovers the Transcendent in the Immanent. The Teacher does not say that man must isolate himself from all activities—nor does he say that he should be carried away by those activities. In life we go to extremes—we either get completely immersed in the indulgence of activities—or we show forth an utter indifference through a denial of those activities. The Teacher says that the man who neither indulges nor denies, who neither accepts nor rejects, who neither justifies nor condemns, he alone knows how to be a witness in the midst of participation. He talks of awareness in action —not awareness away from action. The Teacher speaks here of the Infinite Rest in the midst of Infinite Motion, of relaxation in the midst of tension. When the consciousness is relaxed in the midst of tension then does the arrow hit the mark—for relaxation in the midst of tension seeks not a reconciliation of opposites—it brings one to the transcendence of opposites—it leads one to the experience of non-duality—to the experience of Brahman. The Teacher says:

> Brahman cannot be seen by the eye, and words cannot reveal It. It cannot be reached by the senses, or by austerity or by good actions. By the grace of wisdom and the purity of mind, It can be seen, Indivisible, in the silence of non-distraction.

The Teacher is quite clear on the question of knowing Brahman. He says that neither senses nor speech can know It. But even austerities and humanitarian actions are of no avail. Austerities indicate a withdrawal from the world of actions, while humanitarian work indicates a participation in the world of activities. Neither by introversion nor by extroversion—neither by *Pravṛtti* nor by *Nivṛtti* —neither by retirement nor by active participation does one come to the experience of Brahman, the experience of Truth or Ultimate Reality. He says it is only by "grace of wisdom and the purity of mind" can It be found. This experience comes to human consciousness like grace from above—human consciousness cannot go to it. But such grace comes only when the mind is rendered pure. The purity of mind is obviously a state of utter negativity. The pure is that to which nothing clings. The mind that clings to nothing and nothing clings to it is a pure mind. Such a mind is totally free, for, it has no commitment whatsoever. It is a mind which has no distractions, for, that which distracts is the commitment of the mind. A mind committed to nothing is perfectly open—it can wander anywhere, for, nowhere can it be caught. It can move everywhere, for, nothing can hold it. It is to such a mind of purity that the grace of Wisdom comes. Wisdom is the Higher knowledge—the *Parā Vidyā* . A mind that stands in a state of utter negation, repudiating all its positive knowledge, is alone qualified to come to the understanding of *Parā Vidyā* . And this Wisdom comes as a grace—unasked, for the mind that asks is impure, it is still attached to its knowledge, it is still caught in its commitments. He who asks, never receives. Where the very asking is negated, there, in that condition of immaculate purity, man is initiated into the secret of Higher knowledge. This is man's true initiation—an entry into a higher life, an entry into a new house—"a house not built by hands, Eternal in the heavens."

The Teacher says:

> As rivers flowing into the ocean find their final place and their name and form disappear, even so the wise becomes free from name and form, and enters into the radiance of the Supreme Spirit who is greater than all greatness.

Is not the river merging into the ocean a state of annihilation? Is not the disappearance of name and form a condition of total destruction? Is the end of spiritual life utter annihilation? The mind of man seeking sustenance through a play of the opposites cannot understand that there can be existence without Identity. In fact, existence begins only when identity is gone. In identity, man moves with a false name, for identity is the product of a nature acquired through the process of time. When the identity is gone, when the name and form disappear, then alone begins for man his true existence. He exists in his true nature—not the nature acquired by the reactions of the mind. An acquired nature is a compound. The Lord Buddha said "Impermanent are all compounded things." An Identity is a compound and so is impermanent by its very nature. To guard one's identity is to defend something that is transient, something that is impermanent. He who loses his identity constantly, he alone knows what immortal existence is. Did not Jesus say:

> Whosoever will save his life shall lose it; and whosoever will lose his life shall find it.

To find life by losing it—this is indeed a paradox. But like Jesus, the Teacher of the Muṇḍaka Upanishad also speaks in paradox. He who is free from name and form enters a new life! But who is there when the name and form are gone? Is there any one left who will enter the new life? Yes, the entry into new life is possible only when there is none to enter! Who enters then? Ask the Wise who have found an answer to this question in the illumination of the Higher knowledge. But the Wise declare that the answer cannot be communicated either in thought or speech. To find an answer to that question, man must himself come to that experience where there is existence without Identity. The Muṇḍaka Upanishad ends with that high note, for, it utters a profound statement when it says that *Brahmavid Brahmaiva bhavati*—the knower of Brahman himself becomes Brahman. The *Parā Vidyā* is not knowledge by ideation—it is knowledge by Being. He who knows Brahman becomes Brahman—there is no duality of the knower and the known. The knower has become the known. The identity of the knower is gone, but in the very merging of the identity of the Knower into the Known, the knower has known his true nature. When the knower knows that he is not other than the known, then he steps out of his impermanent identity and enters a realm of Immortal existence. Has the dew drop slipped into the sea—or has the sea entered the dew drop? For an answer to this question—ask the Wise. But with what shall the wise explain? Not by speech, not even by mind, the wise can answer only in silence. He who knows how to commune with Silence knows that Supreme Existence which has neither name nor form, which has neither identity nor continuity, for, It is Immortal and Imperishable—it lives even when all else perishes.

VI

THE NAMELESS BEING

As one studies the history of Western Psychology, one is struck by the fact that there has been an increasing deviation on its part from the ground of philosophy of which it was once an integral part. This deviation is probably because of the fact that its roots were never very deep in the soil of philosophy. And once the deviation began, the distance between philosophy and psychology has tended to increase, so much so that today Western Psychology regards itself more as an ally of science than of philosophy. The history of Indian Psychology has been completely different, for, it was deeply rooted in the ground of philosophy. The beginnings of Indian Psychology are to be seen in the Upanishads. From there it has grown to great heights and depths as one witnesses its growth and development in such books as the *Bhagavad Gitā*, the *Yoga Sūtras of Patañjali*, the *Viveka Cūḍāmaṇi* and the *Yoga Vāsishṭha*, Nowhere do we find any attempt on the part of Indian Psychology to deviate from the ground of philosophy. This has given to it both a purpose and an effectiveness which one misses in the modern Western Psychology. The Western Psychology, has no doubt, achieved admirable results in analysis and synthesis—it has made much progress in the technique of diagnosis. But its very rise, in its modern form, has been from the abnormal conditions of man's psyche. As the great educationist, Madame Maria Montessori says: "The new psychology was in large measure built up on personal deductions drawn from abnormality." Psycho-analysis which had been the instrument of modern psychology for dealing with psychological aspects of man's life began as a new technique for the cure of mental diseases. To quote once again Madame Montessori: "It has brought to light the secrets of the unconscious, but it has brought no practical solution to the urgent problems of life." This is because modern psychology has not known what mental health is—it has drawn its conclusions only from mental diseases and therefore what it regards as mental health is the absence of mental disease. But health is not an absence of disease—it is something positive. Modern psychology has remained a stranger to the secrets of mental health because of its deductions based on the abnormalities of man's psyche.

The picture of Indian Psychology is completely different. It has taken into consideration the factors of mental disease for it has dealt with the problems of mind's distractions in a manner hardly to be seen in modern psychological treatises. But while diagnosing the disease, it has given an instrument which each man can wield for himself. It does not make man dependent upon a psycho-analyst for the cure of his mental ailments. There is a place for the psycho-analyst—but his role must be to help a patient to come to right diagnosis. It is to help the patient to understand his own psychological problems. This, a good modern psycho-analyst or a psychiatrist no doubt does—but the question is: What next? A mere diagnosis without an effective cure may lead man to morbidity. And this is what very often happens.

In any psychological understanding of man, three factors, namely, the Personal Unconscious or more truly Subconscious, the Universal Unconscious or the Unconscious, and the Super-conscious have to be taken into account. The mind of man is subjected to these three impacts coming from the Subconscious, the Unconscious and the Super-conscious. Among the Western psychologists, Freud, Adler and those belonging to that school, or a modified version of that school, have taken into account the influence of the Subconscious on the Conscious behaviour of man. Carl Jung and others of similar, or slightly modified thinking have indicated the influence of the Unconscious on the Conscious working of man. But the influence of the Super-conscious remains almost un-noticed even to this day except in the halting and over-cautious writings of Pitrim Sorokin and others of his way of thinking. This halting recognition of the Super-conscious will not be able to gather speed, for, it faces a blind alley in its further movement. This is due to the fact that the Super-conscious is sought to be understood in the same manner as the Sub-conscious and the Unconscious—in other words, its effect is sought to be measured by the so-called scientific processes which have assumed new respectability in the modern psychological world. So long as psychology regards science as its only ally, so long the secret of the Super-conscious cannot be comprehended—and without its comprehension the understanding of human psyche must remain incomplete. Without listening to the voice of the Super-conscious, any evaluation of man based on the findings of the Subconscious and the Unconscious is bound to be erroneous. It will be like trying to understand the Whole by a process of speculation based on the knowledge of the parts. The Whole, in the psychological sense, is greater than the sum of the parts. Human personality which is a Whole cannot be understood by a summation of the parts—not even by a speculation based on the summation of the parts. Psychology through its alliance with science may know about the parts. But for the comprehension of the Whole it must form an alliance with Philosophy. Without psychology finding once again its roots in philosophy, it can have no understanding of the Super-conscious. Now the Indian Psychology took all the three factors of the Sub-conscious, Unconscious and the Super-conscious into consideration. And nowhere is this complete approach of Indian Psychology seen so clearly as in the Māṇḍūkya Upanishad.

The Māṇḍūkya Upanishad is the shortest among all the Upanishads—but its teaching is very profound. This Upanishad takes its name from the Teacher by the name Maṇḍūka who has given the teachings contained in this Upanishad. This Upanishad is also a part of the *Atharva Veda* and has the same invocation as appearing in the Praśna and the Muṇḍaka Upanishads. It begins with the following verse:

> The Eternal Word OM is all; what was, what is and what shall be, and what is beyond the three-fold time—all is OM. Brahman is all—and Ātman is Brahman.

Here in this verse we come across the famous Upanishadic statement—one of the *Mahāvākyas* —namely: *Ayamātmā Brahma—Ātman is Brahman.* In this opening verse of the Māṇḍūkya Upanishad the Sacred Word, OM, and Brahman have been used as synonyms. To denote what Brahman is, there is hardly any other illustration more apt than the Sacred Word, OM. This Word indicates the co-existence of the articulate and the inarticulate sounds—of the heard and the unheard melodies —of the sound that is struck and the sound that is unstruck—the *Anāhata Nāda.* Sound may be described by its three-fold nature—The Audible Sound, the Inaudible Sound and the Imperishable Sound. The Audible Sound is one which the human ear can hear, the Inaudible Sound is one which belongs to such octaves as are either too high or too low for the human ear to respond to. They may become audible to those who have particular paranormal faculties such as clairaudience. This sound may also be picked up by very sensitive scientific instruments. But there is a third category of sound which is Imperishable. Sound obviously consists of vibrations, and all vibrations have a beginning and an end. Thus sound which is audible as also the sound which is inaudible are perishable in their nature. When the medium through which sound travels ceases to vibrate then the sound has to come to an end. It is needless to say that it is only the struck sound that is perishable—it is the heard melody which has an end. But if there could be a sound which is unstruck—the *Anāhata Nāda* —then surely there could be no end to it as there is no beginning to it. The unstruck sound has no vibrations and so it belongs to no octave. To talk of a vibration-less sound is indeed to indulge in a paradox. In the Sacred Word, OM, there is such a paradox. It is both heard and unheard, struck as well as unstruck, it is both Perishable and Imperishable. It is in its perishable nature that it belongs to time—the past, the present and the future. But in its imperishable nature it is beyond the three-fold time as the above verse says. It is both manifest and unmanifest. In OM one contacts the resonance of articulation, but also the mystery of inarticulation. The Sacred Word, OM, represents both the Perishable as well as the Imperishable Sound. In its Perishable aspect it covers all the audible and the inaudible octaves of sound—but in its Imperishable aspect it signifies the Soundless Sound. The Soundless Sound is indeed the *Nāda Brahma.* Not only was the Word with God, the Word was God. The Word being with God signifies manifestation, emanating from God—but the Word being God is the Unmanifest state. What is with a person can be differentiated, but what is the person himself cannot be differentiated. Now a differentiation is a state with attributes, while a condition without differentiation is an attributeless state. But it is the state of non-differentiation which is the cause of all differentiation, Brahman without attributes is the cause of Brahman with attributes. Now Time is the field in which attributes exist. But how can there be attributes in a condition of Timelessness? The above verse speaks of Brahman in Time and Brahman beyond Time—and this is beautifully illustrated by the articulate and the inarticulate sound which resides in the Sacred Word, OM. If the Sacred Word is all and if Brahman too is all—then the Word and the Brahman are identical. The Word is Brahman. But again the Upanishad says that Ātman is Brahman—and so the Word is indeed the Ātman. The articulate word indicates Ātman in manifestation, but the inarticulate sound represents Ātman in its unmanifest condition. Here one is reminded of the verse of the Bhagavad *Gītā* appearing in its Second Discourse which says:

> Beings are unmanifest in their origin, manifest in their midmost state, and again unmanifest in dissolution.

The beginning and the end of OM are in the letters *A* and *M* respectively—and the letter *U* represents the midmost state. The entire manifestation of OM is in the midmost state, for the sound *A* and the sound *M* are more inarticulate than articulate—they are more unheard than heard. The Ātman which is identical with the Sacred Word has to be experienced both as manifest and as unmanifest. The Māṇḍūkya Upanishad shows us the way by which the manifest and the unmanifest Ātman can be discovered.

But why has Ātman to be discovered? Is man different from Ātman? If so, what caused this separation of man from himself? Man's instrument of knowledge is his consciousness. This consciousness functions in time—and therefore in the course of time it acquires numerous modifications. These modifications are like dust resting on the smooth surface of the mirror. It is not the movement which causes modification in consciousness—it is the grooves established in this movement which are the cause of all modifications. When the grooves are formed then the movement is not free but restricted by the formation of grooves. Instead of consciousness functioning in the open spaces, it moves along the grooves—and every movement in the groove makes the groove deeper. Soon the horses that pull the chariot of life lose their capacity to run in the open spaces—they are not aware of their own strength and capacity. They feel lost when the grooves are not there. It is thus that human consciousness gets conditioned and thereby loses sight of its own nature—of its strength and capacity. Man is separated from himself due to the grooves of modifications. He has forgotten his own nature, he regards himself as a being eternally cribbed, cabined and confined in the restrictions which he has imposed upon himself and to which he is completely addicted. He is so used to moving in the grooves, that this movement has become his second nature—and the second nature has completely eclipsed the original nature. Man has created his own bondage—but he blames others for keeping him in bondage! Man can be free from this bondage by being aware of himself. In fact, the awareness of oneself and the breaking of the bonds are not two different things. The moment of awareness is itself the moment of freedom. The problem of man's freedom is not the problem of acquiring something—on the contrary, it is the problem of negating what he has acquired. Man's consciousness is covered up with various layers—as layer after layer is negated then there is seen consciousness in its pure and unmodified condition. And to the Pure consciousness the perception of Ātman comes, even as the mirror reflects a clear image when all dust is removed. The perception of Ātman comes in the deepening of awareness. The Māṇḍūkya Upanishad is mainly concerned with this problem of deepening consciousness, of arriving at that state where human consciousness is free from all its modifications, a state where it has come to its pristine purity. This process of uncovering or de-conditioning of human consciousness is considered by this Upanishad in its four-fold aspect The Māṇḍūkya Upanishad says that:

> The first condition is the waking life of outward moving consciousness.

This condition of consciousness is described as *Vaiśvānara* who beholds the external objects. Now, one of the meanings of the word *Vaiśvānara* is the general or normal consciousness. It is needless to say that the normal consciousness is outgoing, stimulated by external objects. This is the Waking state—the *Jāgarita* the characteristic of which, according to the Upanishad, is *Āpti* or attainment. It is during the Waking state that man works for various attainments. But this Waking state is not to be mistaken for the Awakened state. The *Jāgarita* or the Waking is the normal consciousness of man—a condition in which he makes his choices, he comes to decisions. It is a condition in which he evaluates and in terms of this evaluation plans for various attainments and achievements. This Waking state, obviously, is made up of the patterns of action as also the motives of action. All actions in the Waking state are impelled by certain motives. The above verse says that man is outgoing in the Waking state. In this outgoing state man wants to appropriate to himself whatever he considers essential for his existence and expansion. This process of appropriation naturally involves choice—and choice implies both acceptance and rejection. But how does man do this choice? What is the standard by which he is guided in this process of choice? How does he decide what needs to be accepted and what needs to be rejected? It is hardly necessary to point out that this choice is determined by the norms and standards maintained by man's Personal Memory. Everything that impinges from the external world is measured in the scales of Personal Memory and when the latter gives its approval then the act of acceptance begins. The outgoing activities of the normal consciousness are thus controlled by the factors that reside in the Personal Memory. But what is the abode of Personal Memory? Obviously it is the Subconscious. It is true that there are certain aspects of memory that reside at the conscious level—but these are of a very superficial and immaterial nature. The impelling power of memory resides in the Subconscious. And so what we call the Waking state is a combination of the conscious and the Subconscious layers of the mind. The conscious layer supplies the patterns and modes of behaviour—but it is the subconscious that gives the motive or the impelling power of action. The conscious and the subconscious are in close collaboration with each other. The subconscious gives the raw material and the conscious mind produces a finished object out of that raw material. The designing of form and pattern is obviously of the conscious mind. Sometimes this design has to be of such a nature that it completely hides the raw material out of which it has been fashioned. In the psychological school of Freud, Adler, and others of similar persuasion, we see a special study of the subconscious—a study of the contents of Personal Memory. The respectability of the conscious mind has within it the ugliness of all suppressed desires. It is the suppressed desires which constitute the substratum of respectable conscious actions. Through respectable actions the suppressed desires very often find their release. In the Waking state that which is awake is indeed the subconscious. In fact, the subconscious never sleeps, for it is seething with restless impulses. It is true that in the Waking state, we make choices, we take decisions, we evaluate and judge, we determine our lines of actions. But the question is: Are our choices and decisions free or conditioned and restricted by the motivating impulses of the subconscious? It is true that the Waking state constitutes an awareness with choice—but the choice is determined by the subconscious. And so the Waking state in which *Vaiśvānara* beholds the external objects is not an Awakened state. The waking-ness of the Waking state is controlled by the motivations of the Personal Memory, by the impelling pressure of the subconscious. Unless one awakens from the Waking state there is no freedom from the conditioning factors of Personal Memory.

The Teacher of the Māṇḍūkya Upanishad then speaks of the second layer of consciousness under which the real nature of Ātman lies covered. This he describes in the following verse:

> The second condition is the dreaming life of inner moving consciousness.

From the *Jāgarita* or the Waking state the Teacher now moves on to the *Svapna* or the Dream state. Here it may not be out of place to mention that the Waking and the Dream states are not to be considered in their physical aspects. It is not the physical waking or the dream arising in the condition of physical sleep that is being discussed. We are concerned with something more fundamental than merely the physical expressions of human consciousness. We saw earlier that the Waking state is that condition in which the conscious and the sub-conscious are in close collaboration. The Waking state is an outward-moving consciousness, for, here all activities arise because of the stimulus arising from the external objects. It may be asked—how does the sub-conscious come into the picture? We act by the stimulation given by external objects—but how does this stimulation arise? The external objects stimulate certain centres of Personal Memory—and the Personal Memory resides in the subconscious. We say Personal Memory because with each object there are memory-associations which are peculiar to each man. The same object does not arouse same stimulation for every one. Each stimulation is personal to each man. We know the external objects in terms of the memory-stimulation. And so in the Waking state while we choose and decide, our evaluation is not free because it is the sub-conscious that dictates to us its judgment through Personal Memory. This is how our normal consciousness functions—this is how *Vaiśvānara* beholds the external world of objects, of persons and of ideas.

The Dream state constitutes a different level of human consciousness. In the Māṇḍūkya Upanishad it is described as *Taijasa*, meaning shining or bright. What is this Dream state about which the Upanishad speaks? Modern Western Psychology has made a special and intensive study of dreams. There is the dream interpretation by Freud and others of his school, according to which dreams contain elements drawn from the subconscious where suppressed desires are located. As suppressed desires represent those factors of man's psychological life as are contrary to accepted norms of respectability, they follow the path of dreams to seek their fulfilment. And so in dreams appear these undesirable elements which are denied all scope of expression during conscious life. However, this interpretation of dreams has been challenged by other psychologists, notably among them Carl Jung. In his interpretation, Carl Jung maintains that dreams contain many other factors whose presence cannot be explained in terms of the sub-conscious. According to him dreams are not merely the safety valves for suppressed desires. He introduces a new factor of the Unconscious which according to him displays its tendencies in dreams. This Unconscious contains Racial Memory because of which it may be called the Universal Unconscious. This Racial Memory influences man's consciousness and appears in the form of Myths and Symbols during the dream condition. Carl Jung maintains that these myths and symbols cannot be explained away in terms of the sub-conscious—to do so would be utterly unwarranted, for, it would result in misinterpreting the dream language. Thus Carl Jung has given to dreams a wider context than was given by Freud and others. He has indicated that man comes into contact with a larger world in dream state for he is able to draw upon the vast store-house of Racial Memory. The contents of the Personal Memory are extremely limited, and so all dream interpretations that confine themselves to the influence of the sub-conscious are utterly restricted in deciphering the dream code. The Unconscious or the store-house of Racial Memory is naturally unlimited in its contents. It contains the experiences of the whole human race—it has factors which are both good as well as bad. While the Sub-conscious has within its store-house only the undesirable characters, the Unconscious is not so. Through the Unconscious man comes into contact with the vast store-house of racial experience and draw from it freely for his own enrichment. According to this the experiences of the human race are not lost—they lie embedded in Racial Memory. It is in the Dream state that man can get easy access to this Racial Memory from where he can bring the message of the unconscious in the language of myths and symbols. It has however to be noted that these myths and symbols reach the conscious level through the subconscious. In this passage they do get mixed up with much that the subconscious imparts. Much sorting out is necessary at the conscious level before the myths and symbols can become intelligible. In fact they have to be transformed if man is to derive any benefit out of them. What interests us here is the Racial Memory which seems to be playing an important part in the Dream state.

We stated earlier that the Dream state is described in the Māṇḍūkya Upanishad as *Taijasa*, or that which is bright and shining. Why is it described thus? The Māṇḍūkya Upanishad says that the experience of the Dream state is like *Utkarsha* or upsurge even as the *Jāgarita* experience is *Āpti* or attainment. From where does this upsurge come in the dream condition? It comes from the Racial Memory which is unlimited in its contents. The upsurge indicates something that comes from beyond one's range. The Racial Memory is indeed beyond the range of Personal Memory. To be able to come into contact with the experience of the entire human race is verily something to be described as *Utkarsha* or upsurge. The Upanishad says that the Dream state is an "inner-moving consciousness". The *Jāgarita* is the outward-moving, meaning stimulated by external objects. The Dream state is inner-moving which means not moved by outer objects but by inner factors. Even ordinarily in dreams man is not moved by outer objects, but by inner modifications. A dream may not have any relationship with objective reality—and yet it is as real as an objective experience. And the more vivid a dream is the greater is the reality felt. From where is this reality derived? If its source had been merely the subconscious or the Personal Memory then surely the experience would not have been such as could be described as *Utkarsha* or upsurge. In a Dream state, of which the Upanishad speaks, there is an exhilaration because of a contact with something that is outside one's range. The experience is like upsurge because an impact has come from the Racial Memory. A dream that arises only from the sub-conscious level may give to man an excitement, an exciting sensation, but not an exhilaration. Such dreams of the subconscious level do not give to the dreamer a feeling that he had had an experience, a fresh or a new experience. In subconscious dreams there may be a reliving of an old experience—but not a feeling of a fresh experience. Such feeling comes only when there is an *Utkarsha*—an upsurge from the Racial Memory, when there is an impact from the Unconscious. It is this impact from the Unconscious or the Racial Memory that brings to the Dream state an element of *Taijasa* –a feeling of brightness.

As we are dealing with Dream state not in its superficial aspect of the happenings during physical sleep, it is necessary for us to note that the *Taijasa* or the *Utkarsha* of the Dream state has nothing in common with the ecstasy of mystical experience. The experience of the Dream state is only psychic in nature—not to be mistaken for that deeply mystical experience which brings to man a sense of ecstasy—a sense in which man steps out of himself. An ecstasy in an experience of self-transcendence. In Dream state nothing of this happens. It has to be remembered that the Dream state is within the frontiers of Racial Memory. The Waking state functions within the confines of Personal Memory.

There is thus an element of continuity maintained both in the Waking as well as the Dream state. In the Waking state this continuity is given by the factors of Personal Memory. In the Dream state it is the Racial Memory which provides the ground of continuity. And so the experience in the Dream state, however exhilarating it may be, is within the confines of continuity. An ecstasy is an experience, not of continuity, but of discontinuity. In the Waking state the circle of continuity is naturally small because it is formed out of the factors of Personal Memory. In Dream state, however, there is to be seen an emergence of Extended continuity. This extension is due to the fact that man in the Dream state can draw upon the vast resources of Racial Memory. But memory by itself signifies a sphere of continuity. In fact, it is memory which casts a screen of continuity on all that happens. And so the experience of the Dream state has no content of originality in it. Here the human consciousnesss is given a sphere of extended continuity within which to function. But sometimes this extension of continuity is mistakenly regarded by man as discontinuity. Just as the ever-lasting is very often mistaken as the Eternal, in the same way Extended continuity is misconstrued as Discontinuity. In the Dream state there takes place an extension of consciousness, but not an expansion of it. Here human consciousness grows in breadth, but not in depth. From Personal Memory to Racial Memory, from subconscious to unconscious, is a movement in breadth of consciousness. It is true that in the Dream state there is no limit to the extensions of human consciousness, for the vast Memory of the entire human race is available to man. However, in practice it is not from the entire human race that man draws—he draws only from those sections and groups in Racial Memory to which he is mentally and emotionally attracted. If this were not the case man would be utterly dazed and confused as a result of extensions brought about in the

Dream state. In the sphere of man's attractions, the Dream state affords a possibility of infinite extension. But an infinite extension in continuity is not Discontinuity.

Let us not forget that by Dream state we are not referring to a state coming into existence as a result of physical sleep. We are also not referring to a condition known as day-dreaming. The Dream state has nothing to do with physical sleep even as the Waking state has nothing to do with physical waking. Here we are concerned with states of consciousness. In the Waking state, all activities are coloured by the projections of Personal Memory. In the Dream state, there are the projections of Racial Memory. Thus the experiences of the Dream state are conditioned by the factors imparted to them by the Racial Memory. Let it be remembered that what constitutes the Dream state is a contact with the Racial Memory—where such contact is not there, the Dream state does not come into existence. The experiences of Dream state come to man in moments of deep absorption—it does not matter what the field of absorption is. It may be prayer or meditation, it may be events full of joy or sorrow, it may be the proximity of nature, or it may be the influence of music or painting or any of the arts, it may be an act demanding great adventure and risk or it may be a sudden accident—it matters not what the happening is—what is of supreme importance is absorption—a condition where there is awareness without choice. Even in our ordinary dream experiences, we know how a vivid dream holds our interest—it keeps us completely absorbed. Wherever there is the element of absorption there the consciousness of man experiences a Dream state. In the Waking state there is a determination born out of choice; in the Dream state there is absorption born out of choicelessness. In personal memory man can pick and choose—but with reference to the Racial Memory there is no process of choice, but of *utkarsha*—an upsurge, as the Māṇḍūkya Upanishad says. This *utkarsha* or upsurge comes like a blinding light because of which the Dream state is described as *taijasa*. However, this upsurge of the Racial Memory is most often regarded as spiritual or mystical experience. When in meditation or prayer a man sees visions of the deity or the Person whom he adores then he begins to believe that the vision is the real experience. Is it not significant that in such visions the deity or the Person appears in the traditionally accepted form? This traditionally accepted form is the projection of the Racial Memory. People find exhilarations in religious gatherings or in meetings of spiritual organisations or places of worship or in ceremonial performances—and they regard such experiences as real, amounting to mystical or spiritual communion. But such is the experience of most people that these exhilarations are short lived —and once their effect is over, man craves for more and more of these experiences. A real spiritual experience has a shattering effect because it destroys the very base of continuity. A consoling experience gives a feeling of security—and such is indeed the case with experiences emerging from the Unconscious—for they give to man security of continuity. The infinite extension of continuity gives a sense of exhilaration—but behind this sense of "uplift" there is a consolation of security. The effect of such experiences is only a modification—not a revolution. A revolution and continuity are contradiction in terms. The Dream state is concerned only with a modification of one's pattern of living—and this modification is induced by the projections of Racial Memory. Man's aspiration under this impact is to become like somebody—like some one who has been regarded as great in human history or in human mythology. The Dream state induces a change —but a change in the image of some one who is the Hero of Racial Memory.

The Dream state, as has been stated above, brings about an extension of consciousness—and such extension is greatly useful, for, it brings a breadth of consciousness. To contact, from time to time, the sources of Racial Memory is indeed a worth-while experience. To be able to tap the sources of Racial Memory is indeed to show forth traits of true education and true culture. The man who acts only from the base of his Personal Memory may be educated, but he is not cultured. He who makes the Racial Memory as the base of his actions is a cultured man, for he is mellow and considerate, not aggressive and self-opinionated as a man moving under the dictates of Personal Memory is.

But it may be asked: Is not Racial Memory a storehouse of good as well as bad influences through which the human race has passed? It certainly is—but then how is man to assure himself that in his Dream state what is projected are the good, the noble, influences of Racial Memory and not the unpleasant ones? We have stated earlier that the intimations of the Unconscious reach the level of the conscious mind through the subconscious. In other words, the intimations of the Racial Memory get distorted as they pass through the field of Personal Memory. And so the heights of the Dream state can be experienced only when the centres of Personal Memory are made inoperative. A true Waking state is that in which man becomes aware of the limiting factors of Personal Memory. Such a man sees for himself that the choices and decisions of his conscious life are not free at all because they are motivated by the impacts of the sub-conscious. To be aware of this limiting influence of Personal Memory is to make its centres inoperative, at least for the time being. When this happens then is man enabled to come to the Dream state where he can come into contact with the ennobling influences of the Racial Memory. In this contact man enriches his feeble effort with the influences drawn from that vast store-house. To his limited experience he gives an extension—almost an infinite extension so that he is able to draw closer to the image of some one whom he adores and worships.

But drawing closer to an Image is utterly different from communing with that Person. The Unconscious contains the memory of the Person—not the person himself. In Racial Memory, at best, one comes into contact with the manifested aspect of the Person, not with the Unmanifest. It is here that one sees the limited scope of what is being attempted in such schools of Western Psychology as are concerned with altruistic behaviour. There is apparently an effort to contact the Super-conscious—but in fact, it is only a contact with the ennobling influences of the Unconscious or the Racial Memory. To understand merely the effects of mystical experience is to contact only the memory of mystics as contained in the Racial Memory. An effect signifies a result—and all results are only the memories of the past. Let us be clear in our minds that the ennobling influences of the Unconscious do not represent the Super-conscious. A Continuity because it has been extended into infinity does not become Discontinuity.

A question may arise: How can we be sure that by eliminating the factors of Personal Memory we shall contact only the good of the Racial Memory and not its bad—since this Memory contains both good and bad of human experience? In the earlier part of our discussion we had mentioned that the Māṇḍūkya Upanishad is concerned with finding the Good or the Auspicious. The problem of good and evil is very interesting but also very intriguing. Let us see how we determine good in the Waking state—which is our normal state, the state where *Vaiśvānara*, beholds all that is happening.

In the Waking state, we declare something as good and something else as evil in terms of what the Personal Memory or the subconscious dictates. And what is the criterion by which the Personal Memory decides? Obviously by the standard of Pleasant and Unpleasant. In the Waking state, where our motivations are determined by the sub-conscious, the values of life are sorted out by labelling them as Pleasant or Unpleasant. This is so because the continuity of Personal Memory depends upon our pursuing that which is pleasant and avoiding that which is unpleasant. Needless to say, for the Personal Memory, the good is that which maintains its continuity. Anything that disturbs its continuity is regarded as evil. Thus the likes and dislikes of the Personal Memory are the determining factors regarding the evaluation of Good and Evil at the Waking state. But if the factors of Personal Memory are made inoperative and man comes to the Dream state, how is the evaluation of good and evil done? When this happens then the Racial Memory or the Unconscious can speak directly to the conscious level of the mind without the intervention of Personal Memory. In this direct communication with the conscious mind, the Unconscious indicates what it regards as good and evil. Now the security of the Unconscious depends upon an un-interrupted continuity of Racial Memory. And so it is the Racial Memory which dictates its norms of good and evil to the conscious mind. The good and evil to the Racial Memory are the Proper and the Improper even as the Personal Memory declares them to be Pleasant and Unpleasant. A continuity of Racial Memory requires an adherence to that which is Proper and the avoidance of that which is Improper. How can the continuity of Race or Group be maintained if improper patterns of behaviour are indulged in? The voice of the Unconscious is the voice of morality which is always concerned about the continuity of race or group. That which strikes at the root of continuity is to be regarded as immoral. Here we are not referring to merely physical continuity—we are concerned more with the psychological or ideological continuity. When the factors of Personal Memory—the pursuit of the pleasant and the avoidance of the unpleasant—are made inoperative then is man able to see clearly the values dictated by the Racial Memory—the moral imperatives on the maintenance of which depend the security and continuity of the Race or the Group. But in both the above cases the good is relative to the continuity of Personal and Racial Memory. But a relative good is fleeting for it changes with the changed circumstances of life—it depends upon the vagaries of the Personal and Racial Memory. Without knowing the Absolute Good, are not the pursuit of relative good a mere groping in the dark? If the relative does not reflect the Absolute, then the former will reduce itself to mere expediency and opportunism. Are we to equate the good with the expedient? Obviously not, for expediency is guided by the doctrine of end justifying the means. But for this the end must be inquired into—for if the end is impure the means are bound to be unclean. The Personal Memory says that the pursuit of the pleasant is good, for it fulfils the end of maintaining its continuity. Similarly the Racial Memory declares the pursuit of the proper as good for thereby its security is guaranteed. But here the ends have been taken for granted. The end of Personal Memory lies in its motives, while the end of Racial Memory lies in its ideals—the ideals and the objectives of the race or the group. If the ideals and the objectives are thrown overboard then the psychological continuity of the Race is threatened. But how can the voice of the Absolute be known without the relative becoming silent? We saw that the intimations of the Unconscious can come to the conscious mind only when the voice of the subconscious is silenced. But for this man must become aware of the motives of his actions in which he indulges during the Waking state. In this awareness of motives, the Personal Memory is rendered inoperative, at least for the time being. In this pause of the Personal Memory, the voice of the Racial Memory can be heard. This is what is meant by the Dream state.

But in the intimations of the Unconscious or the Racial Memory, one finds not the Absolute Good but only the relative good. Here the sphere of relativity is larger—nevertheless, it is relative, and being relative, it is fleeting and changeful. From Personal Memory to Racial Memory there has been an extension in the field of relativity but even an infinite extension of the relative does not bring us to the Absolute. The relative lives in a world of duality—but the Absolute is one without a second. The Māṇḍūkya Upanishad speaking about the Dream state says that it is characterised by *Ubhayatvam*, meaning "bothness" or duality. And so in the Dream state there is no answer to a non-dual experience. All its exhilarations are within the compass of duality—and so the joys of the Dream state are short-lived. Its experiences have no relationship with the ecstasy of the mystic. But how does one come to the realization of Absolute Good—the Good which is not the opposite of evil, the Good which is incomparable, not to be found by a process of comparison and contrast? This is possible only when the Dream state ends. But how can it end? And what lies beyond the Dream state? We saw that one moves from the Waking to the Dream state by being aware of the motives of one's conscious actions. This is necessary in order to release the human consciousness from the thraldom of Personal Memory. The motives and their contents are to be found in the Personal Memory. This Personal Memory associated with external objects and happenings serves as a compulsion under which we act in our conscious life. All actions under compulsion are reactions. But here in the Waking state the compulsion is outer, arising out of the stimulation given by external phenomena. In being aware of these motives and their contents, the pull of the Personal Memory is gone, for, one realizes in this awareness that behind the beautifully planned patterns of behaviour, there is the ugly motive which is securely hidden. One who has become aware of this cannot be a tool of the subconscious. Even though this freedom may be momentary, in that moment, when the Personal Memory has been made inoperative, man comes to the experience of the Dream state. But here too he is subjected to the influences of the Racial or the Group Memory. The sphere of continuity has been enlarged. There is no stimulation from the external objects—but there is an elevating influence or *Utkarsha* arising from the Unconscious. These come in the form of symbols and myths—or it may be described as the influences belonging to the realms of Ideals—very often personified ideals, but sometimes abstract ideals. These ideals become attractive—the meaning of the word *Utkarsha* is attractive—because they are regarded as the achievements of the race. It is said that men rise to higher states of consciousness to the extent to which they contact the orbits of those who have reached such states. And so there is the ideal of the super-man. And the experiences of these super-men are stored in Racial Memory. Their impingement on the conscious life comes in the form of ideals. The Racial Memory projects an image of these super men showing how they had translated great ideals into their behaviour-patterns. And so man begins to worship the images cast by the Racial Memory and invests them with great halo. In the Dream state one is attracted by the halo of these images. The good that is indicated by the Racial Memory is this image—and one is told that to imitate the image, to endeavour to translate it into one's life, would be the greatest good that man can ever hope to achieve. To reproduce the image, stored and nourished by the Racial Memory, therefore becomes the supreme task of man in the Dream state.

But man must release himself from the hypnotic influence of the Racial Memory if he is to come to the understanding of the Good that is Absolute. How can man find his freedom from Racial Memory? By observing the process in which he is engaged during the Dream state. What is this process? It is the translation of the Image into patterns of behaviour. In this observation he is bound to realise that he is trying to establish a link between two divergently opposite things, for, while the Image is static, the living of daily life is intensely dynamic. The daily living involves ceaseless change. How can any link ever be established between one point that is static and another point that is continually in a flux? In this observation, man realizes that the image is devoid of any living quality—it is only a creation of memory. The creation of an image is like taking still pictures of something that is moving at a terrific pace. Such a still picture is obviously lifeless. The image created by Racial Memory is exactly of this nature—it matters not whether the image is of super-men, or of a great Master or of a great Genius. The Image is not the man, the Word is not the thing—it is this realization that frees man from the thraldom of Racial Memory. The worship of image demands a constant adornment of that image, for otherwise the image ceases to be attractive. On man's consciousness must come newer and newer impacts from the image, as otherwise the process of translating the image into daily action becomes even more frustrating. Here there is a craving for more and more lest the glamour of the image may go. The dressing up of the old is the constant activity in which man is engaged in the Dream state. Without this dressing up, the image would look stale and unattractive. In order that the hollowness of the image may not be found out, the mind of man takes out new clothes from its wardrobe with which to cover the image. This covering of the image goes on at all levels—physical as well as mental. Having dressed up the image, one feels the hypnotic influence of the image. And man in the Dream state wants to remain constantly under the spell of hypnotic influences of the image projected by the Racial Memory or the Group Memory. In the very awareness of the process of linking up the image with the act of daily living, the spell of the image is broken, and man experiences freedom from the hypnotic enslavement of the image—and therefore of the Racial or the Group Memory.

The man of so-called spiritual discipline very often declares that his discipline is not the result of any outer or external pressure or authority. He is completely free from outer authority, be it of the scripture or of the guru. He very proudly declares that he follows the inner discipline—that which has been evolved out of inner perception. He forgets that the inner authority is only the authority of the Image. It is the Image that has dictated a discipline and under its hypnotic influence he follows the dictates of that inner authority. It is the projection of the Racial Memory that determines his so-called spiritual discipline. This discipline will keep him moving in a circle, for, that is what happens in all moral efforts. Unless morality arises from a spiritual vision, its movement is like dog chasing its own tail. This spiritual vision is not to be found either in the Waking state or in the Dream state, neither by pursuing the Pleasant nor by giving one's allegiance to that which is Proper. It is not by acting under the compulsion of the Personal or the Racial Memory that one comes to the perception of the Good, the True and the Beautiful. The Māṇḍūkya Upanishad says that in the Waking state the consciousness is "outward-moving", while in the Dream state it is "inner-moving". But Truth is found not by a movement that is outward or a movement that is inward. It is to be found only when there is no movement of consciousness, neither outer nor inner. It is to this that the Teacher of the Māṇḍūkya Upanishad refers as he speaks about the third state of consciousness. The verse of the Upanishad says:

> The third state is of Deep sleep, of silent consciousness where there is no acquiring—where there is no beholding even of dreams. It is a state of oneness.

Speaking further about this state of *Sushupti* or Deep Sleep, the Teacher of the Upanishad says that it is characterised by *Āptii* or final end. The literal meaning of the word *Apiti* is entering into or approaching. The state of Deep sleep is indeed a state where man is approaching the Portal of Truth. It is a condition where man is entering a new realm—a realm where continuity comes to a final end. The portal of discontinuity is known to the mind only as a final end. The state of Deep sleep is indeed the final end of the mind—it is *Apiti* for all processes of mentation. This third state of Deep sleep is also described as containing *Miti* or measure, for, it corresponds to the third sound of the Sacred Word—namely, the sound *M*. It signifies that all the measurements of the mind have come to an end. The verse of the Upanishad says:

> Who knows the Third state, measures all with the mind and attains the final end.

Here the mind has measured all it could measure—and its measuring has come to a final end. In the Deep Sleep condition there is nothing which the mind can measure. The question is: Why has the measurement of the mind come to a final end? After all what is the instrument with which mind measures? Needless to say, the measuring rod of the mind is Memory. So long as memory functions, mind is able to give its measurements. It is memory which keeps the standard of measurement, the norm of evaluation. Both in the Waking and the Dream states, it is memory that functions and dictates its judgments. In the first, it is the Personal Memory, and, in the second, it is the Racial Memory. From Personal to Racial Memory is a movement of the mind towards extensive measurement. Memory is the store-house of experience. In the Waking state one acts in terms of one's own past experiences. In the Dream state one is enabled to draw upon the experiences of the Race or the Group. But experiencing is possible only when one is freed from the shackles of experience. In memory lies the accumulation of experience. But living is possible only when there is no accumulation of experience. Now experience without accumulation does not mean the forgetting of the facts—it does not signify that one must gather all the facts afresh. What is needed is to have the facts of life and yet to divest them of all their compelling influence so that they do not colour the perception of new facts. To have personal memory but to divest it of all its compelling influences is to render it free from likes and dislikes. It is the likes and dislikes rooted in Personal Memory that condition our movement at the conscious level. To have the Racial Memory but to divest it of all its compelling power is to free it from the halo and spell that it casts over the actions of man. Freedom from memory is not a state of amnesia—it is a condition where it remains merely as a record of the past, causing no limitation to the actions in the present. It must remain a record and not arrogate to itself the task of measuring the contents of life. Both in the Waking as well as the Dream state the measuring activity of the mind goes on and that is why man does not come to the perception of the Good, the True and the Beautiful. Through mind's measuring he knows only the relative good, not the Absolute Good. But the relative has meaning only in terms of the Absolute. The relative, divorced from the Absolute, has no significance at all—it is devoid of a living quality. It is the Absolute which imparts to the relative a living quality. But the Absolute cannot be found by the measuring practices of the mind. Mind's measurement must come to a final end—must come to *Āpti*, and this is what happens in the state of Deep Sleep.

The State of Deep Sleep is characterised by silence

where there is no disturbance even of dreams. The inhabitants of the Dream state are the Images, the contents of Racial Memory. In the state of Deep Sleep no image can find admittance, for, the very presence of the image would cause disturbance. In the Dream state are negated the motives of the sub-conscious. In Deep Sleep are negated all the images of the unconscious, with all their decorations in terms of myths and symbols. In Deep Sleep there is no movement at all—neither outer nor inner. In fact, in Deep Sleep there is no duality of the sleeper and the sleep. There is only sleep—there is no sleeper. If the sleeper were present he would disturb the sleep, for, the sleeper is no other than the mind. In our ordinary experience of sleep we know how we are unable to sleep when the mind is active. The thought-processes of the mind do not allow us to sleep. These thought-processes conjure up image after image and thus keep us awake. It is only when all the activities of the mind cease that one can come to a condition of Deep Sleep. In ordinary sleep we are concerned with the quiet of the brain. For when the brain is quiet one is able to sleep easily. But when the brain is quiet, and the mind is active, then the sleep is disturbed by dreams, sometimes by nightmare dreams. When the brain is quiet, the Waking state comes to an end, but if the mind is active then the activity of dream continues. And the dream activity prevents the arrival of Deep Sleep. In Deep Sleep there is no movement of consciousness—neither due to the stimulation from without nor due to the welling up from within—neither in terms of *Apiti* nor in terms of *Utkarsha*. There is a silence, unbroken even by dreams. The verse of the Māṇḍūkya Upaniṣhad says that here there is "oneness"—not *Ubhayatvam*—"bothness", as one finds in the Dream state. Thus in Deep Sleep there is no duality—and how can there be any movement where duality does not exist?

But what is that state of consciousness where all movement has ceased? All movement denotes time. And time can exist only where there is a past and a future. In fact, time is a movement from the past to the future.

The world or *saṃsāra* which displays a procession of events appears to point to a flux where things seem to come from the past and move towards a future. This procession does not seem to stop even for a moment; there is a continuity of movement from the past to the future. That is our experience in terms of our consciousness—nothing stays, everything moves. Things come from somewhere and disappear into somewhere. Man wants to know what this thing is which seems to be all the time moving. But how can he know unless he holds that thing in his hands—and this is what man attempts to do with his mind. The mind wants to hold—but that which is living cannot be held. But man must know it, because it is a constant challenge to him—the mystery of the thing that seems to move must be solved. Man believes that either by going into the past or by contacting the future the thing will be known. For, he argues that the past is the beginning and the future is the end—and so at either of these points he must be able to come to the comprehension of the thing that seems to be in eternal flux. It is knowing in terms of the past and the future that is being done in the Waking and the Dream states. In the Waking state there is the identification with the past—the subconscious; and in the Dream state there is the identification with the future—the unconscious, with its images fashioned out of myths and symbols. But a consciousness moving at the behest of the past or the future is unable to find the Good, the True and the Beautiful.

When one realizes the futility of a movement motivated by the subconscious and a movement towards future induced by the images of the unconscious, then does consciousness come to a stop, for, no further movement is possible. It is the accumulations of the past that create anticipations of the future. The subconscious contains the accumulations of the past and the unconscious is beset with the anticipations of the future. The accumulations and the anticipations cause a compulsion—man acts from compulsion, either outer or inner. It is only when the compulsions, both outer and inner, cease that there can be the vision of the Thing that seems to be in constant flux. Sometimes it is said that Truth compels. Be it noted that Truth never compels. It only exists—and that too in utter silence. It is the motives of the sub-conscious or the images of the unconscious that compel. How can a spiritual state arise under compulsion? There can be no compulsion whatsoever—not even of Truth. The *Apiti* or the approach of human consciousness, has to be free from all compulsions—it must be an approach of a complete free will and accord. But does not an approach suggest a movement? It may seem paradoxical—but in Deep Sleep there is an approach of no-approach. The Deep Sleep state is described as the "silent consciousness". Just as *Jāgarita* or Waking is described as *Vaiśvānara*, just as *Svapna* or Dream is described as *Taijasa*, the Deep Sleep is described as *Prājña* or the Wise. The Deep Sleep condition is indeed the state of Wisdom. Wisdom is not arrived at through the inter-action of the opposites—it comes into being when the play of the opposites ceases. The play of the opposites is the movement of time—from the past to the future. But Deep Sleep arrives where the past is not and where the future is not. The Deep Sleep is a state where consciousness has come to that Interval where the past and the future have been negated. This Interval is the Present—the Present is the moment of discontinuity—a moment where the continuity of time has come to a stop, may be for a split second or may be for a longer duration. Man wants to know what is it that is in flux—but how can this be known unless human consciousness comes to the moment of the present? Experience without accumulation is a state of experiencing—but this experiencing is possible only in the moment of the present—not the chronological present, but the psychological present. The moment of present is free from all pulls of memory—both the personal as well as racial. It is when the consciousness is freed from memory that the state of Deep Sleep arrives—for there is no memory to disturb it. It is in the conduction of Non-memory, and there alone, that the whisper of the Super-conscious can be heard. And it is the intimation of the Super-conscious which brings about an integration in human psyche, almost effortlessly. In Deep Sleep, where duality has dropped away, there is no conflict, there is no effort to become anything, there are no anticipations born out of the unfulfilment of the past. The moment of the Present can be known in utter silence where all movement of consciousness has stopped. There are no modifications induced either by the subconscious or the unconscious.

But in this present moment what does man see? Is he able to see the Thing that seems to be in eternal flux? If he sees it what is its nature? And why is it in flux? A strange question arises: Is there any thing in a state of flux? Is there a flux at all? The great European philosopher, Immanuel Kant, said that "we create time ourselves as a function of our receptive apparatus". In other words, time is one of the categorical imperatives of the mind without which it cannot perceive anything. Mind creates time in order to perceive what is—but, curiously enough, it is this time which prevents the mind from seeing what it wishes to see! Is not flux a projection of the mind? If time is the creation of mind then surely flux is also the product of mind. Are we to conclude that there is no flux at all? To say that there is flux is wrong, but to say that there is no flux is equally wrong. Flux has no intrinsic significance or existence—it has a derived or projected existence. How can one say that the image in the mirror does not exist—and yet the image has no intrinsic existence. One has to use the paradoxical language and say that the Image exists and yet it does not exist! The same is the question about flux that one sees and in which things seem to be moving away.

Are things moving away at all? If they are not, then why do we see the eternal flux of things? The experience of flux is induced by the Intangibility of things. As life is intangible, as it cannot be grasped by the human mind, its elusive nature is interpreted as time, as movement, as the eternal flux. How can Reality be moving away? If It moves away then surely it exists in time—and that which exists in time is perishable. Why does Reality which is changeless appear as changeful? The flux of things is mind's effort to interpret that which is Intangible and Ungraspable. So long as the movement of consciousness continues so long the Intangible is not seen—what is seen is only the movement—the movement projected by the mind. If the mind could come to a pause then in that very pause the movement would come to a stop—the flux is no more, the Thing is perceived as it is. Mind attempts to grasp the Intangible in the net of time—but because time cannot grasp it, it points to the past where it believes the Thing has gone or points to the future where the Thing is supposed to have vanished. The Thing in its absolute nature can be seen only in Deep Sleep, for, here the consciousness of man has come to silence, to the cessation of all movement.

But how does man come to the comprehension of the real nature of things in the state of Deep sleep. It is not man who arrives at comprehension, it is Truth that appears in the silence of Deep Sleep. This arrival of Truth, where Truth reveals itself is what the Māṇḍūkya Upanishad calls the Fourth State—the *Turiya* state. All things exist in their original nature in the Fourth or the *Turiya* state. When man knows his own original state then alone is he truly integrated. There is no integration possible in terms of the past or the future. The original nature of things is the Absolute Good. When man knows the Absolute Good then is his movement in the relative world significant and meaningful. The Teacher of the Māṇḍūkya Upanishad says:

> The self resting in its own real state is the All-powerful, the Omniscient and the Immanent—this is the source of all, the beginning and the end of all things.

The beginning and the end of all things—this is what time is. When the self or the Ātman is known in Its true and original nature then the mystery of time is solved. One has to come to the source of all things. But the perception of the Ātman comes in a state which we have termed the Super-conscious—a state where the mind is freed from the pulls of the past and the anticipations of the future. It is in the pin-point of the Present that the revelation of the original nature of things comes. The Māṇḍūkya Upanishad describes this as:

> The Imperceptible, the Indescribable, the Unnamable—the negation of the phenomenal world.

How can consciousness by its effort know this? That which is known by consciousness through its own efforts is surely Nameable. It is also Perceptible and Describable. For mind knows a thing by defining it and by naming it. It is only when the very naming by the mind ceases that the Original can be known. The condition of Deep Sleep is indeed characterised by the cessation of all naming. The naming is the verbalization of the mind. And mind's verbalizations are either in terms of the past or in terms of the future. Mind can give names about the past and the future. But the Present is for ever Nameless. The moment the present is named it is no longer the present. In Deep Sleep all names disappear, all verbalization ceases —it is only then that the Nameless reveals itself. It is because of this that the experience of the Fourth State, coming in the Deep Sleep condition, is called *Advaita*—Non-dual. And this indeed is the experience of Love. In the state of Love only the Beloved exists. And is not the Beloved for ever Nameless? Who shall give the name of the Beloved? The giver of the name is no longer there. And so long as the giver of the name is there, so long what is known is the Beloved with Name. But how can the Beloved be called by any name? No name can contain the Beloved—and so the Beloved is for ever Nameless. To know the Nameless is to come to an ecstasy—it is the very bliss of life. When all names are negated and there is no name to give, then it is that the Unnamed and the Unnamable Truth reveals itself to the gaze of man. When man perceives this Truth then can he go into the endless processes of time—but there he goes as a different man. With the ecstasy of the Nameless he goes into the realm of name and form. But he transforms the name and form of all things. To each he gives a new name—but each name becomes a symbol of the Nameless. He transforms the phenomenal world into a mighty symbol of the Noumenal. What is the nature of the Nameless? Who can tell? It is something which each man must discover in the moment of Deep Sleep. And when he comes to this discovery, he indeed joins with the great saint and mystic of India, Kabir, who declared in one of his immortal songs that:

> There is an endless world, O, my brother
> And there is the Nameless Being
> Of whom nought can be said.
> Only he knows who has reached that region—it is other than all that is heard and said.
> No form, no body, no length, no breadth is seen here; How can I tell you what it is?

VII

THE BLISS ETERNAL

One of the great contributions of Indian civilization has been in the field of education, covering not only the philosophy of education, but the system of education as well. The philosophy of education was not different from the philosophy of life which the seers and sages have given. This is to be seen in its purest form in the Upanishads. There was a system of education, known as the Gurukula system, which was one of the boldest experiments in education and which remains even today as one of the finest contributions of India to the field of education. There are two aspects of Gurukula education that need to be emphasised here. The first is the type of education imparted at the Gurukula, and, the other is the Method of education which made the Gurukulas unique institutions for educational experiment, perhaps nowhere surpassed in the world. The Gurukulas gave liberal education to its students—truly liberal, in the strict sense of the term. It was not liberal because of the variety of subjects taught—it was liberal because it instilled among the students a liberal outlook—an outlook of utmost catholicity. The purpose of the Gurukula Teacher was to awaken intelligence among his students—not to stuff their minds with a mass of information. This awakening of intelligence meant the development of a sharp intellect but also the development of an intensely sensitive response to men and things. The student who came out of the Gurukula was an inquirer whose process of inquiry never ended. His sense of learning was never dimmed—on the contrary, intensified because of all the knowledge that he had gathered in the āśrama of the Guru. The Teacher saw to it that the Flame of Learning and Inquiry was never extinguished. It was because of this that the student who passed out of the Gurukula never displayed dogmatism or arrogance. He never felt that he had come to a finality of understanding—he had gathered knowledge, immense knowledge, but this made him humble and therefore ready to learn. What greater expression of liberal education can there be than this openness of mind and the sensitivity of heart with which the student returned from his Gurukula after completing his studies? In the Gurukulas it was not the subject that mattered, it was the way of learning the subject that was of prime importance. The Gurukulas emphasised not *what* to learn so much as *how* to learn. And the man of true liberal education is one who knows how to learn—he keeps the process of learning pure and unsullied because of which he is open to learn everything and that too with an unbiassed mind. The possession of such a mind is indeed the hallmark of liberal education. As one looks at the lists of subjects one is impressed by the fact that the liberal education did not put sciences and humanities in water-tight compartments—on the contrary, they were intermingled so that a student came to an integral understanding of life.

Perhaps in no other Upanishad do we find such a comprehensive sweep of Gurukula education as we see it in the Taittirīya Upanishad. It is true that in the modern civilization of colossal urbanisation, we cannot have the Gurukula system in the form and structure in which it existed in an age where the tempo of life was slow. But even if we cannot reproduce the form, we can certainly examine the possibility of impregnating our modern systems of education with the spirit and content of the ancient Gurukulas. We can certainly explore the feasibility of laying an emphasis on *how* to learn—and not merely *what* to learn—so that the Flame of Learning may remain ever bright in the life of students whom we send out in thousands each year from the Universities all over the world. If only the Flame of Learning could be kept bright—then everything else will follow—everything that contributes to the integration of man and the integration of society. Let us turn to the Taittirīya Upanishad in order to know some of the unique features of the Upanishadic education.

The Taittirīya Upanishad derives its name from the teacher Taittiri. It belongs to the Yajur Veda and has mainly three sections, known as Vallis. These three sections deal with the Social, the Intellectual, and the Spiritual education of the student. They are known as *Śikshā Valli, Brahmānanda Valli* and *Bhṛgu Valli* respectively.

It is most interesting to see how while the Upanishadic teachers could soar into dizzy heights of philosophical understanding, they could remain firmly planted on earth. They were not impractical visionaries. Here in the Taittirīya Upanishad one sees the Teacher laying down the fundamental principles of the science of education. It is true that man's first contact with the external world is through the senses. But among the senses the first to respond to outer impacts is the sense of hearing—after that come touch, sight, taste and smell. It is in this order that the senses become active, capable of responding to the outer stimuli. In some of the Vedic hymns this order is given when they speak of *Śabda, Sparśa, Rūpa, Rasa,* and *Gandha*—meaning Hearing, Touching, Seeing, Tasting and Smelling. Thus it is in hearing that the basic factor of learning lies. If the student can hear—can know how to listen, even in the physical sense, then he would learn very quickly. When the student's hearing has been left unattended in the basic years of education then he has to undertake the journey of education with many handicaps. If one watches the growth of the little child in the first years of its infancy, one notices how it is the sense of hearing that gets stimulated first. The animal that is closest to man—the dog—has a very sharp hearing. In hearing lies the foundation of man's growth and therefore the foundation of true education. In spiritual life, too, man begins by being a *Śrāvaka* —that is, one who belongs to the Order of Hearers. The Order of Hearers is the first step on the journey to spiritual heights. But in hearing, two factors are essential the one who hears, and, also the one who speaks. If the speaking is not clear, how can the hearing be effective in laying the foundation of true education? While the hearing is to be done by the pupil, the speaking is the function of the teacher. The teacher in this Upanishad explains the science of hearing—but the science of hearing depends upon the science of pronunciation. If the articulation is not proper, how can the hearing be proper? Both the teacher and the student must know the science of articulation. But since articulation is the primary responsibility of the teacher, in this Upanishad, the teacher begins with an invocation in which he says:

> Let there be fame for both of us. Let there be the lustre of spiritual knowledge for both of us.

He asks for illumination for both the teacher and the student. With this invocation begins the instruction given by the teacher, Taittiri. Education is obviously meant to give to the student a capacity to communicate. A truly educated man is he who can communicate to others effectively what he has experienced. It does not matter what the medium of communication is—what matters is the effectiveness of communication. Now the most common means of communication is the speech—the spoken word.

In this connection the Teacher refers to the six limbs of speech—it is not with the content of speech that he is concerned, it is to the form of speech that he directs the attention of the student. Even in the form of speech it is on voice production that the teacher focuses the entire discussion. Without a correct production of voice the form of speech is weak and feeble. For an effective communication a proper voice production is essential. The Teacher says that there are six components of voice production. They are *Varṇa* or Quality, *Svara* or Pitch, *Mātrā* or Measure, *Bala* or Emphasis, *Sāma* or Modulation and *Santāna* or Combination. It is doubtful whether such scientific and clear classification of voice production is to be found anywhere else. The Teacher says that in voice production the attention must first be paid to the *Varṇa* or the quality of voice. A man must speak with his own quality—and not with assumed or imitated quality. One must maintain the natural quality of one's own voice. Any distortion of this quality, in order to appear like some one else, strikes at the very root of voice production. Then comes *Svará* or note or the pitch of the voice. It is necessary that one discovers his own pitch—the natural range of one's own notes. The next in importance is the *Mātrā* or measure or pause, meaning an equal or a harmonious distribution of one's voice so that it remains clear all throughout and does not suddenly drop towards the end as happens very often. In voice production, *Bala* or emphasis is also of great importance. With a wrong emphasis the pronunciation becomes distorted, and, sometimes due to this an entirely different meaning is conveyed. Then comes *Sāma* or modulation. One must know one's own pitch but one must also know the range of one's pitch so that while speaking one modulates one's voice within that range so as to convey effectively the emotional content of speech. And the last component of voice production is: *Santāna* or combination. The combination of words and thereby creating compounds of words is very necessary for the clarity of pronunciation and for the conveying of meaning. Thus the six limbs of voice production are very essential to any effective educative process. When the teacher and the student master the technique of voice production then they are able to communicate with each other effectively. It is of the highest importance to realize that voice production must be natural and not artificial or affected. For this, one must discover the quality and pitch of one's own voice. It is in this natural background that other factors of voice production should be introduced.

From the voice production the Teacher moves on to language, the structure and combination of words. This is but natural as voice production by itself has no meaning. It becomes meaningful only with reference to words. Voice production deals with articulation—but, then there must be something that is to be articulated. The last of the above six limbs of voice production speaks of *Santāna* or combination. It is this *santāna* or *saṃhitā* to which the teacher now turns—for, proper combination of letter and words is greatly conducive to effective articulation. Now *saṃhitā* really means proximity of letters and words. When letters are in close proximity there comes about a natural combination. This combination is known as *sandhi* or joining together. When the letters of the alphabet are lying scattered there arises no meaning—but when the letters are joined together, then, by that *sandhi* or combination a meaningful utterance becomes possible. When the parts are lying about helter-skelter then there is no significance—but when the parts are brought together or they come together, then a significance or a purpose is imparted to them. In the combination of parts there is something more that is added—and it is that more, which, in joining the parts together, gives to that combination a meaning which was not there. But the combination has to be natural. Ordinarily in *sandhi* or combination, what is needed is the proximity of two letters or words. But does combination come into existence by the mere proximity of these two letters or words? Now, there has to be a *sandhāna*— the inducer of a union, the factor which brings about the joining of the two. Without this *sandhāna*, the joiner, the mere *sandhi* or joining is mechanical and lifeless. When the inducer of a union is present then the union becomes meaningful. The inducer of union awakens an urge to unite—and it is only when the urge is there that the two opposites come together in happy union. The combination that arises is a whole where each part is occupying its rightful place. It is the inter-relationship of the Part and the Whole which is indicated in this whole subject of *saṃhitā* or combination.

The *Sandhi,* or the union of letters and words, is taken only as an illustration by the teacher. For, from this base he enters the larger field of *sandhi* or union needed for uttering effectively the language of life. In enlarging upon this theme of *sandhi,* the teacher speaks of the union of Earth and Heaven, of Fire and Sun, of the Teacher and the Pupil, of the Father and Mother, of the Lower Lip and the Upper Lip. The teacher says that out of a union of earth and heaven comes the vast space which we call the sky. Out of a union between Fire and Sun comes water. From the union of the teacher and student comes knowledge and from the union of the father and the mother comes the progeny. In the union of the two lips is the birth of speech. What is the meaning of water arising out of the combination of fire and sun? Here fire denotes sacrifice—and all sacrifices are performed keeping sun as a witness. In the Third Discourse of the Bhagavad Gītā there is a verse which says, "out of sacrifice cometh rain." The combination of fire and sun is indeed the sacrificial rites performed in the presence of the sun—and it is this which is considered as the begetter of rain.

It may be noted in the above illustrations that the product of the union is completely different from the nature of the two units that come together in the act of *sandhi*. The real *sandhi* is not two parts put in juxtaposition nor is it the forced union of the two. In *sandhi*, which is natural, the parts are integrated and the result of integration is something entirely new. It is not the sum of the parts—it is more than the sum of the parts. But this depends upon whether a *sandhi* is just a synthesis or it is an integration. A synthesis breaks up under an external impact—but integration never breaks, for, while in the former the opposites are balanced, in the latter they are transcended.

But why should there be a difference in the *sandhi*? Who determines this difference? Why should it be synthesis in one case and integration in the other? That which determines the nature of *sandhi*, is *sandhāna*— the inducer of the union. And so it is to the Inducer of the Union that we must turn in order to understand the secret of *sandhi*. It may be noted that the teacher has given a wider context to *sandhi* by bringing in five illustrations. By these illustrations he indicates that he is dealing with the Language of Life, and not merely the language of words. In the language of words what is needed is proper articulation—but to this articulation, it is *sandhi* that supplies a meaning—without it the letters and words lie about in utter disorder. To the disorder of words, *sandhi* gives a design, an order, a meaningful existence. In the Language of Life too we need a meaningful articulation. In life, communication is of prime importance, but communication must be both effective and meaningful. One must know the science of articulation as also the art of *Sandhi*—the art of relationship. For the effective articulation of the language of life, there must be one's own quality and the proper striking of one's own note, there must also be the right emphasis and the correct pause. And these must be well modulated so that a sense of proportion is maintained. The effectiveness of any communication depends upon the maintenance of a sense of proportion. But these constitute the technique of communication. The language of life needs a means of communication—but of what use is a technique of communication if there is nothing to communicate? This demands a richness of language. We have seen above that a language has a structure and this is built by the harmonious blending of letters and words. This is what the Upanishad describes as *sandhi*. If the letters and words are well blended then the articulation is easy and the communication is effective. But sometimes the rules of *sandhi* are observed with meticulous care and yet the language seems to be missing something. When the *sandhi* rules are correctly observed, the articulation is also clear and precise—and yet why does the language miss something? What is it that it misses?

We saw above that *sandhi* represents a union—whether in the language of words or in the language of life. But the question is: How has the union been induced? Who is the inducer of the union? We have called the inducer of the union as the *sandhāna*. What is the nature of this *sandhāna*— for the quality of *sandhi* or union depends upon the nature of the *sandhāna*. A *sandhi* is a union of two opposites or at least it is a union of a duality, it is the bringing together of the dual elements. What induces the dual elements to come together? Why do they join to form a union?

In the above five illustrations of *sandhi*, the Upanishad gives an example of the Father-Mother duality with the child as the *sandhi*. The above illustration says that the urge to unite is the *sandhāna*. But the question is—what is the nature of this urge? Has only a biological urge brought the father-mother together? Or is the urge the outcome of deep love and affection? It is quite obvious that the quality of *sandhi* or the child will depend upon the nature of the urge. Without *sandhāna* there cannot be *sandhi*—but the quality of the *sandhi* will obviously depend upon the nature of the *sandhāna*.

Now *sandhi* in the larger context, in the language of life, evidently means relationship. The Teacher of the Taittirīya Upanishad is explaining to his students the problems of human relationship. In man's life communication with fellow human beings is a prime necessity. But how can there be effective communication without relationship? A communication without relationship is like articulating words which have no meaning. The meaning to words is given by language—for language weaves words into a unity. It is *sandhi* which makes the language, for, without it, it would be only a jumble of words having no cohesion. Thus effective and meaningful communication is possible between human beings when there is a relationship between man and man. This relationship is *sandhi*. Unless there is a coming together of two individuals, how can there be communication between them? But once again the effectiveness of communication will depend upon the nature of relationship. A communication between two strangers is of a very superficial nature. The cause of this superficial relationship is to be found in the nature of the *sandhāna* which brought about this *sandhi*. The two strangers come together by sheer accident—the *sandhāna* is superficial and so the relationship too is superficial.

The Taittirīya Upanishad is concerned with the problem of relationship. Communication is most effective only when it takes place at the same time, at the same level and with the same intensity between two people. But such communication can exist only in communion—it is only the Intangible that can speak with such effectiveness to the Intangible. But the Taittirīya Upanishad is concerned with all aspects of relationship. It deals with the relationship of social obligations as it speaks also of the relationships based on intellectual understanding. It also indicates to us the relationship of spiritual communion.

This Upanishad is well-known for what has come to be known as the convocation address given by the teacher to the pupils who were about to leave the āśrama.. Ordinarily studies in the Gurukula were spread over a period of twelve years. During this period the students studied many subjects, both sciences and humanities—but apart from that they were a part of the teacher's household. And so one can imagine that the valedictory addresses of the teacher could not have been dry and impersonal. In their addresses there must have been present an emotional content because of the intimate and personal relationship existing between the teacher and the student. In sending the student out into the world after his graduation, the teacher must have felt that he was sending someone belonging to his own family. In modern universities, because of the largeness of number and because of a lack of personal touch between the teacher and the student, the convocation addresses delivered at the time of graduation seem so dry and impersonal that they hardly create any lasting impression upon the students. Having seen the student grow up in his own family, when the teacher sends out his pupil from his gurukula, he sends him not merely with the stamp of learning but also with his personal blessing. One of the glaring defects of the present-day educational system is the complete lack of a personal touch between the teacher and the student—but what will the teacher of today impart to the student if he were to be given an opportunity of coming into closer contact with him? In personal attention it is not mere learning that counts—what is needed is something more than learning. The Upanishadic teachers had that "something more" because of which they were in the true sense of the term friend, philosopher and guide to their students. In the Convocation address forming part of the Taittirīya Upanishad, one sees the considerateness of the teacher for the welfare of his student. In his final instruction the teacher takes into account various aspects of life—he imagines diversity of situations in which the student is likely to be placed and so gives him a word of advice lest the student be led astray by the social forces that would impinge upon him. Knowing well that the student was leaving the sheltered existence of the āśrama and plunging into the fast moving stream of outer life, the teacher in his valedictory address speaks to him about his social obligations. The first duty of the student will be to the society in which he was entering—and so the convocation address of the Taittirīya Upanishad deals with the relationship of social obligations. The address of the teacher begins with the following words:

> My dear child, your study of the Vedas is over. Now go forth into the wide world. Speak the truth and practise Dharma or Law. Do not falter in the study of Veda. Study more, but, never less than the portion assigned to you.

The teacher tells the student that he must keep up his studies in the subjects in which he has specialized so that he is in touch with further researches in his particular subject. He indicates to the student that his learning process must never come to an end. His graduation is not the end of learning—in fact, it is the beginning of learning. In the gurukula the student must have specialised in some branch of learning. But in every branch of learning there take place new discoveries, there come to one's gaze new facts—these must be studied. Any slackness in keeping up with the latest developments in his own subject would render his studies at the gurukula ineffective. The teacher tells the student—Speak Truth. This seems so platitudinous—but it must have had a strong impact on the student leaving the gurukul because of the personal touch of the teacher. The teacher wants his student to have the courage to speak truth—and not be corrupted by the exigencies of the time. But the teacher also says to him—Follow Dharma. Very often we speak out the truth but by deviating from dharma. Dharma is the law of human relationship. The truth that is spoken must not be an act of aggressiveness—it must be within the bounds of decency and courtesy. When truth is spoken without any consideration of human relationship, then it becomes bitter and carping. The speaking of truth would always remain within the limit of courtesy if the law of human relationship is not forgotten. The law of human relationship implies reverence to elders, friendliness towards equals and compassion towards those who are unable to stand on their own. If truth is spoken within the limits of this law—then it would be truly beneficial.

The teacher tells the pupil that while he may show his respect and devotion to his preceptor in whatever measure he can, he must enter the life of a house-holder with full understanding of his responsibilities—and with no neglect in discharging them. He tells him that as a householder his duty must be to engage himself in doing good—never to neglect such duties by performing which there may be greater prosperity. The central theme of this Convocation address is: Do not deviate from Truth: Do not deviate from Duty. And the teacher gives a detailed description of what his duties would be. He says:

> Do not neglect your health. Do not be neglectful in those acts that would lead to prosperity and well-being. Do not show forth any idleness in learning.

In the above instructions the teacher refers to physical, material and mental aspect of the student's life. He asks him to lead a balanced life in which there is time both for material as well as intellectual pursuits. But in engaging himself in these two pursuits he must be careful to maintain good health. One sees here the anxiety of the teacher —the extraordinary considerateness on his part regarding the well-being of the student. Here one feels that it is not merely the teacher that is speaking, it is the father instructing the son out of deep concern and affection.

In any relationship based on social obligations, the element of continuity plays a very important part. This finds its expression in the respect and regard that one shows for the past. When one considers one's obligations to society, one must take into consideration the forces emanating from the past so that what is essential may be maintained and what is non-essential may be eliminated. In the growth and development of human civilization one sees three factors at work—Continuity, Modified Continuity and Discontinuity. Continuity and modified continuity constitute the *sandhi* of a human society—the question is which is the *sandhāna* —it is on the nature of the *sandhāna* that the quality of social change depends. If it comes from Discontinuity then the society, through the retention and modification of its organisations, will be able to show forth a high quality in the different aspects of its activities. But for this, first the factors of continuity must be understood. It has to be remembered that the student, after his graduation, is entering the world—from the *brahmacarya* he is moving to the state of *gṛhastha*. The *gṛhastha* is a house-holder. He must be conversant with the factors of continuity, for, he must be true to his social obligations. It is for the *Vānaprastha* to bring in the element of modified continuity even as the *Sannyāsin* brings the refreshing air of discontinuity. However, we must understand that these four orders are psychological states. The student, having completed his studies, is now entering a new psychological state—that of a house-holder or gṛhastha . The house-holder must see to it that healthy factors of continuity are maintained and nourished. For this he must be respectful to the past—for in understanding the past, man is able to find the meaning and purpose of those factors that give sustenance to continuity. The teacher is not oblivious of the other two factors of modified continuity and discontinuity. He turns to them in the second and the third sections of the Taittirīya Upanishad. But first the student must bring to bear upon the factors of continuity the light of knowledge that he has gained in the Gurukula. And so the teacher says in his convocation address:

> Let there be no neglect in offering what is due to gods and the ancestors. Give reverence to your father and mother. Treat your guests with honour and dignity. And above all to the teacher be supremely dedicated.

Here the teacher enjoins upon the student the desirability of establishing a right relationship with the past. While it is true that the past must not be allowed to condition and restrict our actions in the present—but at the same time it would be suicidal not to take full advantage of the harvest that the past offers. As one who enters the gṛhastha state, the student must learn to draw full advantage from the harvest of the past. During the stage of *brahmacarya*, he has been enabled to develop a logical mind, capable of examining pros and cons of any situation. In the *Brahmacarya* state a person is instructed how to clearly define the opposites so that the mind moves along the path of flawless logic. In the *gṛhastha* state he is asked to maintain a movement between the opposites as smooth as possible so that the process of continuity may go on unhindered. In the *Vānaprastha* state man brings about necessary and essential modifications in this continuity. But it is in the state of sannyāsa—and there alone—that he comes to the vision of discontinuity—the source of all fundamental changes, the fountain-head of true spiritual revolution.

The teacher in his valedictory address tells the student that his task now is to maintain the stream of continuity as clean and as smooth as possible. For this he must draw on the past—but draw with a mind that is alert and active, seeing clearly the two opposites. The above verse deals with this harvest of the past. The gods and the ancestors, the father and the mother—these represent the factors of the past. Even the guest symbolizes the past, for, who would come as a guest unless he has an association with the past of the family? The word used for the guest is *atithi* one who comes without giving any notice. Surely he alone will come without notice and yet receive hospitality, who has been familiar with the family. But a question may arise here: Does the teacher too represent the past? The gods and ancestors, the father and the mother, and even the guest—one can associate with the past—but how can one consider the teacher as symbolizing the past? Here the word used for the teacher is *ācārya*. Now ācārya is one who invests a boy with the sacred thread and instructs him in the Vedas. The instruction in Vedas represents a continuity of knowledge even as the investing of the sacred thread symbolizes a continuity of tradition and a passing on of a secret from one generation to the other. Thus the whole of the above verse indicates a right relationship with the past so that a proper continuity may be maintained. The *gṛhastha* represents that state of human consciousness where a movement between the opposites goes on with as little friction as possible. It is to this state that the student now becomes initiated. The Teacher then goes on with his instruction and says to the departing pupil:

> Be devoted to such deeds as are regarded blameless. Adopt all such customs as are good—not others.

The above verse talks of deeds that are blameless. However, the word used for blameless is— *anavadyāni*—the teacher says to the student that he should do such things as do not become the subject matter of talk or gossip by others. He elucidates the point further by saying that he must adopt all good customs—customs that are regarded good by people. Surely the student, after all his training and instruction in the ashrama, must be able to distinguish between good and bad—which means what is good for the continuity of the human race and what is not good for such continuity. He must adopt all such customs whereby society can move on without friction or conflict. The teacher is confident that the instruction that he has received in the āśrama will enable the pupil to sift the good from the bad.

But the teacher is considerate and is aware of many pitfalls that the pupil may have to face so that he tells him what he should do in case he is in doubt about finding out what is good and what is not good. He says if there is any doubt in your mind then

> You should conduct yourself in a way in which those learned people, who may be living there, who are competent to judge who are not led by others, who are not cruel and who are lovers of virtue, conduct themselves in such cases.

The teacher asks the pupil to turn to learned people in case of doubt and difficulty—but who are these learned people to whom he must turn? They must be capable of judging for themselves, not those who are led by others. The teacher says it does not matter whether they hold any official position or not—but he says that such learned persons should not be *alūksha,* which means dry, devoid of feeling. He says—do not go to such dry people, for, their learning will be of no avail to you. Go only to such learned people whose feelings and emotions are alive—who have the sensitivity of heart along with head-learning. Watch such people and do as they do. Do not conduct yourself as do the dry and emotionless people who are proud of their learning—but adopt the ways of those who, in spite of learning, have preserved the delicacy and sensitivity of heart.

The last word of advice that the teacher gives to his pupil about giving what he has to others who may be in need. Social obligations demand that a person must know how to receive from the community—but he should also know how to give to the society to which he belongs. He who receives but does not give has not known his relationship to society. He must accept from society gracefully but he must also give to society equally gracefully. The teacher tells the student:

> Give always with faith—do not give if you do not have faith. Give generously—but let your generosity be tempered with modesty. Give with sympathy but also give with propriety.

How significant it is that the teacher tells his pupil to give generously and yet with modesty. These two seem so utterly contradictory. If people give generously they wish to display their generosity—but the teacher says give generously but without any display of generosity. A display of generosity very often causes humiliation to the person who receives. Even while giving generously, the giver must have a respect for the one to whom he gives. In modesty lies this respect for one who receives. In such giving there is grace and there is dignity. The giver gives with grace and therefore there is utmost respect for the dignity of the receiver. When giving is done without faith it is no giving at all—it is a ceremonial giving—it is charity without any compassion in it. It is a giving without sympathy and therefore has no propriety in it. The giver must give in terms of the need of the person who receives. To be aware of the need of the other person is to bring in one's giving the element of sympathy as also the element of propriety. When the giver gives in order to satisfy his own pride and position then the giving may have generosity—but it has no modesty in it. The giving must be such where the giver is in the background—it is only the giving that exists. When giving is without the giver then there is generosity with modesty. The teacher wants the student to give and to give generously—but never with any display.

The teacher says to the student that "This is my instruction. This is the secret of knowledge that I have imparted to you. See to it that you never deviate from this path". Throughout this address one sees the teacher of the Upanishad though deeply learned and yet extremely tender with emotions. In fact, in this valedictory address we are reminded of the great Sanskrit play, *Śakuntalā*, where the great sage Kaṇva bids farewell to the daughter of the āśrama with heart filled with deep emotion. The Upanishadic teachers were *alūksha*—deeply learned and yet filled with feeling of love and tenderness. One feels that in the going away of the student a part of the teacher also seems to be going—such was the intimate relationship of the teacher and the pupil in the gurukuls of ancient seers and sages.

From the Convocation address, the Taittirīya Upanishad moves on to its second section known as Brahmānanda Valli. One wonders why the Upanishad did not end with the Convocation address. This is probably because the teacher desires to place before his pupil the entire picture of life—not just the stage into which he enters on the completion of his studies. And so while technically the convocation address ends with the first section, it continues in the second and the third sections also. We have already stated that the four stages in man's life are really the four psychological states, called the student, the house-holder, the hermit and the ascetic. In an integrated human being all the four states co-exist. While the stages come one after the other—the states exist simultaneously. The state of the student signifies an alert mind which is capable of formulating and defining the opposites. The state of the house-holder represents a vigilant mind observing the play of the opposites, keeping the stream of continuity between the opposites unbroken and unimpeded. The state of the hermit indicates a negative mind recognising the limitations of all mental efforts and therefore slowing down the flow of continuity. The state of the ascetic symbolizes a silent mind where the stream of continuity has come to a stop. While in the student state, man is enabled to clearly formulate the opposites by virtue of the sharpening of the mind, in the other three states he is concerned with the relationship that must subsist between the opposites. If the opposites are not clearly seen then the question of relationship is bound to get utterly confused. The teacher has trained the pupil in the formulation and clear perception of the opposites. It is with this equipment of the mind that man enters the world of relationships. In his convocation address, the teacher has dealt with one aspect of this relationship—the aspect which is concerned with the house-hold state. It is an aspect where relationship is sought to be established on the basis of social obligations. It is a relationship in which the maintenance of continuity occupies a predominant place. But very often it happens that this continuity gets disturbed and the possibility of its re-establishment on the old basis seems out of sight. In other words, occasions do arise when the patterns of continuity need a modification, if relationship is not to break down. A relationship of mere social obligation is not enough. When social and conventional norms do not satisfy then does a need arise for man to seek a new basis of human relationship. It is a relationship based on Intellectual Understanding—it is a relationship of common ideals. In the relationship of social obligations, it is the common past that serves as a binding link. But sometimes this link proves too weak, unable to stand the strain of changed circumstances. Then does man seek a new basis of relationship—not of common past, but of common future. When common ideals are discovered then the relationship that comes into existence is that of Intellectual Understanding. This is what is represented by the *Vānaprastha* or the Hermit state. And the Brahmānanda Valli speaks to the student about this *Vānaprastha* state—for when modifications in continuity are needed it is the *Vānaprastha* state that helps him. He must be aware of this lest he get confused and baffled in the problems of relationship.

If modification of continuity is needed then it must not be haphazard or eccentric—it must arise from solid ground. It is with this solid ground of modifications that Brahmānanda Valli is concerned. What can be the solid ground of modifications? The Taittirīya Upanishad says—it must be the knowledge of Brahman. Now Brahman that can be known is the manifested Brahman and it is with the manifested Brahman that this section of the Upanishad is concerned. It describes the knowledge of the manifested Brahman as veritable Bliss. But the bliss of knowledge is not to be mistaken for the ecstasy of realization. The latter is the subject matter of Bhṛgu Valli which forms the third section of this Upanishad.

What is this bliss of knowledge with which the second section is concerned? When man evolves an intellectual frame-work in which all things can be fitted in, or when he formulates an intellectual philosophy which can seemingly give explanations of everything, then he naturally comes to a bliss of knowledge. To act on the problems of relationship on the strength of this bliss is indeed to establish a new basis for relationship—it is a relationship based on intellectual understanding. In the relationship of social obligation, it is Duty which is the keynote, in the relationship based on common idealism it is Understanding which forms the keynote. It is understanding which becomes the *sandhāna* for the new basis of *sandhi*—the urge to unite is Understanding. This is the base from which the *vānaprastha* or the hermit acts. Brahmānanda Valli is indeed concerned with this base of action.

In the very opening verse of this section, the Upanishad speaks of Brahman as *Satyam, Jñānam, Anantam*—Existence, Knowledge and Infinity. Now all the three are attributes belonging to the realm of the mind. Brahman that is Existent—not that which is non-existent—this surely is how mind understands Brahman. Mind can describe It only in terms of Knowledge. And Infinity is endless continuity. Thus Existence, Knowledge and Infinity are mind's conceptions of Brahman. Out of these conceptions it evolves a philosophy which seemingly explains everything. Thus is man enabled to come to an intellectual bliss. It is a bliss of reconciliation—not a bliss of transcendence. For, here in this seemingly perfect intellectual philosophy, the opposites are reconciled, brought into a synthesis. In terms of reconciliation there comes into existence a stream of modified continuity. In the very opening verse of the Brahmānanda Valli, Brahman is described as "the intelligent". In terms of this intelligence, the Upanishad shows how there is a plan and a design in creation. It is the Plan of Creation which forms part of this section. An orderly Plan or Design indicates the existence of an Intelligent Being. This Intelligent Being is Brahman—but obviously Brahman in manifestation. This section says in one of its verses:

> It is understanding that all the gods worship as Brahman.

It is the worship of Understanding that is indicated here—and Understanding is equated with Brahman. The Sanskrit word used for Understanding is *Vijñāna*. This is discriminative knowledge. But with what instrument does man discriminate? Obviously through the instrument of ideals or values. The very basis of one's relationship with the outer world is: Values or Ideals. This relationship becomes intimate where a common-ness of ideals is discovered. A bridge is constructed between the points of common interests or common ideas. The *san-*

dhāna for relationship is the ideal. In the Brahmānanda Valli it is stated that:

> If one knows understanding as Brahman, and if one does not swerve therefrom then he enjoys all his desires.

Once again the emphasis is on knowing Brahman as Understanding. This section deals with the Bliss of Brahman—but from the above verse it is clear that the bliss spoken of is the enjoyment of desires. When there is understanding, the enjoyment of desires must mean not ordinary desires—but the desires considered as noble. Here obviously desires mean the values of life. If one is rooted in Understanding then one can enjoy one's values of life. But what does knowing Brahman as Understanding mean. It means, as was stated above, knowing Brahman as the Intelligent Plan of the Universe. It is knowing Brahman, the creation, not Brahman, the Creator. Understanding implies an existence of duality where the knower and the known are the two opposites. When they come together then there is knowledge. But what is the *sandhāna* for this union? It is ideals, ideations or values. *Vijñāna* is the instrument which brings the knower and the known together. And what is the nature of knowledge? It is the sublime Plan of the Universe. Now a Plan needs a future in which to work out its fulfilment. And therefore men who know Brahman as Understanding are united in terms of that common future in which the Plan will be fulfilled. It is in terms of the Plan that they bring about modifications in their current patterns of life. The second section of this Upanishad says:

> He becomes non-existent if he knows Brahman as non-existent. If he knows that Brahman exists then people know him as existent.

The very existence of man depends upon postulating Brahman as existent—not Brahman as non-existent. Here what is indicated most clearly is the worship of Brahman, the manifest, and not, Brahman the unmanifest. To know Brahman, the manifest, one requires a discriminative understanding. To know Brahman in manifestation is to know Unity in Diversity. This is indeed the function of a *vānaprastha* the hermit. The *gṛhastha* is content to maintain the even flow of diversity. He recognises diversity and accepts it. His task is to eliminate as much friction as possible between the various units of diversity. This he does by invoking the common past. But a conflict between the various units of diversity is bound to arise—when this happens what is he to do? If he is able to discover a unity in diversity then in terms of that unity he can bring about a synthesis of the diverse elements. In the convocation address the teacher had laid emphasis on relationship based on social obligations. Here in the Brahmānanda Valli, the teacher indicates to the pupil that when harmony of relationship cannot be maintained in terms of social obligations, then he must seek a unity in diversity. He must bring to bear upon the problem of relationship the faculty of *vijñāna*. This will enable him to find a new base of human relationship. To find unity in diversity is a process of abstraction. From the diversities of actual life, a common factor is abstracted. It is this which is called unity in diversity. It is a conceptual process. Man has not come to an experience of unity—he has created a conceptual framework of unity—and into this framework he places diverse parts so as to create a plan or a design. It is a plan where parts are brought together—and they are held together by the concept of unity. The Brahmānanda Valli says that he who deviates from this unity is caught in fear—the fear of a never ceasing conflict between the diverse elements. This conceptual unity is indeed the bliss of the existent or the manifest Brahman. It is like discovering the unified theory of the universe. Man would come to intense delight if he were to discover this unity into the framework of which he can give to the vast diversities of life their appropriate places. The dual factors of gravitation and electro-magnetism would find a synthesis in such a unified theory. In the larger sphere of life, too, man seeks this framework of unity. When he finds this he experiences a great delight. Here the Brahmānanda Valli gives a detailed description of what it calls the Bliss of Brahman. But at the end of each description it says that "this is the bliss of the *śrotriya* "—meaning that this is the bliss of the learned, of those who are proficient in the lower knowledge or *Aparā Vidyā* . It is the bliss of knowledge, not the ecstasy of Wisdom. It is a joy arising out of the discovery of a conceptual unity. It is an ideational bliss born out of a dedication to the ideals and aspirations which one may have accepted. In the Upanishad this bliss is described as follows:

> Let us suppose that there is a strong, well-built, virtuous youngman. If he is firm of mind and full of ambition, and if he becomes the owner of this world, then he enjoys full happiness. That may be counted as one unit of full human happiness. But hundred-fold is the happiness of the Gandharvas in heaven. A thousand-fold of that is the happiness of the gods. A thousand-fold of the happiness of the gods is that of Indra. A thousand-fold of that is the happiness of Bṛhaspati. A hundred-fold of this is the happiness of Prajāpati—and a hundred-fold of that is the happiness of Brahman—and this is the Bliss of the *śrotriya*.

The above passage seems quite strange, for, here happiness is sought to be measured in quantitative units. Does happiness lend itself to such measurement? Obviously that which is measured belongs to the realm of the mind, for it is mind that deals with measurable quantities. What the above verse declares is that the happiness of one who has come to the discovery of conceptual unity in the midst of diversity is immense. He feels that this conceptual unity will open all the deadlocks. He can move about in life with a glow of happiness for he has found unity in diversity, Brahman in manifestation.

It is most interesting to note that after describing the Bliss of Brahman, the Brahmānanda Valli ends with a statement which negates that very bliss, for, it says:

> Not having attained whence words along with the mind return.

It says both words and the mind have returned—not after having attained, but without attaining. In the former verse, the Upanishad spoke of the Bliss of Brahman as the bliss of the *Śrotriya*. If the *śrotriya* has not found the bliss, then what is he happy about? The *śrotriya* is the knower of the Vedas—he is a man of deep learning. The knower of the Vedas has a mind which is sharp and alert. He has acquired knowledge and in terms of this knowledge has evolved a framework in which all happenings of life can be easily fitted in. He is happy at his own invention—but the happiness of invention is short lived. That which is quantitatively full can be qualitatively empty also. It is a fullness which depends upon external factors. Life is so unpredictable that suddenly a new fact may arise completely destroying the framework so laboriously built by the mind. The beliefs and the concepts of the mind have their structures built on sand. A tidal wave arising from the sea will in no time demolish these structures, no matter how majestic they may be. Happiness which rests on the sandy shores of the mind must die as quickly as it is born. Neither speech nor mind can find that Eternal Bliss which remains uncorrupt and which the tidal waves of life cannot destroy. A conceptual unity is short-lived—it soon gets over-powered by the floods of diversity. A conceptual unity is something dead—it can never hold in its framework the vitality of life. How can thought which is static contain life which is intensely dynamic? Thought must return along with speech.

It is with this declaration that Brahmānanda Valli ends inviting the student to move further for the exploration of Bliss Eternal. And it is this which becomes the subject matter of the last section of this Upanishad known as Bhṛgu Valli.

From the state of the house-holder, the student has been taken to the understanding of the state of the hermit. But the hermit, after all his efforts at synthesis and conceptual unity, declares that mind cannot find the ultimate truth. And without this ultimate truth man cannot find his true integration. It is true that life consists of continuity and modified continuity—but from where do these two factors of evolution draw their sustenance? What is it that impels them to go on? What induces modification? If modification has its roots only in a desire to continue then it will bring the evolutionary stream to a dead-end.

The urge for modification must arise not from conceptual unification but from elsewhere. It is from the realms of discontinuity that the vital life-force of continuity and its modification must emerge, for, then alone the evolutionary stream will show forth new qualities of life, new orders of existence. This is indeed the function of the state of *sannyāsa*, or, of the ascetic. The ascetic is one who has completely broken away from the past—he has no fears or anxieties about the future. He lives in the present—and the Bliss of the Eternal can be found only in the present. The ascetic represents that state of the mind which has no distractions of the past and no commitments regarding the future. It is a mind bereft of all pulls and agitations. It is completely open and therefore receives the full impact of the present—a present which is free from all corruptions of time. Such a mind finds a new level of relationship—a relationship arising from no base at all—neither the base of Duty nor the base of Ideals. It acts not from social obligations nor from the ground of ideals. It does not act from the base of something which is common—it is not afraid to establish a link from the uncommon to the uncommon—from the unique to the unique. In every diversity it sees the unique—and the unique is incomparable, it cannot be caught in the network of comparison and contrast. The relationship of the unique with the unique is a *sandhi* without a *sandhāna*. There is no inducer nor is there any inducement—for this is a relationship of Love. Does Love require an inducement? Does not the presence of the inducer utterly negate the existence of love? But can mind know this Love? Can mind hold it? It is only when the mind becomes mind-less that into that purified consciousness love is born. It is a condition of utter silence—not the silence of words, but the silence of the mind.

It may be stated that the introduction of the subject of *gṛhastha*. *vānaprastha* and *sannyāsa*, in this discussion of the Taittirīya Upanishad is rather far-fetched. How do these stages or states of life come into the picture? We have to remember that the Upanishad refers to an occasion when the student after completing his studies in the gurukula is about to leave the āśrama. The teacher is giving to him on this occasion certain essential instructions so that he may lead his life both happily and profitably. The teacher opens his instructions with the subject of *sandhi* or relationship. To this subject he gives a wide context describing the various types of *sandhi* both in nature as well as in human societies. Thus the main theme of this Upanishad is human relationship. The student is about to enter the stage of a house-holder. We have regarded these stages as really states of consciousness. The state referring to a house-holder is one where the student will have to understand the first layer of relationship—that which is based on social obligations. The whole of the Convocation address deals with this subject in detail. But a relationship of mere social obligations would become utterly conventional—sometimes even superstitious. Such a relationship would naturally lead to frustrations. The teacher, so considerate about the welfare of his pupil, would certainly like to see that his life is not wrecked on the rocks of frustration. The entire Upanishadic education is based on the integration of man. It is but natural that the teacher would give to the pupil an integral approach to the whole problem of human relationship. This he does by giving to the pupil instructions given in the Brahmānanda Valli and Bhṛgu Valli. These two sections refer to those states of consciousness which can be described as *vānaprastha* and *sannyāsa*, for, they give a new basis to *sandhi* or relationship. A life of social obligations is concerned with the maintenance of social continuity—it is interested in preventing forces of social disintegration from having an upper hand. But human society is so dynamic that it cannot be kept confined to rigid patterns of behaviour. These patterns need to be changed from time to time. What will be the basis of this change? A mere expediency—or an idealistic vision? Surely it must be the latter. Society must be reformed from time to time—and this reform must be the expression of great and lofty ideals. But a reform tends to become a mere patchwork if there is not behind it the spirit of revolution. It is in the state of *Vānaprastha* that one plans for reforms. But from where will the inspiration for reforms come? From the continuing stream of the mind? If so, then the reforms will be very halting containing mere patchwork. If the reforms are to be vital and dynamic then they must draw the inspiration from realms beyond the continuing sphere of the mind. It is from the realms of Discontinuity that the inspiration for modified continuity be brought. Modified continuity represents *Yuga Dharma*—the Law of life for a particular period. But *Yuga Dharma*, if it is to be real and vital must reflect the *Sanātana Dharma*—the Law of Eternal Life. It is in the realm of Discontinuity that the Law of Eternal Life can be found, for it is timeless. The teacher speaks to the pupil about the traditional law of life, about the *Yuga Dharma* and about Sanātana Dharma. These three categories of the Laws of Life are covered by the states of consciousness known as *gṛhastha*, *Vānaprastha* and *sannyāsa*—the house-holder, the hermit and the ascetic. It is for the *Vānaprastha*—one who has come to that state—to give the fundamental principles of Yuga Dharma. But he can do this effectively only if he draws his inspiration from *sannyāsa*—that state of consciousness where the mind is rendered mind-less. If Yuga Dharma does not reflect the vision of Sanātana Dharma then the former is but a change devoid of meaning and significance. Thus the teacher has shown to his pupil a completely integral approach to the problems of human relationship. It is the individual that is the crux of the social problem. The society is static, it is only the individual who can bring fundamental changes. The teacher of the Taittirīya Upanishad is concerned with the creation of the New Individual—an integrated individual. It is in the Bhṛgu Valli that we find the very source of man's integration—for *sannyāsa*, is indeed a state of integration. Here a reference is made to the father instructing his son in the highest knowledge. It seems Bhṛgu, the son of Varuṇa, approached his father and said: "Venerable sir, teach me about Brahman." The father said "Food, vital breath, mind—this is Brahman"—but he further added saying "That from which all things and beings are born, that by which they live and that in which they are dissolved—That is Brahman". In other words, Brahman is declared here as the source of Creation, Preservation and Dissolution. Needless to say that here the teacher speaks of Brahman, the manifest and also the unmanifest. It is manifest during Preservation but in Creation and Dissolution It is unmanifest. Creation comes from the Unmanifest and to the Unmanifest it returns. But Varuṇa says to his son that this Brahman is to be realized, directly perceived. None can communicate what it is. But how to realise Brahman?

The path towards the realization of Brahman that is indicated here is *Tapas*. But what indeed is *tapas*? Is Brahman to be realized by austerity? Is It to be found by mortification? Tapas here means a process of negation. The fire negates the dross and at the end of this process of negation what remains is pure gold. This is indeed the practice of tapas. How can one know the Self, the Ātman? Only by negating the not-Self. How can the Imperishable be known? Only by negating the Perishable. Man knows by his own experience what dies and dissolves—what does not endure. If he brings his mind to a focus and becomes extensively aware of that which does not endure, that which is the not-self, then in that awareness the perception of the Imperishable comes. Varuṇa gives to his son this very process of negation. The father tells his son that Brahman is Food, Breath, Mind and Intelligence. But this information is of no use—the son must know for himself. Father asks him to enter into tapas to find out the real nature of Brahman. The son by negation and quiet reflection comes to the realisation that Brahman is food and declares this to his father. But the father says, "Go again into tapas". The son negates food and declares the vital breath as Brahman. Again and again the father asks him to go through reflection and negation. And so the son says out of his own experience that Brahman is intelligence. To this he comes after negating food, and prāṇa and mind. But the father does not allow the son to settle down in this declaration. The son must continue the process of negation still further, and when he does that he cries out with joy, saying Brahman is Bliss. The experience of bliss is indeed a state of ecstasy. The son says that "Creation comes out of Bliss, it is maintained by Bliss and it returns to Bliss".

The Taittirīya Upanishad says: *Raso vai Saḥ* —Brahman is Bliss. It is difficult to translate the word *Rasa* in any other language. It is delight but it is not just delight —it is delight that comes in the moment of a deep experience of Love. The bliss that arises from love—this is *Rasa*—and the Upanishad says this is indeed the nature of Brahman. The entire creation is Its delight—but it is Love that maintains the Creation. Bliss has no separate existence from Love. It is the overflowing of love. It exists so long as the experience of Love lasts. Love is indeed the source of all true human relationship. It is a union without any inducement. It is a union without any goal or purpose. For, can there be a goal or purpose in Love? As Poet Rabindra Nath Tagore says:

> Love is an endless mystery,
> For it has nothing else to explain it.

When all explanations of the mind fade away then is one aware of the great mystery of Love. Brahman is indeed that endless mystery—for there is nothing to explain it. Man must perceive It for himself and convey It to others in the joy and ecstasy that he carries into the world of human relationship. When love approaches, all problems fade away, for, indeed it is true that Love conquers all.

VIII

THE DESCENT OF THE SPIRIT

In the whole of human history there is nothing so stirring as the triumphal march of science moving from height to height, bringing under its increasing control both man and nature. In this march, we see such giants as Galelio and Newton, Darwin and Einstein. The long strides of science have covered enormous distances. Science has revealed to us the great wonders of the expanding universe; it has also revealed to us the challenging mystery of the atom. As one studies the growth of science, one is struck by the fact that when it comes face to face with dead ends in its onward journey, there appears a genius of scientific insight who by a startling discovery of new laws and theories gives a different turn to the march of science. One such revolutionary thought came towards the latter half of the 19th century—it came through a great scientific gesius, Charles Darwin. His book the *Origin of Species* must be regarded as one of the epoch making books of all ages. By his doctrine of evolution, Charles Darwin, gave to the erstwhile disorder in the happenings of nature a connected theme—a unity indicating order and design in the immense diversity of nature and man. The doctrine of evolution gave a new turn to the scientific thought, and even today science is discovering newer and newer facets of this revolutionary principle of Evolution.

The idea of evolution was not quite foreign to the religious thought of the world. All the great religions have their Cosmogonies. These deal with the creation and growth of the universe. Whether one looks at the Genesis of the Christian scriptures or the Buddhist or Hindu cosmogonies, one finds in these, indications of the idea of evolution—but in a form almost unintelligible to the common man. In Hindu mythologies, as depicted in the Purāṇas, one comes across stories of creation and the narrations of the earlier periods of man and the universe. The Purāṇas contain legends and stories of creation and dissolution. In *sarga, pratisarga, vaṃśa* and *manvantara,* constituting the various sections of the Purāṇic narrations, one finds comprehensive accounts of the universe, even of cosmography. But these are in stories and parables so that while people who read them find great entertainment, they are unable to piece them together to create a connected story of Evolution. It is in the concept of the Hindu Avatāras—the Divine Incarnations—that one sees an effort to give a connected story of evolution.

The Hindu mythology speaks of ten avatāras out of which eight seem to indicate great periods of evolutionary history. These are described as Fish, Tortoise, Bear, Man-Animal or Narasiṃha, Dwarf, Paraśurāma or the Giant, Rāma, the Perfect Man and Kṛshṇa, the Divine Man. Modern science tells us that life must have appeared on the earth first in waters. This is indicated by the Fish. And then we see Tortoise, a creature both of water and earth. This is followed by Boar, an animal entirely of the earth, unable to live in waters. And then we see the transition between man and animal in the Narasiṃha incarnation. Then comes the first man—the Dwarf. History bears witness to this fact. The next to appear is Paraśurāma, the giant man. We then see the stature of man as he is in the person of Rāma. But man is a meeting place of biological and psychological evolution. In the incarnation of Kṛshṇa we see man showing forth divine characteristics. Here in rough outline we see the story of evolution as it has been depicted in the Hindu Purāṇas. This shows that the ancient seers and sages had intimations of the great principle of evolution. It remained, however, in parables; it was left to modern science to give a detailed story of evolution from the beginnings of life to the present stature of man. The Purāṇas came much later in the growth of Indian civilization. The Upanishads preceded them by many centuries. And it is in the Upanishads that we find first intimations of ancient cosmogony. In many of the Upanishads we find mention about Creation, about the beginnings of the Universe. But it was given to the teacher of the Aitareya Upanishad to enunciate in greater detail the story of creation and the beginnings of the sentient life.

The Aitareya Upanishad derives its name from the teacher, Mahidāsa Aitareya, the son of Itarā. It forms part of the Aitareya Āraṇyaka of the Ṛg Veda. One of the verses of the Ṛg Veda appearing in the Aitareya Āraṇyaka says:

> Truth is the flower and fruit of speech; and he will become a master, a man of renown, one of excellent repute, he who speaks this flower and fruit of speech, Truth.

This idea is reflected in the Invocation with which the Aitareya Upanishad begins. It speaks of a perfect accord between Mind and Speech.

It is in this beautiful background that the teaching of the Aitareya Upanishad begins. The Upanishad in its story of creation begins at the very beginning. In its opening verse it says:

> The One self was all at the beginning, nought else winked.

Not even a wink in that vast undifferentiated space! This is a state prior to the first flutter of awakening manifestation. There was not even a flutter in that Universal Space. One is reminded of the description of this state given in that old, pre-historic, archaic manuscript known as the *Stanzas of Dzyan*. These stanzas describe this state where "nought winked" in the following words:

> Time was not, for it lay asleep in the infinite bosom of duration. Universal Mind was not for there were no celestial beings to contain it.
>
> Darkness alone filled the Boundless All, for Father, Mother and Son were one, and the son had not awakened yet for the new wheel and the pilgrimage thereon.

It may be interesting to note that in the archaic books, Space is known as the Eternal Parent. It is Space which is the parent of all creation—but it is Pure, Undifferentiated Space—it is Space without an object, without even a wink or a flutter. But how does creation come out of this Pure Space where Nothing exists! The Aitareya Upanishad says that the Spirit brooded over the Space and thought: "Let me create the worlds." But who created the Spirit? The Spirit is *Svayambhū*— —self-created. But how did He create Himself? What was the material out of which He created Himself? The answer to this question is with the Spirit Himself—and each must find the answer from Him. The self creation of the Spirit is a mystery—the greatest mystery in all the universe. It is only when the questioner is merged in the Spirit—when he becomes the Spirit, that he can know the secret of this Great Mystery. The mind of man can know that which has a beginning and that which has an end. The Beginning-less and the End-less cannot be known by the mind. This can be known only when the mind is transcended—for, in such transcendence, the questioner, which is the mind, ceases to exist.

And into the vast Space, devoid of anything, there came the first stirrings of creation as the Spirit brooded over the Space. It was the thought of the Spirit which became the creation. But why did the Spirit brood over the Space—why did It think of creation? Probably because the Spirit could not help creating. Out of its immeasurable Fullness, creation came naturally and spontaneously. The creation came not because the Spirit felt lonely—but because the Fullness found its natural expression in creation. The Upanishad says that into the vast space, the Spirit created the Field. He demarcated the areas in that vast space—He defined the Fields into which He would pour his expressions. The Aitareya Upanishad says:

> The spirit created four fields of influence or *Lokas* by the name Ambhas, Marīci, . Mara and Āpaḥ

Strictly speaking Lokas that were created were three —and the third Loka was filled by the spirit. This filling of the Third Loka was essential as necessary conditions for the emergence of life must be created. This filling in of the Third Loka is *Āpaḥ* and the very word really means filling. How was the Third Loka filled? It was filled with water. But what are the three Lokas? The Upanishad seems to be dealing with the lower end of creation—that stage of creation where physical life came into existence. It has not dealt with the subtler realms of creation as perhaps a description of them would be too abstruse and obscure. At the lower end of creation it speaks of the three Lokas—*Ambhas*, *Marīci* and *Mara*. *Ambhas* is the sky or the heaven. It is the Heaven world or the world of the Mind. *Marīci* signifies light and so the second world is the Astral or the Shining world. Mara is the physical world—the world of old age and death. Thus the Upanishad says that the Spirit created the Mental, the Astral and the Physical worlds. These are worlds not in a static sense—they are really the fields of influence. These are indeed names of matter in three different states. When physical matter itself is regarded as a wave of probability—much more so must this description become applicable to the astral and mental states of matter.

But the mere creation of Lokas or Fields would be meaningless. There must come about the Peopling of the Field. But how can people arise in the field unless proper conditions for their existence emerge. So long as earth remains a seething mass of fire, nothing can arise there. It must cool down. And the above verse indicates that the Spirit created water on earth—and the first signs of life appeared in water. The Upanishad speaks of the beginning of life on earth in the following verse:

> The spirit thought Here are the worlds
> Let me now create the guardians of the worlds.
> From the waters themselves, he drew forth a person and gave him a form.

In the story of creation we see three phases—the creation of the Field, the Preparation of the Field and the Peopling of the Field. In the former verse we saw the creation of the three fields and the preparation of the field with the emergence of water. Now the Upanishad speaks of the peopling of the Field. The above verse says that the process of peopling the field began in the waters. This is in accordance with what modern science tells us regarding the beginnings of life on earth. It believes that life must have appeared first in the waters. The above verse of the Upanishad says that the spirit drew forth a person from the waters and gave it a form. Here the person is not to be understood as a human being. The verse says that a person was drawn and then a form was given. The person here obviously means a life impulse. The sentient life began in water and the spirit gave form to this sentient life. Here the Upanishad lays down a fundamental principle of creation, namely, that life precedes form. First there came the stirrings of sentient life—and then form was given to this life-impulse. A question may arise—What was the nature of the life-impulse without a form? We may ask another question—What is the nature of life-impulse before the biological form comes into existence? Just because it is invisible to the physical eye, one cannot doubt its existence. And so first came the stirrings of life impulse and then a form was created. But the scene of the first emergence of sentient form was the Waters. That the Person in the above verse does not indicate a human form is made clear in the following verse of the Upanishad. It says:

> The spirit brooded over this Form. By this brooding, into this Form a mouth burst forth as if it were an egg.

Here the Upanishad seems to refer to the Egg-born. In the course of vast periods of evolution we see different methods of re-production. The first is by Fission and Budding as we see in creatures like the amoeba. A part of the body extends and then there takes place a fission—the part so extended separates itself from the parent body and begins to live its own life. Then came the sweat-born, the hermaphrodite, the bi-sexual of evolutionary history. From the sweat-born arise the egg-born—the pre-mammalian creatures. It is with the arrival of mammals—and man is also a mammal—that we see the method of re-production where the child is nourished in the womb and comes out of the womb. The Aitareya Upanishad does not give the whole story of evolution in all its details. And so it takes up the story with the egg-born. The above verse says that the form over which the Spirit brooded burst forth like an egg and in this bursting forth the mouth appeared accompanied by sound. And then there appeared the two nostrils indicating the breathing process of the creature that had been thus created. The verse gives a very detailed description of how the various organs of the body appeared. The verse says that the bursting forth of the egg took place because it was *abhitapta*—heated up. What does this mean? How is the hatching of eggs done by the hen? She broods over the egg and in this brooding gives it the warmth of its own body. The spirit by brooding over the form gave it warmth—and the warmth resulted in the bursting forth of the egg. Here by the egg-born probably the author of the Upanishad means the creation of the kingdom of birds—the coming into existence of what is traditionally known as the angelic kingdom. The creatures of the angelic kingdom constitute the elementals. The above verse indicates the birth of the elementals. Since the creatures of the angelic kingdom are comparable to birds, the Upanishad has used the simile of the egg in the act of creation. The mammals have not yet come on the evolutionary scene. The Upanishad says that these "elementals were associated with hunger and thirst." The elementals were naturally imbued with desires—they were pulsating with energy—they clamoured for the satisfaction of their urges. The Aitareya Upanishad says that they:

> Demanded an abode for themselves so that they could nourish themselves.

The verse says that they asked for *āyatana* —a resting place where they can quench their hunger and thirst. These elementals needed avenues of expression. For these devas and elementals, the spirit must make a provision for their feeding. The Upanishad says:

> For them the Spirit brought a cow. But they replied this is not enough for us. The Spirit then brought a horse—but again they said—this is not enough for us.

Here there is a clear reference to the arrival of the mammals on the evolutionary scene—it is a movement further from the egg-born to the womb-born. First comes the cow and then the horse. In the story of evolution given by science, horse is a perfect example showing all the various stages of mammalian growth. In fact, it is by studying the horse that one is able to perceive the movement of nature in the creation of more and more perfect forms of mammals. But the devas and the elementals say that these are not enough. Their energies cannot find full satisfaction in such forms of mammals as are represented by the cow and the horse. The evolutionary stream must move still further. And so the Upanishad speaks of the arrival of Man—the *homo sapiens*. The story of evolution as depicted by science tells us that life appeared first in the waters. And then after millions of years there came serpentlike creatures. From these creatures arose a bifurcating line of evolution—one moving towards the creation of birds and bird-like creatures—those that were egg-born, and another line proceeded towards the creation of mammals—the creatures that are womb-born. The Upanishadic teacher seems to have been aware of the order in which these creatures arose. For it is after the egg-born that he speaks of the womb-born. And even among mammals, he comes to men only after showing the emergence of such creatures as the cow and the horse.

Finding that the elements did not feel completely satisfied with the cow and the horse, the spirit created man, the highest among the mammals. The verse of the Upanishad says:

> For them the Spirit brought a Person.
> They said: "This is well done indeed."
> The Spirit told them: "Now enter the Person according to your distinctive functions."

Here the Spirit asks the elementals to take up their own distinctive abodes in the body of Man. The elementals are asked to occupy appropriate places in the bodily organism of man. One of the interesting features of evolutionary growth is that it moves from the unicellular to multi-cellular, from homogenous to heterogenous and from simple to complex. In this movement, a remarkable thing happens, and that is, the differentiation and specialization of functions. In the amoeba there is no differentiation and therefore no specialization of functions. It seems to be doing everything with its entire body. It even eats with the whole body. But as life-stream advances and greater and greater complexity of structure arises, the need is naturally felt for specialization of functions. Man is a very complex creature in his structure and functions. This complexity of structure demands great deal of specialization in its functioning apparatus. The Upanishad speaks of the various elementals entering their appropriate places in the bodily organism of man so as to discharge their respective functions. It is to functional differentiation and specialization that the Upanishad makes a reference when it speaks of Agni becoming speech and entering the mouth and *Vāyu* becoming breath and entering the nostrils. We find a detailed description of the various functions occupying their respective places.

But then Hunger and Thirst cry out saying "What about us—where do we go?" The Upanishad says that the Spirit consoled them by saying that they will occupy their places within the functional elementals themselves—they will not be separate from any of the functions. This denotes that if hunger and thirst are present in all functions then they will be induced to act. Hunger and thirst represent the urges that impel the functioning organism to act. Without the impelling power of these urges the bodily organism would tend towards laziness and indolence. And so very wisely, the Spirit asks Hunger and Thirst to take their places in all the functioning agencies of the body.

But having created the field and the entities to people the field, the next task before the Spirit is to find food for them. The Upanishad says that the spirit created food to feed the entities. But an interesting situation arose. The different senses, urged by hunger and thirst, desired to grasp food by their own functioning powers. The tongue and the nose, the eye, the ear and the skin and even the mind (being one of the senses) tried to grasp food—but they all failed. If they had succeeded then the sight of food and the hearing of the word food, the smelling of food and the uttering of the word "food" or thinking about food would have been the means to satisfy oneself. But surely none of these could have assuaged the hunger of man. Man would have remained hungry even though he may have seen food or heard about food, or smelt and spoken the word "food" or even if he had thought about food. None of these senses could hold food. Food eluded their grasp. At last food was grasped by the *Apāna Vāyu* —the vital breath operating in the lower regions. It is the proper function of *apāna vāyu* to handle food and to see that it is turned into energy because of the elimination of waste. In this illustration of food being grasped by various senses with no result, and the *apāna vāyu* holding it within its powers, we are given an understanding of the differentiation and specialization of bodily functions. The eye must do its appointed task—it cannot arrogate to itself the functions of the digestive organs. Each must do its appointed work, for, each function has its own specialized apparatus which can do the work given to it efficiently—but which cannot take over the functions of another. Here we witness the great development which comes in the wake of evolutionary progress, namely, the specialization of functions. This becomes necessary because of the complexity of structure.

But would not differentiation and specialization by themselves lead to chaos and disorder? How would the various functions remain within their bounds? Surely with specialization there must come co-ordination. Without such co-ordination each functioning agency would do as it pleases. It may demand more for its nourishment than is due. Since each agency would function within the narrow field of its own specialization, who would think of the entire body? This thought came to the spirit and it decided to enter the body. The entry of the spirit in the body, after the development of specialized agencies, clearly signifies the need for co-ordination. Human body functions because of specialization and co-ordination. But how does co-ordination come into existence? The Upanishad says that the Spirit thought "By which door shall I enter the body—through the feet or through the head?" The Spirit decided to enter through the head. The Aitareya Upanishad says:

> After opening that very end of the head, through that as door It entered the body. This is the door that is called *vidṛti* or cleft. This is the joyous entry.

The entry of the Spirit into the body through the head has many layers of meanings. It denotes the role of the brain as the co-ordinating factor in the whole functional realm of the body. The specialized centres of the body function with a wholeness because of the Brain. Without this co-ordinating factor the different functions of the body would pull in different directions. And so the presence of the Spirit in the Body is a unifying force, giving to the bodily organism a cohesion, a harmony, a synthesis. But the entry of the Spirit in the Body has a deeper meaning too. The verse of the Upanishad says that this spirit entering the body has three abodes—they are the Eyes, the Throat and the Heart. The abode in the eyes indicates the Spirit that is visible, the abode in the Throat symbolises the Spirit that is invisible—only heard but not seen, but the abode in the Heart points to the fact that the Spirit is beyond the visible and the invisible—the Intangible. It cannot be seen, nor can It be heard—It can only be felt. The entry of the Spirit through the head not only points to the co-ordination of functions in the bodily organism—it means the existence of the spirit in manifestation both as visible and as Invisible. But above all it gives an indication of the fact that It is Unmanifest and as such can only be felt by him who has the sensitivity to commune with the Intangible. With the entry of the spirit, man becomes aware of Brahman, the Manifest. With this entry, man says: "I have seen this." The verse of the Upanishad says that the perceiver of this is known as Idandra—one who has seen this. This refers to the spirit that is seen, Brahman that is visible. The visible is always seen indirectly for here there is the duality of the seer and the seen. The entry of the Spirit in the body is visible Brahman and the knowledge of it is indirect.

We said earlier that the entry of the Spirit in the body has more than one meaning. Another category of its meaning becomes clear as we turn to the second part of this Upanishad. Here there is a reference to Vāmadeva who released himself from the bonds of birth and death.

Here the Upanishad speaks of three births of man. These three births of man refer to his journey from the Manifest to the Unmanifest—from the visible through the invisible to the Intangible. In the Upanishad, the three births are referred to as born in the Seed of the Father, in the Womb of the Mother and the Body of the Child, these three really constitute the states of consciousness—they are the *Jāgarita* or the waking, the *Svapna* or the Dream and *Sushupti* or the Deep Sleep. The birth in the seed of the father is the Waking state, the birth in the womb of the mother is the Dream State and the birth in the body of the child is the Deep Sleep state. The state of Deep Sleep is the condition of innocence, a condition free from all corruption. If one could maintain this child state then in that condition one would come to the understanding of Brahman, the unmanifest. The Deep Sleep is a condition of Wisdom, of *Prajñāna* as the Upanishad declares. Since the real nature of Brahman can be known only in this condition of Wisdom, the Aitareya Upanishad gives out that famous Upanishadic statement—one of the *Mahāvākyas* namely, *Vijñānaṃ Brahma—Brahman* is Wisdom. The Upanishad speaks of the freedom of Vāmadeva. This is stated thus:

> A hundred iron cages hemmed me in, down here, a hawk, with speed did I burst forth.

The freedom of the spirit—the spiritual freedom—is not a gradual process. It is an experience of bursting forth with speed like the fast moving bird. In the state of Deep Sleep this experience of freedom comes suddenly and instantaneously. In this condition one knows the Immortality of the Spirit—one communes with the spirit that is Unmanifest—one knows what lies beyond birth and death. Vāmadeva having gone through the experience of three births—the experience of the three states of consciousness—knows what Immortality is—what Deathlessness indicates. In the third and the last section of this Upanishad the inquiry into the nature of the self or the spirit is carried further. The Upanishad asks the following question:

> Who is this whom we worship as the Spirit? Is it that whereby one sees, or whereby one hears, or whereby one smells, or whereby one utters speech, or whereby one knows what is sweet and what is not sweet? Which of the two is the Spirit—one subject to birth and death or one that is free from birth and death?

In the whole Upanishadic thought there is an emphasis on two aspects of Brahman—Brahman in itself and Brahman in the Universe. Brahman in Itself is Brahman without attributes, it is Brahman, the Unmanifest. Brahman in the Universe obviously means one that is manifest. In the above verse the same two aspects of Brahman have been mentioned. The Aitareya Upanishad has laid stress on the manifest Brahman more than on Brahman, the Unmanifest.

We saw in the earlier verses a description of the Spirit entering the body. This is indeed an indication of Brahman manifesting in the Universe. This Upanishad says that Brahman or the Spirit entered the body and stayed there. And with the entry of the Spirit in the body there came about a co-ordination of all bodily functions. In the scientific studies of evolution there are thinkers who are beginning to accept two main factors of Evolution—one is the factor from below, and the other is the factor from above. They say that the factors from below by themselves are unable to explain the whole phenomena of evolution. There are a number of evolutionary problems that remain unexplained in terms of the factors from below. We have to take into account the arrival of factors from above. This becomes all the more evident when we witness a phenomenon like biological mutations. Some factor from above, or from the Unknown, seems to be responsible for this mysterious event in the story of evolution. Now the entry of the Spirit in the body is indeed the arrival of a factor from above, giving a new turn to evolution. This factor from above serves like a magnet so that different parts in the magnetic field remain naturally attracted to the magnet. This is exactly what happens when the Spirit enters the body—for we see that the different and specialized functions come into a pattern of co-ordination. In evolution, while specialization denotes factors from below, co-ordination indicates the factors from above. When factors from above come then the co-ordination becomes almost effortless—there is a natural coming together of diverse and specialized functions. This is Brahman in the universe about which the Aitareya Upanishad speaks.

But this Upanishad speaks not merely of the co-ordination of physical functions. It speaks of the co-ordination of psychological functions as well. The presence of Brahman or the Spirit in the universe serves as a unifying force. It has a magnetic influence over all different parts whether at the physical or at the psychological level. The verse of this Upanishad says that the Spirit is not only That by which one sees or hears or touches or smells or tastes. Brahman or the Spirit is also that by which the mind and heart function. In the realm of man's psyche too the spirit acts as a magnet affording a co-ordination of the functions of the mind. The following verse of the Aitareya Upanishad makes this point clear. It says:

> The spirit is that which is heart and mind too. It is consciousness, perception, discrimination, intelligence, wisdom, insight, steadfastness, thought, thoughtfulness, impulse, memory, conception, purpose, life, desire and will.

Here is given a complete statement of the functions of the mind—the composite process known as thought-emotion. One wonders whether modern western psychology has come to such perfect analysis of the functions of the mind. The mind has a greater diversity of functions than the body. These functions not only show the differentiation of mind in its functional aspect but also specialization. For each function of the mind is a specialized agency for the discharge of specific work. These functions can be grouped together to form an intelligible pattern. One can see here five functioning groups of the mind—they are conception or *Saṅkalpa,* Thought or *Mati* and Thoughtfulness or *Manīshā*; Consciousness or *Sañjñāna,* Perception or *Ājñāna,* and Discrimination or *Vijñāna.* steadfastness or *Dhṛti,* Impulse or *Jūti,* and memory or *Smṛti,* Purpose or *Kratu,* Life or *Asu,* Desire or *Kāma* and will or *Vaśa* —and finally Intelligence or *Prajñāna* Wisdom or *Medhā* and Insight or *Dṛshṭi.* If one examines these five groups, one realizes that the functions of the mind can be stated as Thought, Awareness, Continuity, Imagination and Intelligence. The forming of concepts and the building up of the logical structures of thought constitute the first of its functions. The second function denotes a process of selectivity whereby the mind discriminates between good and bad, between true and false, between the beautiful and the ugly. In the third function we see mind's continuity through memory and impulse or mind's instincts. Thought gives a wide material to the mind from which to make a selection through discrimination. Having selected, having regarded something as good and something as bad, mind wants to establish a continuity of that which it declares as desirable. This is naturally done through memory and impulse or instinct. Then comes the fourth function of the mind wherein the mind generates through imagination, energy for the maintenance of a continuity of that which it has declared as good or true or beautiful. The energy is sought to be generated through purpose, through desire and through will or imagination. And the final element of mind's functioning is Insight or Intelligence. The last is indeed the co-ordinating element of mind's functioning. If the mind accepts the guidance of Insight, Intelligence or Wisdom then its thinking is clear, its selectivity or discrimination is proper, its field of continuity is free from conflicts and it has immense energy to deal effectively with the situations of life. In other words, mind would find its various functions discharging their duties well and truly if there is the acceptance of the guidance of Intelligence or Insight. It is Intelligence which is the unifying factor of the mind. The unifying factor of the body is brain but since brain can function only as an instrument of the mind, it is mind which controls the functions of the body. And so it is Intelligence which controls the mind and through the mind all the bodily functions. But if the mind does not take the guidance of Intelligence then there is disintegration of the mind and disease in the body. Thus Brahman in the Universe is Intelligence or *Prajñāna*.. Thc Aitareya Upanishad declares that "all are appellations of Intelligence or Prajñana". The Upanishad sums up its entire teaching in the following concluding verse:

> He is Brahman; he is Indra, he is Prajāpati, he is all these gods; and the five gross elements, namely earth, air, space, water, light, these things and those which are mingled of the fine, as it were; origins of one sort and another, those born from an egg, and those born from a womb and those born from sweat, and those born from a sprout; horses, cows, persons, elephants, whatever breathing thing there is here—whether moving or flying, and also what is stationary.
>
> All this is guided by Intelligence, is based on Intelligence. The world is guided by Intelligence. The basis is Intelligence, Brahman is Intelligence.

The Upanishad says—all is guided by Intelligence. But then why are there sorrow and misery in the world? This is because while the guidance of Intelligence is available, man refuses to be guided by It. And the refusal of man comes because of the acquired characteristics of the mind. The desire of the mind comes into conflict with the purpose towards which Intelligence directs. The mind raises a thick cloud of dust and behind this cloud remains hidden the light of intelligence. The dust raised by the mind must settle down and the mind must refrain from raising fresh dust—it is then only that the vision of Intelligence can come for the guidance of man. The mind's process of thought and evaluation, its continuity and its energy lead to greater and greater frustration because the light of Intelligence has been shut off. The mind has closed its doors to the light of Wisdom. When the intellect of man is illumined by the light of Intelligence then it is that man sees Brahman in the Universe. In the light of this Vision, in the ecstasy of this experience, man discovers that neither space nor time is a bondage. He is indeed utterly free, for nothing can ever bind him. In seeing Brahman as Intelligence, in perceiving Brahman in the Universe, man comes to the realization of his intrinsic freedom—not freedom at the end of soul's journey—but freedom in the very beginning—for if there is no freedom in the beginning, there can be no freedom at the end.

IX

THE FULLNESS OF THE VOID

It must be said of the Forest University, constituted by the great Upanishads, that it fulfilled its tasks with great efficiency. It was concerned both with the deepening of the experience of the individual as with the imparting of such skill and technique by which the base of human expression may be widened. It addressed itself to the task of Experience as also to the task of Expression. Its interest was both in Culture as well as in Civilization. In the Chāndogya Upanishad we see this twofold nature of the Forest University, perhaps, more clearly than in any other Upanishad. The dialogue between Nārada and Sanatkumāra, appearing in the Chāndogya Upanishad, indicates to us very clearly the task to which the Forest University, constituted by the great Upanishads, addressed itself. The story runs as follows:

It seems Nārada once approached sage Sanatkumāra requesting him to show to him the Path of Real Knowledge —the Path of Wisdom. The Upanishad says that Sanatkumāra addressed Nārada thus:

> Let me first know what you have already learnt. I shall then teach you whatever may be further than that.

Sanatkumāra asked Nārada to bring into his mental focus all that he had learnt—he must first be clear as to what he knows. He thus asked Nārada to first of all bring system and order in his own mind so that he can clearly state what he already knows. Here sage Sanatkumāra indicates the fundamental principle of right education, of moving from the Known to the Unknown. And so he asked Nārada to tell him what he already knew. And this is how Nārada replied:

> Sir, I have learnt the Ṛg Veda, the Yajur Veda, the Sāma Veda, the Atharva Veda, history and traditional stories which together

> are called the fifth Veda, the method of remembering and repeating the Vedas, the technique of śrāddha ceremony, grammar, philosophy, mathematics, astronomy, astrology, science of augury, jugglery, logic, ethics, music, science of dance, poetry, science of animals, science of war and many other branches of knowledge.

Hearing this long list of subjects which Nārada had learnt in the course of many years of study, Sanatkumāra said:

> Dear Nārada, all that you have known is but mere name and verbiage, mere words. You can by your present knowledge achieve only what words can achieve and nothing more.

Then Nārada said to Sanatkumāra:

> What is it that is greater than name and words? Please teach me that.

This indeed is the subject matter of Chāndogya Upanishad. The list of subjects learnt by Nārada is very impressive—almost staggering. How could one person learn all these various subjects forming part both of the sciences and the humanities? The list clearly indicates that in ancient India education was truly integrated. But there is something more than that which we see in these subjects—it is the capacity to learn on the part of the student. The student must have known how to learn because of which his learning must have been quick and precise. The student was obviously free from all outer distractions, but that alone cannot account for such quick and effective learning. The problem of distractions is both objective and subjective. The gurukulas being situated far, far away from the din and the noise of the outer world must have supplied a setting free from objective distractions. But what about the subjective distractions—those that arise from within?

It is quite possible that like Pippalāda of the Praśna, Upanishad, the teachers in the gurukulas must have asked students to spend one year in the teachers' āśramas for orienting themselves to the requirements of intensive education. Perhaps the same technique as employed by Pippalāda was used by other teachers for the purposes of orientation. This must have been the Pre-university period for training and equipment as also for subjective orientation so that the actual years of study may be without any impediment. The technique used by Pippalāda was *Tapa, Brahmacarya* and *Śraddhā*. The Upanishads have said — *Nāyamātmā balahīnena labhyaḥ* — Ātman cannot be found by one who is devoid of strength or energy. The technique of *Tapa* and *Brahmacarya* is for the release and the conservation of energy, so that when Faith or Śraddhā brings one face to face with the Unknown, one does not falter. It demands great strength and energy to face the Unknown. The Forest Universities prepared their students for this by *tapa* and *brahmacarya*. The energy locked up in the framework of the known was released and conserved. It is in this condition that Faith was born—it was the faith of the strong, not of the weak. It was in this orientation that the student was enabled to plunge into his studies with tremendous physical and mental energy. No wonder, that the student could learn quickly and yet effectively.

A question may arise: If Nārada had learnt so much, why was he striving to learn still more? Was he not satisfied with what he had learnt? If not, why not? Nārada was indeed not satisfied with what he had learnt—the Flame of Learning had not been extinguished after he completed his gurukula training. The beauty of the gurukula system was that while it taught many subjects, it sent out students, from its campus, not as self-satisfied individuals, feeling that they had learnt all that could be learnt and that therefore their learning had come to an end. The gurukula system impressed upon the student that the training by the guru was over—but the period of self-training, of self-education, had just begun. The student must engage himself in this self-education after the completion of his studies in the gurukula. He had become proficient in the *aparā vidyā*, but now he must embark upon the journey that takes him to the land of *Parā Vidyā*. The student had acquired knowledge, but now he must travel, alone and unaided, along the path of wisdom—for, no teacher can instil wisdom into the mind of the student. These can be a School of Knowledge, but surely not an institute of Wisdom. Nārada had acquired knowledge, but he was not satisfied. He missed something in his life, and it is to this that he gives utterance when he addresses Sanatkumāra thus:

> Sir, I feel that I merely know the *mantras* or patent words but I do not know the Ātman or the soul or the spirit of things. I have heard from men like you that he who knows Ātman goes beyond all sorrow. Sir, I am full of sorrow and grief and remorse.

It is to this Nārada, who had come to the realization that knowledge acquired by him was inadequate, that Sanatkumāra spoke those words in which he declared that his knowledge was merely words—it was nothing but verbiage, a collection of names. Is this not true of all knowledge that is acquired by the mind? If mind is asked to explain a word, it places before us more words. It explains one thing by greater verbalization of that very thing. Asked to explain the significance of a name, it weaves a chain of more names. What Sanatkumāra tells Nārada is —Realise that the Word is not the thing—that the thing is not identical with the name that is given to it. The Word God is surely not God—the Word Beauty is not Beauty—the name given to Truth is not Truth. One can proceed further from knowledge only after this realization that the word is not the thing. The words of Sanatkumāra were almost shattering—but Nārada was not disturbed by what he said because he himself had seen the inadequacy of knowledge. And so to this disciple who was ready he says—Realize that the Word and the Thing are different. The identification of the word and the thing is done by the mind. The word is superimposed upon the thing—and with this, man begins to live in a world of projected things—not a world of real things. To know that one is living in a projected world is to shatter one's own abode—it is, indeed, to become homeless. It is verily an experience of Void. And the fundamental theme of the Chāndogya Upanishad is the unravelling of the mystery of the Void, the mystery of Nothingness.

The Chāndogya Upanishad belongs to the Sāma Veda. It is one of the longest Upanishads as it discusses the subject of Reality from diverse standpoints. Its invocation is the same as found in the Kena Upanishad. This invocation speaks of non-denial of Brahman by man and non-denial of man by Brahman. There is a denial so long as something stands between man and Brahman. That something indeed is the projected image of the mind; that something is the Word, the name, the verbalization of the mind. If there has to be a non-denial of Brahman by man and of man by Brahman then the veils cast by mind's verbalization must be rent asunder so that there may be a direct perception. It is in the negation of the word and the name—the negation of the entire process of verbalization by the mind—that man experiences that supreme state when the Ātman discovers Brahman in the very cave of his heart. The invocation prays for more strength and energy—for how can the Ātman be found without knowing that secret whereby energy never gets depleted—nay, it increases from moment to moment.

The Chāndogya Upanishad begins with the narration of the glories of the Sacred Word OM. The Upanishads again and again refer to the Sacred Word because it is the purest symbolization of Brahman. It is the sublimest manifestation of Brahman. While other aspects of manifestation are like compounds, arising out of the combination of several things, the Sacred Word, OM, is the simplest and yet the highest expression of Brahman.

> As all leaves are held together by a spike, so all speech is held together by OM.

The Chāndogya Upanishad, being a part of the Sāma Veda, naturally approaches the whole subject of Brahman through speech or, more truly, through sound. In this Upanishad, OM has been indicated as *Udgītha*—the Sacred Word that is sung. Obviously there is a reference to the articulate sound of OM—but as the articulate has its root in the inarticulate the Upanishad deals both with the manifest and the unmanifest—but clearly indicating that the manifest derives its meaning and significance from the Unmanifest.

This understanding is indeed the elixir of life—the

Amṛta a as the Upanishad says. The Unmanifest in Manifest is indeed like nectar which nourishes the *vasu* or the earthly substances, *rudra* or the vegetable life, the forces of nature as represented by the *Ādityas* and *Maruts*, and finally the animal and man. The Upanishad says that this secret, or, the elixir of life, is indeed *Madhu Vidyā* —the sweetest of all knowledge. It is communicated by the teacher to the disciple, by father to the son—but such communication is done only to the disciple who is worthy, to the son who is inwardly ready. The Upanishad says:

> Even if a disciple were to give to his teacher land rich with wealth and surrounded by sea, the teacher may not impart that secret to him. For this Madhu Vidyā is more precious than the wealth of all the world. It can be communicated only to a worthy disciple.

It seems long long ago there was a king called Jānaśruti who ruled over the kingdom of Mahāvṛsha. He was very charitable in disposition, known for his vast philanthropy. His generosity was on the lips of all. He naturally felt proud of what he had done and he felt that he had surely accumulated much religious merit by his numerous charities. He measured his merit by the amount of money and gifts he had distributed. One evening, after the hard work of the day, he was resting on the terrace of his palace. Just at that moment two swans were flying, speeding their way to a well-earned night's rest. As they were flying, the male bird rebuked his mate saying: "Don't you see the bright beam of light emanating from King Jānaśruti? Do not cross that beam as otherwise you will get burnt. The king sheds that light because of his numerous charities". The female bird laughed and said: "Why do you threaten me like this? We are wanderers of the sky. And besides what is the merit of this king compared to that of Raikva, the cartman?" The king heard this conversation and became restless. He decided to contact Raikva and to find out what made him more meritorious than himself inspite of all his charities. After much search, Raikva, the cartman was spotted in a very small village. The King proceeded to meet this poor cartman in his village and took with him numerous gifts. His generosity was all the more lavish on this occasion. When the royal party arrived, Raikva, was greatly surprised to see the king loaded with all types of gifts. The king made obeisance to the cartman and requested him to accept the gifts he had brought and also instruct him in the way of peace and happiness. Raikva, the cartman, said to the king:

> O royal friend, why do you waste these precious things on me? All these and a hundred kingdoms cannot buy spiritual knowledge. It is not something that can be bartered and bought in a market. These trinkets that you have brought are worth nothing to me.

The king felt greatly hurt by these words of Raikva and returned to his palace utterly disappointed. But Raikva had cast a spiritual spell upon him and so he returned to the cartman with humility and supplication. Raikva saw that the king was now ready to receive spiritual instruction. Raikva told the King:

> Various are the gods that people worship. The sweeping wind, the flaming fire, the breathing vital force are all worshipped as god by man. But the Spirit itself uncreated, creates all and supports them. The Spirit eats not anything, that is, it does not stand in need of anything. It is self-supporting and self-sufficient. All belongs to the Spirit—all are but instruments of its will.

The cartman asks the king to turn to the Uncreated which creates everything—he asks him to move away from the diversity of gods to the One, without a second. He draws his attention to Brahman in itself—for by knowing this he will be able to perceive Brahman in the Universe. To the king, this poor, but enlightened cartman said that he who is rooted in this understanding behaves absolutely differently. He told the king that if he understood what he was saying then:

> Go thou, great king to thy palace. Give but not with pride. Give generously but not with egotism. Give freely but not with an eye to fame. Give but not as something that is yours—but as something given to you by the Spirit for giving to others. He who sees this truth becomes a seer and to him nothing is wanting —he becomes the enjoyer of all things.

The enjoyer of all things—this is the state of one who has come to spiritual illumination. He enjoys whatever is given to him. The manifest as the instrument of the Unmanifest—that is the great teaching which Raikva gives to the king. He does not ask him to give up his palace and his kingdom—he does not ask him to give up his position. He indicates to him that all that he has are but symbols. Let not the symbol be regarded as the substance. So long as one regards symbols as symbols there is no difficulty—it is the mistaking of the symbol for the substance that creates misery and sorrow and remorse. The Word, the Name, is only a symbol. To know that Word is not the thing, to know that Name is only a symbol, is to come to that great secrets of secrets—the secret of seeing the Unmanifest in the manifest, of discovering Brahman in the Ātman.

In this illustration of the king and the cartman we see the teacher testing the readiness of the pupil. The pupil coming with many possessions is indeed unworthy. These possessions refer more to the mind than to the body. A pupil leaving all possessions behind, approaching the teacher in utter humility is truly worthy to receive spiritual light. The worthiness of pupil is judged by the condition of the mind—and not by outer patterns of behaviour. The readiness of the pupil does not depend upon the discarding of the normal dress and putting on of a special regalia. The putting on of a regalia is as much of a show as the king bringing lavish gifts to overwhelm the teacher. The approach to spiritual life has to be simple. But very often simplicity also becomes a matter of display and ostentation. A tendency to display anything, whether material wealth or the so-called spiritual acquisitions, is a distinct disqualification on the path of true spirituality. The mind that displays is a shallow mind—it does not matter what it displays. It is the simplicity of mind that endows a person with true worth in spiritual life. But so long as a simple person thinks that he is simple, so long is he away from true simplicity. It is the mind which is naturally simple—not simple by a process of cultivation—that is ready to receive spiritual light. In the Chāndogya Upanishad we see the example of a truly simple mind in the person of Satyakāma Jābāla.

Once Satyakāma went to his mother and said "Mother, I wish to enter upon the life of a religious student: of what family am I"? The Upanishad says that the mother answered thus:

> I do not know, my child, of what family thou art. In my youth I was poor and served as maid many masters, and then I had thee: I therefore do not know of what family thou art. My name is Jabālā and thy name is Satyakāma. Thou mayest call thyself Satyakāma. Jābāla

The boy then went to the Master Hāridrumata Gautama and said: "I want to become a student of sacred wisdom. May I come to you, Master?" The Master inquired of him as to what was his family. Satyakāma told the teacher what his mother had told him. He did not hide any fact, and said "I am Satyakāma Jābāla." After hearing the story of Satyakāma, the teacher said:

> Thou art a Brahmin since thou hast not gone away from truth. Go therefore and bring *samidhā* or sacrificial fuel and I shall initiate you into *brahmacarya*, You have not departed from truth, but clung fast to it, happen what may.

Here we see the Upanishadic teacher completely free from social traditions and norms of social respectability. Having heard the story of the boy, an ordinary teacher would have sent him away saying that one born of a mother of questionable character could not be admitted in the ashrama of a guru. But here was a guru who was *Brahmanishṭha* —he was not merely learned in the scriptures, he was a man of deep spiritual realization. He must have been, indeed, a very courageous man. This incident also gives us an insight into the conditions of freedom that must have prevailed in the ancient Indian society. For the admission of Satyakāma in the gurukula shows that there was no stigma of birth or caste attached to a person. The teachers of the Upanishads were truly catholic in their outlook, completely free from the false standards of social respectability. But here too was a young man utterly simple and honest, not afraid to speak the truth. For seeking admission Satyakāma could have spoken a lie as most people in his circumstances would do. But Satyakāma was made of a different mettle. One is filled with great respect for his mother—the mother could have kept concealed the unpleasant fact. Evidently she had the strength to tell the truth—and Satyakāma too had that character by which he refused to deviate from truth—it is this utter truthfulness on the part of Satyakāma that must have impressed his teacher—so that he was immediately accepted as a pupil and initiated into the state of *brahmacarya*.

But the teacher of Satyakāma was a hard taskmaster. He knew that the boy was utterly truthful—but was he ripe enough to learn the great truths of life? The teacher must test him before he initiates him into the secrets of higher knowledge. And so the teacher gave an assignment to Satyakāma. He told him to take charge of four hundred lean, weak and poorly-fed cows. He told him:

> Take this whole lot of cows to the forest and do not return to the āśrama till they become a herd of a thousand.

And so Satyakāma went into the forest driving the lean, weak and poorly-fed cows—he took the assignment gracefully, to live with the cows and the bulls, far far away from the āśrama. The story says that Satyakāma spent his days happily in the forest, never for a moment keeping aside his urge to know Brahman, to come to the experience of the Ultimate Reality. This urge to know Brahman made everything alive so that the whole nature became his teacher. Then the trees and the flowers, the sun, moon and the stars, the rivers and the streams, the light of day and the darkness of the night—all these spoke to him of the nature of Brahman. He felt that all was Brahman. He heard of Brahman in the songs of birds, he felt the presence of Brahman in all things that surrounded him. He realized that the eye that sees and the ear that hears does so because of Brahman. He felt that the pulsating life around him as also the mind that raises innumerable questions all these are but aspects of Brahman. Satyakāma tended the cows and the bulls—but in the midst of this seemingly mundane work, he communed with nature—and in this communion realized that which filled him with joy indescribable. When the herd of cattle had swollen from four hundred to one thousand, he moved towards the āśrama. Reaching the āsrama he went to the teacher and bowed before him. The teacher received him with joy, but was wonderstruck to see the face of Satyakāma He said to him:

> Dear young man, you look like one who has known Brahman. Who was it that taught you? How is it that some agency other than the human has taught you this knowledge? For no one was with you in that wilderness except these dumb cattle and the dreary tumult of the forest?

If man is sensitive enough then he can learn from nature the highest truths of life—such is the experience to which Satyakāma bears witness. But it is to the utter simplicity of mind and heart that the doors of nature are opened revealing the secrets of life hidden in her bosom. The teacher realized that Satyakāma was indeed a worthy pupil—his doors of perception were wide open, his mind was sensitive, his senses were responsive to the subtle beauties of nature—he realized that the house of Satyakāma was open for Truth to walk in. The Upanishad says that the teacher gave to Satyakāma highest knowledge—for where could he find a pupil so honest, so sincere, so worthy as Satyakāma ?

These two instances of Jānaśruti and Satyakāma reveal to us the fact that the readiness of the pupil was a factor on which the Upanishadic teachers laid great stress. The esoteric knowledge was not kept hidden because it was a close preserve of some teachers—it remained esoteric because there were few pupils of such maturity and sensitivity as Jānaśruti and Satyakāma . But when such pupils came, the teachers of yore opened the whole treasure house before them. In the mystery schools of the Upanishads, esoteric knowledge lay open for all—but only the sensitive in heart and mature in mind could understand its significance. They who understood the significance went into the wide world as truly inspired people, imbued with the elixir of life.

It is said that Satyakāma became a great teacher himself and had many pupils under him. He sent out into the world pupil after pupil after the completion of their studies but there was one student by the name Upakosala Kāmalāyana whom he did not send out—his graduation ceremony was postponed year after year. He was a very brilliant student and yet he was kept back in the āśrama without graduation. The wife of the teacher pleaded with her husband to have the graduation ceremony of Upakosala performed, but Satyakāma would not agree to this. He went away on some important work and so was away from the Āśrama. Upakosala then stopped eating all food. The wife of the teacher asked him why he was undertaking this fast. Upakosala replied that there was disease in his body. Asked to explain the nature of his disease, he said he was not yet free from the desire to know and to achieve. What greater disease could there be than this desire? Man comes to the realization of Brahman only when he is free even from the desire to know Brahman. So long as such desire lasts, that very desire becomes an impediment for coming to a realization of Brahman. He probably felt that his guru had not declared him as a graduate because he was still full of this desire—he was learned in the Vedas and the various limbs of the Vedas—but he had not come to the realization of Brahman. Of what use is mere learning without realization? The fast was symbolical as an awareness of this desire, serving as an obstacle to the direct experience of Brahman.

The story says that seeing this young man fasting, the Lords of Fire decided to initiate him in the mysteries of Brahman. They said "Brahman is life, Brahman is Joy and Brahman is Void". Upakosala declared that he knew Brahman as Life. But how could Brahman be declared as Joy and how could Brahman be described as Void? The Lords of Fire said that Brahman is Joy because It is Void. It is very significant that the Upanishad places Joy and Void together. It indicates that the experience of Joy arises only in Void. Life seems to many utterly joyless because they do not come to the experience of Void. Without Void one may know the pleasures of life—but pleasures are the begetters of pain. Joy can come only in

Void. Void is indeed the negation of all that mind has accumulated. Mind's accumulations keep us for ever chained to pleasure and pain. When the mind is completely free from all its possessions and accumulations, then, in that mind, joy is born. Joy cannot be sought after—it comes when human consciousness stands face to face with Void—with that Absolute Nothingness in which everything that life has accumulated is negated. What greater joy there can be than the meeting of the Lover and the Beloved—but such meeting is possible only in Void. It is in the Night of Nothingness that the Lover and the Beloved can meet—and be united with one another. It is in the Void that Brahman is perceived—and this perception is the highest joy of life. When all positive concepts and ideations of Brahman cease then in that Void is revealed the very nature of Brahman. Upakosala must come to this experience of Void, if he is to be a *Brahma-nishṭha* and not merely a knower of the Vedas. Without this Void, learning is mere knowledge; in the Void learning becomes direct perception. Our story says that at this stage, Satyakāma Jābāla returned from his tour. Seeing the face of his disciple, Upakosala, he was intensely happy. He said that while the Lords of Fire had given him an intellectual understanding of the Great Void, he would himself show the way to that Supreme Bliss. Satyakāma found the pupil ready, free even from the desire to know and to find. Having come to that Void within he was initiated into the mysteries of the Great Void Without. In that great Buddhist book, *The Voice of the Silence,* the author instructs the disciple thus:

> Thou hast to study the voidness of the seeming full, the fullness of the seeming Void.

Upakosala had come to the understanding of the voidness of the seeming full. He must now come to the realization of the Fullness of the seeming Void. It is in the Void of the mind that the experience of Fullness comes. In giving further instruction, Satyakāma speaks to his disciple about Communion and Communication. Communion demands a particular state of the mind; Communication requires an effectiveness of speech. For communion as well as for communication, a process of purification is needed. The teacher here speaks of Mind and Speech. He refers to Vāyu and says that Vāyu is the great purifier. The teacher says that it purifies because it is always moving. It is the very movement that purifies. Mind is purified by its very movement. But then should not a restless mind be considered very pure? A restless mind has no movement—it revolves round certain fixed points of the mind. A mind that moves round about its own conclusions or ideations is caught up in a stagnant pool. Its waters do not flow—they revolve in a circumscribed area. A restless mind is like a stangnant pool. It has agitations, but no movement. It is committed to certain conclusions and ideations. It is only a mind completely free from all commitments that knows what movement is—and it is this movement that keeps it pure and unsullied. The speech that emanates from such a mind is not only pure—it is potent. Its communication has a strength and an intensity which cannot be found when the mind is impure—when it knows only agitations and no movement. It is the mind, not only un-corrupt, but incorruptible, that comes face to face with the Void or the Unknown. For, so long as mind is engaged in its process of projections, so long it is restless. It is these projections that corrupt the mind. But the mind in which the process of negation is present is a mind that is pure—and remains pure because of that movement of negation. The process of projection renders the mind impure; the process of negation makes it pure and incorruptible. The movement of negations brings the mind constantly to the experience of Void. This experience can be constant but not continuous. For, a negation which is continuous is no negation at all. Truly speaking, a movement of negation is a contradiction—it is a paradox. A movement of negation is a pure movement, for it is a movement not of something. If something moved then it would be a movement induced by a conclusion. The process of negation does not allow anything to exist in the movement—and so it is a movement where nothing moves.

It is not a movement of something, it is indeed a movement of Nothing. It is interesting to note here what Robert Lissen, the author of Living Zen says:

> Pure movement is not movement of anything. For in pure movement all dualities and distinctions have died out. Only pure movement in the observer can recognise pure movement in the object observed. In this paradoxical perspective, observer, observed and observation are integrated in the ever-present reality of pure movement which from moment to moment is Unthinkable.

This Pure Movement can be described as Thinking without Thought. If thought enters the movement, then is movement rendered impure—for, then there is something that is moving. Usually our thinking is from thought to thought—and therefore it is an impure movement, it is like agitations in a stagnant pool. The experience of Void is the experience of Thinking without Thought. It is experience without accumulation—it is indeed the state of experiencing. It is the verbalizations of the mind, arising out of its thought-process, that render all experiencing impure and corrupt. For, verbalization seeks to give a continuity to an experience. To give continuity to anything is to confine it within the limits set by the mind. It is not mind that has to be destroyed—it is the continuity of the mind that must be eliminated. And when mind's continuity is gone, then man faces the Void—the Great Unknown. It is to the significance of Void that the Chāndogya Upanishad turns, as it relates the story of Uddālaka and his son, Śvetaketu..

When Śvetaketu was twelve years of age, his father asked him to engage himself in studies at the āśrama of a guru. And so the son went to a gurukula and remained there until he was twenty four years of age. The father welcomed him warmly and greatly appreciated what he had learnt at the feet of the Master. The father told him " Śvetaketu , I am glad you have learnt all these sciences and arts, but did you receive that instruction?"

> Whereby what is not heard becomes heard, what is not thought about becomes the subject of thinking, what is not known becomes known?

Śvetaketu then said to his father, "O venerable sir, how can there be such instruction?"

Śvetaketu's question is indeed very pertinent, for, how can there be any knowledge by knowing which that which is not heard can be heard and that which is not known can be known? Can there be any knowledge which unlocks the secrets of all knowledge? The father tells his son that if one could know the original substance then its modifications, however numerous they may be, can be known immediately. It is not necessary to examine each modification separately in order to find out of what substance it is made. The substance is the ground in which all modifications arise—and so by knowing the ground, the variations can be easily understood. The father tells his son:

> My dear Śvetaketu, just as with one lump of clay all that is of mud becomes known, the change being only a name, the product of speech, and the truth is that it is all clay.
>
> Just as with one grain of gold all that is of gold becomes known, the change being only a name, the product of speech, and the truth is that it is all gold.

The father is here instructing the son in the knowledge of the Original and its modifications. He says that all modifications are only names, they are only verbalizations, the product of speech. But sometimes the name becomes all-important with the result that the original substance is completely forgotten. When man gets caught up in the network of verbalizations, then is he ignorant of the very substance itself. There is an identification with the name and so the original is lost—nay, sometimes, its very existence is denied. In the Yoga Sūtras of Patañjali this is described as *Asmitā* or false identification and this arises because of *Avidyā* or ignorance. When there is ignorance about the original nature of things, then is man caught in the process of false identification—he becomes a slave to the name, to the verbalized product. Needless to say, without knowing the original nature of things, mere name is meaningless. The Many arise out of the One—they are the modifications of the One. Without knowing the One, how can one understand the significance of the Many. When all modifications caused by verbalizations cease, then there remains only the One, the One without a second, the One without any name. When all the names drop away, then what remains is the Nameless Being; the Origin and Source of all things. To Śvetaketu, the father says:

> My dear, these rivers of the east flow eastward, those of the west, westward—they arise from the ocean and to the ocean they return. As all is absorbed in the ocean and the rivers do not have the feeling "I am this or I am that", even so my dear, all these beings spring from *Sat*, but know not that they have sprung therefrom.

The rivers are indeed the modifications of the ocean. The ocean is the source, the origin, from where the rivers arise and into whom the rivers merge. In most religions there is a practice of repeating the names of God. In Hinduism the devout followers of the faith repeat one thousand names of Vishṇu. But of what use is the repetition of a thousand names if the Original is not comprehended? The names are mere modifications, they are verbalizations by mind and speech—but when the modifications are seen without the experience of the One or the Original, then they create divisions and conflict. One notices in the history of religions how men have fought for the defence of the Name of God. When the name is repeated over and over again, it takes the place of the original. Then it is that the word is mistaken for the thing, the name is identified with the person, the symbol takes the place of the substance. But if the original is without a name then how can It be identified? How can one know a thing without its name? Is it possible for one to know the Original without its modifications?

Here the Chāndogya Upanishad discusses a very interesting topic—of Being and Non-Being. Is the original state to be known as Being or as Non-Being? Do all modifications arise from Being or do they arise from Non-Being? The father says to Śvetaketu :

> In the beginning, my dear, this world was just Being (Sat), One only, without a second. To be sure some people say, "In

the beginning this world was just Non-Being (Asat), One only, without a second—from that Non-Being, Being was produced."

But verily, my dear, whence could this be? How from Non-Being could Being be produced. On the contrary, in the beginning this world was just Being, One only, without a second.

It is from Being that non-Being comes into existence. Thus the manifestation is Non-Being—it is the Unmanifest which is the Being. The manifest constitutes all the modifications, the variations, the names and the verbalizations—which according to the above, is Non-Being. The emergence of the Many is indeed the modifications of the One. The modifications thus represent the Non-Being. But is Non-Being the negation of Being? How could this be? The very existence of Non-Being rests in Being. Without Being, Non-Being would have no existence whatsoever. Are Being and Non-Being opposed to each other? Surely, this is inconceivable, for, Being can have no opposite, what then is the relationship between Being and Non-Being? It is the relationship of the Whole and the Part. The Part is not the Whole, and, yet, it is not separated from the Whole. The Part would have no existence without the Whole. The Being and Non-Being of the above verse may be restated as Being-without-attributes and Being-with-attributes. The modifications of the Being are the attributes. The naming or the verbalizing is the giving of attributes to the attributeless Being. But since Non-Being exists in the Ground of the Being, it must contain, in an imperceptible manner—in an intangible manner—the very essence of Being. It is this which gives harmony and cohesion to the various attributes, as otherwise they would fly in different directions. The Non-Being or the Being-with-attributes has its sustenance in the Being-without-attributes. The latter is the very soul of all manifestation, of all attributes, of all modifications. Without the soul, the body would wither away, would cease to exist. But the soul of things is always imperceptible and intangible. That indeed is the Being of the universe—the Being of all that lives and moves. The father says to Śvetaketu:

This true Being, this subtle source of the world, that is the soul of everything; That is Truth, that is Self, That thou Art, O Śvetaketu.

Here we come across one of the most famous of the Upanishadic statements—one of the great *mahāvākyas*—*Tattvamasi* —That art Thou. The Pure Being, the subtle source of the world, that indeed is Brahman—and that verily is Ātman. The father says to Śvetaketu—That art thou. Man is indeed the intangible being—not the tangible, showing forth modifications and their fluctuations. But once again the intangible is not away from the tangible. It is the subtle source of the tangible—it is the soul that informs and inspires everything. The soul of things is not invisible—it is Intangible. It is there as Infinite Rest in the midst of Infinite Motion. But Śvetaketu asked his father to enlighten him more on this question of the intangible *something* being the soul of everything. He wants to know precisely what that intangible *something* is. Śvetaketu realized that by knowing this intangible *something*, all else can be known—for It is the subtle source of everything.

The father in order to instruct the son further asks him to bring a fruit of the nearby banyan tree. Śvetaketu brings one of the fruits lying on the ground. The father then asks him to cut it into two. He then puts a question to him saying, " Śvetaketu, what do you find on cutting the fruit into two?" Śvetaketu replies that he sees innumerable tiny seeds. The father says, "Take one of these tiny seeds and break it". Śvetaketu does as he is asked. When he breaks one of the tiny seeds, the father inquires of the son, " Śvetaketu, what do you find on cutting this tiny seed into two?" And Śvetaketu says: "There is absolutely Nothing there, sir. Venerable sir, I see nothing at all". The father tells the son:

> My son, from this that you call nothing, there comes into existence this vast banyan tree. Believe me, my son, a subtle and an intangible essence is the Spirit of the whole universe. That is Reality, that is Ātman. That art Thou.

The Chāndogya Upanishad here speaks of nothing as the source of everything—the non-existence as the source of all existence. How can this be? In the earlier part of this section of the Upanishad the father had said: "How could Non-Being be the source of all being—how could nothing give birth to all things"? And yet here he brings Śvetaketu to that very point where he indicates that it is out of nothing that all things have come into existence. Is there no contradiction between the two?

There is—and yet there is not. We stated above that Being and Non-Being should be described as Being-without-attributes and Being-with-attributes. Now the Being-without-attributes is in true sense Nothing—for It is indefinable and indescribable. This must appear to the human mind as nothing. Surely, the mind cannot hold something that defies description and definition. That which is indefinable cannot even be identified. To speak of existence without identification must seem meaningless to the mind. How can one talk of existence where even identification is not possible? The mind of man must declare this as veritable nothing. Now the Being-without-attributes is something indefinable—something un-identifiable. Surely, such a Being can well be equated by the human mind with Nothing or with Non-existence. In the tiny seed of the banyan fruit there was nothing—and yet that nothing was the source of the vast banyan tree. Existence comes out of Non-existence—such is the startling teaching of the Chāndogya Upanishad.

But Śvetaketu is not satisfied with this instruction. He wants to know as to how can one come to the experience of Nothing and comprehend it as the source of everything. His intellect is unable to grasp this point, for, how can Nothingness, how can Void, be the source of all creation? Is it really a Void—or is it a void only to the gaze of the mind? Is it possible that the Void of the mind contains all the Fullness of the Spirit? How to find this out, for, this seems to be the secret of secrets? The tiny seed when broken up reveals utter nothingness—but surely there must be something in that nothingness, for, otherwise how can the big banyan tree come into existence? These are some of the questions that must have intrigued the mind of this young disciple. And so he tells his father to instruct him further about the great Secret of the Void, about the mystery that resides in Nothingness.

The Chāndogya Upanishad here leads us to one of the profoundest teachings of the great Upanishadic vision. It says that one cannot come to the understanding of the Fullness of the Void unless one knows the Void of the Fullness. The world that we see with our eyes and touch with our hands is indeed a world of fullness. We see the universe rich in colour and variety. We are amazed by the numerous attributes that we see in men and things. But the question is—What are these attributes? This question really brings us to an interesting inquiry into the psychology of perception. Dr. Kahn, a noted German physiologist says:

> Vision is not a physical process like photography, but rather a psychological experience. It is not the eyes that see. We commonly believe that we see, but actually we form judgments. The image on the retina bears the same relation to vision as a book to its reader. Just as two people, even when they read the same thing, never have the same thoughts, while they are reading, in the same way their gaze may fall upon the same object, but each one sees something different.

Thus we live in our own private world and the attributes about which we speak are also of this private world. In other words, we perceive what we have projected. The mind of man has imparted to the world a fullness drawn from its vast warehouse. One of the modern thinkers, C.E.M. Joad says:

> What we are actually aware of when we believe ourselves to be making contact with the external world, are not things outside ourselves, but things happening in our own bodies and brains.

If this be true, then the external world is only a projection of our own internal state. It is the internal state that determines the character and attributes of the world in which we live. Strangely enough, the attributes are not outside—they are within us. And so the Fullness of the world is only the super-imposition by our mind. Prof A. N. Whitehead makes a startling statement when he says:

> Nature gets credit which should in truth be reserved for our-

selves—the rose for its scent, the nightingale for his song and the sun for its radiance.

The world of attributes is filled with a fullness—but from where does this fullness come? Obviously from the mind of man. We do not know what the world in itself is. We see only a super-imposed world. Our world is only our image of the world. Strangely enough, we live in a world of images—to know this, to be aware of this, is to realize the utter Void of Fullness. What we call Fullness is no Fullness at all—it is utter emptiness. It is not the intrinsic fullness of things—it is only a projected fullness—and how can the projected fullness be called fullness at all? To realize that we live in a world of projected fullness is to face the startling truth that our fullness is nothing but emptiness. This is indeed the Void of Seeming Fullness—when one sees the Void of Fullness, then is one enabled to see the Fullness of the Void. When the entire process of mind's super-impossition drops away, then is man enabled to see for the first time the intrinsic fullness—the Fullness that resides in the seeming void. The seed of the banyan fruit displayed utter nothingness, absolute void—and yet, this void has a fullness out of which the entire banyan tree comes into existence. It is in seeing the voidness of the seeming full that one comes to the realization of the fullness of the seeming void.

But Śvetaketu wants to understand how is one to come to this realization. His father, Uddālaka Āruṇi., was a great teacher—one of the most brilliant that we come across in the Upanishads and so he asked Śvetaketu.. to get a cup full of water and drop into it a few grains of salt. He told him: "My son, go to sleep and bring this cup to me in the morning". The son took the cup of water to the father the next morning as was the instruction. When he took the cup of water, the father said, "Dear son, take out the salt which you had put in the water". Śvetaketu felt exasperated and said: "Father, what do you mean by this instruction? How is it possible to take out the salt which I had put in the water?" The father said, "If that be the case, then taste the water from the top, how does it taste?" Śvetaketu said: "It is saltish". The father asked him to taste the water from the middle and also from the bottom and asked him: "How does it taste?" Śvetaketu said: "It is saltish all through". With this reply, Uddālaka Āruṇi said to his son:

> My dear child, just as salt pervades the entire quantity of water, so does the Spirit pervade all existence. It is subtle and intangible, even as salt is in the cup of water. This subtle and intangible Spirit, thou art, O Śvetaketu,.

Salt pervades water and yet it cannot be grasped. The same is indeed of the Spirit—ever subtle and intangible and yet pervading the whole universe. There is no point of manifestation where the Spirit is not. If it pervades the whole universe, then surely It must occupy some space. For, how can It be in the Universe and yet not occupy any space? The Spirit pervades everything and yet does not occupy even an inch of space. All-pervasive and yet ever elusive—that is the nature of the Spirit in manifestation. No amount of exploration in the realms of time and space will ever reveal the spirit seated in the heart of all things. Śvetaketu asks his father:

> Dear father, how to find this Spirit? It looks so simple and yet it is so difficult.

The father said that since salt pervades water, salt must be found in water itself and not away from it. But how? The father asked the son to throw the water away and meet him the next day. As the son approached the father, the latter pointed to the spot where the water had been thrown away. On the ground was seen a deposit of salt. How did the salt come there? As water evaporated, what remained behind was salt—the salt that was dissolved in water. The instruction of the father regarding the throwing away of water is very significant. For the finding of the Spirit too, there is no other way. What has one to throw away in order to find the Ātman or Truth or Spirit? In the illustration of salt, water represents the form in which the Spirit remained pervaded. The father asked the son to throw away the form—in other words, he asked him to negate the form. And when the form is negated, then what remains is the Spirit. But the negation of form is not the mortification of form—it is not the performance of austerities nor is it a gospel of denial. We saw in the earlier part of this discussion that man lives in the world of images. The mind of man projects image after image —and it is these images that hide the face of Reality. It is by negating image after image projected by the mind that man can come to the perception of the Real. When image after image is put away, until there is no image left, then does man come to an experience of Void. It is in this void that the Fullness of Reality can be seen in all its majesty. The projections of the mind render us blind. We move in the world blind-folded. Uddālaka Āruṇi tells Śvetaketu:

> Suppose we blind-fold a man and lead him into an unknown forest, away from his usual residence, what would he do? How would he try to find his home? As soon as he is left to himself, he would just remove the cover from his eyes. Then would he start his inquiry about his way back.

In order to discover the Spirit, imperceptible and intangible, hidden in the very heart of manifestation, man must come to a real and serious inquiry. But when can such an inquiry start? A real inquiry is possible only when man removes the cover from the eyes of the mind—when he is no longer blind-folded in his mental perceptions. That which renders the mind blind is the projection of the images with which the world is filled. The world seems full of colour and form—but it is this fullness which imparts to the medium of perception an opaqueness. How can one see through that which is opaque? The opaque must be rendered transparent so that a clear vision may be vouchsafed to man. But the mind becomes transparent only when its images are cast away. It may be asked when can the image be cast away? It can be thrown away, or, rather it can drop away only when one is aware that one's world is filled only with images. It is awareness of the image as an image that transforms mind's opaqueness into clear transparency. A mind that is transparent can enter into deep and serious inquiry, for into such a mind truth will enter. A transparent mind perceives the void of the seeming full—and therefore, it is ready to experience the fullness of the seeming void. When image after image drops away, then does the mind of man face absolute void —it has nothing with which to fill up that void. Into this void of seeming nothingness, Truth appears and fills the entire void with its majestic presence. This is the experience of the Ātman, of Brahman—and it is to this experience that Uddālaka Āruṇi had led his son, Śvetaketu..

In the first part of our discussion, in the Chāndogya Upanishad, we referred to a conversation between Sanatkumāra and Nārada Nārada was told by the great teacher that his seemingly vast knowledge was only words, mere names, nothing but mental verbalizations. It was a knowledge of images—not of living truth. When the teacher addressed him thus, Nārada asked for the higher knowledge—the knowledge that transcends mere name and word. Sanatkumāra told him that he must realize that the word is not the Thing, that the Name and the reality of things are completely different. Unless Nārada comes to this realization, no further instruction can be given to him. Uddālaka Āruṇi, too, led his son to the self-same awareness of the utter void of the seeming fullness. But how to come to this awareness? Sanatkumāra tells Nārada: "Meditate on Name". This seems to be a strange instruction, for, instead of throwing away the Name, the teacher asks him to meditate on Name. Why this strange instruction? For, the name must drop away—it is meaningless to cast it away. One may throw away one name and pick up another. But what is of importance is to see that the whole process of naming drops away. This can happen only when the very content of name is examined. Here Sanatkumāra helps Nārada to understand the full implication of the process of naming. The image of the mind is nothing but the externalization of name. There is much that is involved in the naming process and Sanatkumāra clearly unveils this process. He says that the naming process implies:

Speech thought, determination, sonsciousness, concentration, understanding.

It is obvious that naming results in speech or verbalization. But verbalization indicates a thought process. Thought, verily is the other word for verbalization. But behind thought there is determination or selection—it is a process of acceptance and rejection. But how does one accept or reject? It is only by being conscious of something that one evaluates it. Consciousness is the stimulation of the centres of recognition. These centres of recognition reside in memory and so one becomes conscious of men and things by the activising of memory. But a mere stimulation of memory is not enough—there has to be a concentration of the forces of memory. In other words, the mind must dwell upon that which stimulates the centres of memory, if it is to come to a judgment or an evaluation. But concentration is possible only on the basis of knowledge or understanding. Thus, the whole naming process arises from mind's knowledge. It is concerned with giving a name to what mind has gathered. Man feels a certainty about knowledge only when he is able to give a name to it. So long as name has not been given, there is an element of uncertainty. It is name which gives to man a base for action. The intervening steps between knowledge and name are: concentration, memory stimulation, selection and thought. Knowledge is no knowledge, unless the mind is able to dwell upon it, but the dwelling depends upon the stimulation of memory, for, memory alone gives a continuity to the processes of the mind. But once again, the stimulation of memory is possible only on the feeling of pleasure and pain—the factors of selection. And how does the feeling of pleasure and pain come into existence? Obviously by a thought process—a process of comparison and contrast. It is thought which gives names to things. In the Chândogya Upanishad, Understanding or knowledge is described as *Vijñāna*. But speaking about Vijñāna, it says that by it man can understand the four Vedas. This understanding of Vedas must remain remote so long as man is not able to give to them his own names. The mind of man for ever gives to the unfamiliar a framework of familiarity. So long as the unfamiliar is not put in the framework of the familiar—so long man feels uncertain. The mere understanding of the Vedas keeps the mind on the unfamiliar plane. Sanatkumāra indicates the various steps by which the mind of man gives to the unfamiliar the framework of familiarity. When man is able to give a name to something that he has learnt, then the unfamiliar becomes familiar. Sanatkumāra says that it is by concentration, consciousness, determination and thought that the unfamiliar is sought to be put in the framework of familiarity. This process ends when the mind is able to pronounce the name of that which it has acquired.

Sanatkumāra then speaks to Nārada about Strength, Food, Water and Fire. What do these signify, coming as they do soon after knowledge or understanding? With the certainty of knowledge, which comes in the wake of naming, there comes to man a sense of strength. Naming does give to man a feeling of power. Mind always wants a certainty about the knowledge that it has acquired. This certainty naturally generates a feeling of strength. But the strength has to be maintained by food—and the food of the mind is more knowledge and more naming. How can man be sure of giving the necessary food to the mind so that its strength may be maintained? The continuity of food supply is possible only through water and fire. Water obviously indicates a factor of emotion even as fire signifies a condition of alertness. If the mind is alert and at the same time emotionally alive, then it will find a never-ending supply of food. Its strength will be maintained and so it will be able to move from certainty to certainty in the realm of knowledge. But this certainty of knowledge is circumscribed by three factors—these are the factors of Space, Time and Causation or Movement. These three fundamental factors which condition mind's knowledge have to be understood, as without it, man cannot come to the comprehension of the utter void of mind's fullness. Sanatkumāra speaks of these three factors. He first draws the attention of Nārada to Space or *Ākāśa*. He says:

> Through space one calls out; through space one hears, through space one answers. In space one enjoys himself, in space one does not enjoy himself. In space one is born, unto space one is born.

It has to be understood that mind's knowledge always belongs to the realm of duality. And duality pre-supposes space. Space is always needed for the existence of the two. The name, which is the certainty of mind's knowledge, can be called out only in space. We require name in order to call to some one who is away. All enjoyment or lack of enjoyment is possible only in space—for, enjoyment constitutes right relationship between two units of duality—it hardly needs to be said that lack of enjoyment denotes absence of such relationship. Mind's knowledge, which alone is its certainty, is thus circumscribed by the factor of space. Sanatkumāra says that there is also the factor of Time. And he points to this element of time by speaking of Memory and Hope. These two words denote the stream of time in terms of the past and the future—Memory stands for the past, even as Hope points to the future. Mind's knowledge exists always in this flow of time from past to future. From the unfulfilled experiences of the past, there is always the anticipation of a fulfilled future. Mind never knows a thing as it is—it knows only the thing as it was or as it will be. Thus its knowledge has no base of reality. Time is a great conditioning factor in all the process of mind's knowledge. But Sanatkumāra says there is a third factor which conditions that mind—and that is Causation or movement or *ayana*. The teacher denotes this factor by mentioning about life or *Prāṇa*. The vital breath is in a state of constant movement. And is this not the nature of mind's knowledge? Mind acquires knowledge by movement between the two poles of duality. Its knowledge is the knowledge of the opposite. It knows one as opposed to the other. It does not know a thing by itself—its knowledge is always indirect. The opposite is the image which it strives to translate into actuality. Its whole process of becoming is a movement towards the likeness of the image. The mind puts the image in distant space or in distant time and then organises its movement towards this image. Both time and space are mind's creations. Having created something fictitious, the movement that it organises is naturally frustrating. To know this is indeed to come to the void of mind's fullness. Sanatkumāra has clearly indicated to Nārada three things—first, how does mind arrive at its certainty of knowledge; second, how is a continuity of this certainty maintained, and third, how this certainty is utterly false and fictitious because of the movement of the mind between two imaginary points. How the limitation of space, time and causation makes mind's knowledge utterly uncertain and undependable—this is what Sanatkumāra indicates to Nārada To be fully aware of this is to realise that the Name is not the thing, that the word and the thing are not identical.

He who knows this becomes what the Upanishad calls the *Ativādin* —meaning he is the superior speaker, he speaks with real understanding, for, he has known the hollowness of mind's knowledgc. He has seen the void of mind's seeming fullness. The Teacher says to Nārada:

> When one sees nothing else, hears nothing else, understands nothing else—that is plenum.

The word for plenum as used in the Upanishad is *Bhūmā* . When the void of mind's seeming fullness is experienced, then there comes a plenum—a real fullness in the void. This experience of plenum is described as a condition where "one sees nothing else, where one hears nothing else, where one understands nothing else". In other words, this denotes a totality of attention, with no image of the mind causing any distraction. When man comes to the experience of the void of minds seeming fullness, then all projections cease. There is no more any image of the mind to be projected. And where projections cease, there distraction too comes to an end—for, we are distracted by what we project. And so the plenum—the fullness of the seeming void—is known in the totality of attention. Sanatkumāra says to Nārada that the plenum is indeed the whole world. One can see the fullness of Brahman here and now, if mind's images are negated so that one knows the utter void of mind's seeming fullness. In that void comes the vision of Fullness—the whole world contains this Fullness—the Fullness of Brahman, which indeed is the Fullness of the Ātman.

It may be recalled that Nārada had approached Sanatkumāra because inspite of all knowledge, he was unhappy. He wanted to know what happiness is. The Teacher at the end of this illuminating discourse tells Nārada :

> When one is happy, one performs one's duty, in sorrow one does not—it is in happiness that one does and so one should understand what happiness is. That which is without any limitation is happiness—there is no happiness in the finite—the infinite alone is happiness.

Infinite alone is happiness—this is the culminating point of the great teaching which Sanatkumāra imparted to Nārada. How can mind know what happiness is? Mind moves in the realm of the finite—and the finite is perishable. It is when the finite is put aside that the infinite can be perceived. The infinite comes in the void of mind's seeming fullness. The infinite is indeed fullness of the void—it is the plenum which resides is the heart of emptiness. This is Ātman—and as Uddālaka Āruṇi said to Śvetaketu. one can repeat: That art Thou-*Tat-tvam-asi*. If Infinite alone is Happiness, then surely happiness is to be found in the discovery of the Ātman .

Having heard about this great teaching about happiness through the discovery of the Ātman, the gods and the demons decided that they too should possess this secret of discovering the Ātman . They came to this decision independently of each other, for the teaching about the Ātman was so attractive. And so Indra on behalf of the gods and Virocana on behalf of the demons went to Prajāpati for obtaining this secret about the discovery of the Ātman . Prajāpati asked them to look into a big pan of water—they did as they were asked. Prajāpati asked them: "What do you see in water"? They replied, "We see ourselves—our face and our body in water." Prajāpati asked them to put on their best clothes and to wear rich ornaments. Once again Indra and Virocana did as they were told. Prajāpati asked them again to look into water and inquired saying, "What do you now find in water? They said, "We see ourselves richly adorned and finely dressed". Prajāpati said, "What you see is Ātman ". They went away greatly pleased. Virocanaa said to his colleagues that he had found the way to the Ātman —it was by bodily indulgences. But Indra returned to Prajāpati , as even on his way to the gods, he found doubts arising in his mind. He said: "What I see in water is Ātman. When the body is richly adorned, I see this in water—but if the body is lame or if the eye is blind, then surely I will see the same in water. And if what I see is Ātman , then the Ātman is hurt when the body is hurt. Of what use is such an Ātman "? Indra expressed his doubts to Prajāpati and Prajāpati said, "It is well. I will give you further instruction". And so Prajāpati told him: "He who moves about happy in a dream—that is the immortal, the fearless Brahman. That is Ātman ". Indra went away apparently satisfied but on the way again doubts arose. He said, "It is true that the Ātman remains unhurt even when the body is hurt—but in dream there is the feeling of pain and sorrow, there is even weeping. Surely, that is not an enjoyable state". He expressed his doubts to Prajāpati and the latter promised to give him further instruction. Prajāpati said:

> Now, when one is sound asleep, composed, serene, and knows no dream—that is the Ātman . That is the immortal, the fearless. That is Brahman.

Indra was greatly pleased with this fresh instruction and felt that he had found a final answer to his question. But again on the way doubts arose in his mind and he said:

> Assuredly, this Ātman does not exactly know himself as *I am he*, nor indeed the things here. He seems to become one who has gone to destruction. I see nothing enjoyable in this.

And so once again he returned to Prajāpati , expressing his doubts about the Ātman discovered in the condition of deep sleep. Prajāpati said to Indra that he would give him further and final instruction. He said:

> Indra, this body is mortal, ensnared by death, and yet it is

the lodging of the immortal, un-embodied self, becoming embodied, the self is caught up in the pleasant and the unpleasant; so long as it is in the embodied state, there is no overcoming of the pleasant and the unpleasant, but when it exists, dissociated from the body, the pleasant and the unpleasant alike touch him not.

Here in this story, we find Prajāpati giving instruction to Indra about the three states of consciousness and the fourth—the Waking, the Dream, the Deep Sleep and the Beyond. In the Waking state, Indra and Virocana saw their images in water. The waking state is, indeed, the condition where there is an acceptance and a rejection of images. In the Dream state, there is only the acceptance of images—for there can be no choice or selection in dream. But in the Deep Sleep, there is neither an acceptance nor a rejection of images. Images do not distract the consciousness—there is a totality of attention which is not disturbed by anything. In this totality of consciousness, in this state, devoid of images, there is seen Ātman in its purest form where it is bereft of all forms—the Formless Being. Since it is Formless, it is capable of incarnating in all forms. When the form is mistaken for the Being, then is man caught in illusion—but when form is seen only as an instrument of expression for the Being, then is one transported to the realms of eternal joy. He who knows the Formless in Form, he indeed knows what infinite freedom is. In the seeming void of the formless, myriads of forms of indescribable beauty appear. A new vision is imparted to the manifested universe, for, into the forms of the universe one sees the Formless. And when one returns to the land of forms, it is not the same land—for, into the forms is seen a new beauty—the beauty that was never seen on earth or in the heavens. There is a very significant verse in the Chāndogya Upanishad which says:

Through purity of intellect arises steady memory, and through the attainment of recollection all the knots are completely broken.

Steady Memory—that is the way indicated in the Chāndogya Upanishad. What makes the memory unsteady? It is the plethora of images created by the mind —each image demanding the attention of the mind.

Memory can be steady, only if perception has been steady. It is only as man sees facts—and not the projections of the mind—that there emerges a steady memory of facts. An English poet says that our birth is a forgetting. We have forgotten from whence we have come—we have forgotten our real nature. By the projection of images has been built up an acquired nature. We have lost the root base of steady memory. When there arises the void of mind's seeming fullness, then into that void comes a recollection, the birth of a steady memory. We see what we are—and it is with this knowledge that we return to the world of every day action. He who has seen his real nature, for him the process of becoming is joy indescribable. His journey of life may be long but the end is not far away, it exists in the very beginning. When the end is in the beginning, the journey with all its hazards is a thrilling experience. One is not concerned with arriving. For him there is no arriving, but only journeying. When the tension and anticipation of arrival are gone, every step of the journey becomes a fascinating experience. This journey into a seeming void brings to one an experience of intense Fullness—a fullness that remains full, even with the passage of time. For, it is a Fullness which time cannot touch. It is a Fullness that knows no decay—for, it is not a fullness filled with something. It is Fullness of utter void, of total nothingness, of absolute emptiness. The Fullness of the Void is indeed the Ātman, the immortal and the fearless, the one which incarnates in all forms, yet remains supremely Formless.

X

THE FLAME WITHOUT A FLICKER

The Bṛhadāraṇyaka Upanishad has the same invocation with which the Īśa Upanishad begins. It speaks of the Whole, remaining for ever the Whole, even when divided or multiplied. The whole is Brahman. It suffers no diminution, even when manifested—for, the whole abides even in the tiniest part. The whole is indivisible even when divided, for the quality of things suffers no loss even when split into a thousand bits. That which is indivisible, even in the midst of division, must surely be transcendent, even while it is immanent. Such is indeed the nature of Brahman—and such is indeed the nature of Ātman. Immanent and yet transcendent—Manifest and yet Unmanifest—this is Brahman, and this is the subject of this great Upanishad.

The following verse speaks about it:

> Purusha was afraid. He reflected--surely one who is alone is afraid. But he argued—"When there is nothing beside me, why am I afraid?" Thereupon his fear vanished. Why should he have feared. It is from the presence of the second that fear arises.

There can be no fear when one is alone—it is the presence of the second which causes fear to arise. Here, the presence of the second has to be understood not merely in the physical sense—it is of the psychological presence that the verse speaks. Thus fear arises only where duality is —because each point of the duality wants to possess the other. The desire for possession always generates a fear of dispossession. But when there is no duality, who will possess whom? Where possession itself is negated, there fear can have no abode. In the realm of duality, the solution of the problem of fear is only a modification of fear—from fear of man it may be fear of God. Mind always seeks a solution in terms of modification—it may know reform, but never a revolution. But if the prayer of the aspirant for being led from the unreal to the Real, from darkness to Light, from death to Immortality is to be granted, then there must arise a state of revolution—for a mere reformation cannot bring this great movement from the unreal to the Real into existence. The above prayer of the spiritual aspirant is for knowing the secret of spiritual revolution. And this Upanishad, indeed, shows such a path—not a path of mere moral reformation, but a way to fundamental transformation—it is not a seeking of mere variation or modification—it is prayer for knowing the path to mutation. This Upanishad indeed shows us a way to Spiritual Mutation.

It is most amazing to see in the Upanishads an approach which is utterly un-conventional and un-traditional. The teachers of the Upanishads were not bound by traditions. They lived in an atmosphere of absolute freedom and they instilled into their pupils a sense of complete freedom. Here, in this Upanishad, we find a Kshatriya, one belonging to the warrior class, giving spiritual instruction to a Brahmin. This is contrary to all traditions, for, it was the prerogative of the Brahmin to give instructions in spiritual matters to all. And yet here in this Upanishad, we find Gārgya, a Brahmin, receiving instruction about Brahman from Ajātaśatru of Kāśī, a Kshatriya by birth and by profession. The story says that Gārgya went to Ajātaśatru for imparting to him instruction in Brahman, but all his expositions were of no avail. When he found that his explanations were ineffective, then he approached Ajātaśatru asking him for enlightenment on the nature of Brahman. The instructor was ready to become a disciple—such was the humility of an inquirer and such was the eagerness to know.

The story of the Upanishad says that Ajātaśatru took Gārgya by hand and brought him to a spot where a man was fast asleep. He addressed the sleeping man thus: "O great one, O white-robed one, O radiant one, O Soma etc.", but the sleeping man did not respond. Then the king pushed him with his hand and the man woke up.

Ajātaśatru asked Gārgya, "Please tell me where was the Self when this man was asleep?" Gārgya could not answer that question. To him the king said, "When this man was asleep, the Self had withdrawn from active participation in the body. This condition is known as *svapiti*". Now *svapiti* really means being absorbed in oneself. This indeed is the Dream State. The Dream State is a condition of self-absorption. Ajātaśatru describes it thus:

> When the self thus stays in the dream state, it then becomes either a great king, as it were, or a worthy brahmin, as it were, or reaches high and low conditions as it were.

While the waking state is a condition of Distinctive Differences, the Dream state is a condition of Non-distinctive Differences. When one is in a Waking state one sees differences and gives to them distinctions. The norm of these distinctions resides in memory. It is through this giving of distinctions that man engages in selective activity. But in the Dream state, there is no selection and so it is a condition of non-distinctive differences. Man experiences different conditions in the Dream state—but he does not ascribe to them any distinctions—for he is completely absorbed in what he experiences, be it the experience of a king or of a beggar. Ajātaśatru says:

> Again when the self is fast asleep, it is not aware of anything. Just as a baby, or a great king or a worthy brahmin lives, having reached the very limit of bliss, so does the self remain.

The Deep Sleep is a condition of Non-differentiation. It is a non-dual experience. In the moment of happiness, one is not aware that one is happy—such is, indeed, the state of Deep Sleep. It is in this Non-differentiated condition that one knows Distinctions without Differences. This is the perception of Uniqueness—and uniqueness is incomparable. That is why it is described as Distinctions without Differences. The perception of the Unique is indeed the vision of the Ātman—the Ātman in Its true Being. From this uniqueness it emerges in manifestation. This is the rhythm of creation, dissolution and recreation. This is the Great Rhythm of the Manifest and the Unmanifest. In this rhythm lies the music of the spheres—in this rhythm is the pulsation of life and death. Ajātaśatru says:

> Two are the phases of Brahman—that with Form and that without Form—the mortal and the immortal, the limited, fixed to a place, and the unlimited which is not fixed to a place, the perceptible and the imperceptible.
>
> That which is subtle, immortal, unlimited and imperceptible is the essential.

It is from the Intangible and the Imperceptible, the Unlimited and the Immortal, that the mortal and the limited come into existence. He says:

> As a spider moves along the thread it produces, or as from the fire little sparks scatter, just so from the Self issue all organs, all worlds, all gods and all living beings. Its secret name is Truth of Truth.

The Flame and the Spark are identical in nature—for the spark emanates from fire and shares all the qualities of the fire. In Ātman resides the nature of Brahman—such is the cardinal doctrine of the Upanishadic philosophy. The forms of the Form-less are countless like the "cloth dyed with turmeric or grey sheep's wool or the deep red, like insect Indragopa, or the tongue of fire or white lotus or a flash of lightning." Its forms are so numerous that no one form nor a collection of myriads of forms can ever convey its true nature. And so:

> The indication of Brahman is *Neti, Neti*—Not this, Not this, for beyond saying *Neti, Neti,* there is nothing else possible—for It is Truth beyond Truth.

It is here, that we come across the famous phrase of the Upanishads—*Neti, Neti*—Not this, not this. C. Jinarajadasa, a great mystic and a philosopher, says in his book, *The Divine Vision*:

> As the Muni (or the spiritual man) contemplates all his experiences of the bliss of communion, as he gazes at the divine Vision before him, he must whisper to himself—*Neti, Neti.* Not this, Not this. To rejoice in the splendour of the gods, to worship very God of very God face to face, and yet to say: "This is but the phenomenon, not the noumenon; I seek that which cannot be expressed in Vision"—"this is the greatest teaching which India has given." *Neti, Neti* is India's greatest contribution to the spiritual problem, and how great only a few will ever know.

In the seeming negation of *Neti, Neti,* there is the declaration that the Supreme Experience is so intensely positive that no expression, however subtle, can contain it. It is the experience of *Neti, Neti* that enables one to transcend the realm of forms and enter the land of the Formless. It needs great courage to declare *Neti, Neti,* for, it indicates a condition where the mind cannot settle down anywhere, in no positive description of the Ultimate Reality. The mind which can say *Neti, Neti* is a pure mind, for, there is a movement in it—not the movement of thought, but the movement in which no thought exists. *Neti, Neti* is, indeed, the putting away of thought after thought, it is the discarding of image after image, of ideation after ideation, until the mind comes to a silence, to the condition of a Muni. But what does the mind do there? Nothing, for it cannot do anything. When all positive efforts of the mind cease, then there descends upon human consciousness a supreme negativity—it is this which is conveyed by the words *Neti, Neti.* What happens in this Supreme Moment of Negativity? who can tell? Edwin Arnold, in his *Light of Asia,* says:

> Om, Amitaya, measure not with words,
> The immeasurable, nor sink the string of thought
> Into the Fathomless. Who asks doth err,
> Who answers, errs. Say nought.

Silence is indeed the only speech that one can utter. *Neti, Neti*—that is the highest state to which the mind of man can ascend. Let the mind stand still where its frontiers have ended. Into that stillness will come the whisper of the soul, the Voice of Silence, the Vision of the Formless, the soothing touch of the Intangible.

It is to this Vision of the Formless that the Bṛhadāraṇyaka Upanishad takes us through the teaching which the great teacher, Yājñavalkya imparted to his wife, Maitreyī. It seems Yājñavalkya was about to retire from the world and wanted to make a property-settlement between his two wives, Maitreyī and Kātyāyanī. He expressed his intentions to Maitreyī, who after listening to his illustrious husband said:

> Dear one, you are talking of property and its partition. But

> what would it avail me even if the whole world full of wealth were mine own? Would it make me immortal, and take me beyond all sorrows and suffering?

Here one is almost reminded of Naciketā asking deeply searching questions to Yama. Maitreyī says to Yājñavalkya , "Of what use are wealth and property, if I cannot go beyond the realms of pain and suffering?" Yājñavalkya replied saying:

> My dear, no, not at all. Your life would be as comfortable as material means and wealth can make it. There is no hope of immortality through wealth.

Yājñavalkya here makes a distinction between comfort and happiness. He tells his wife that wealth and property can give her comfort—but not that condition which is beyond sorrow and suffering—not a condition of immortality. The answer of Yājñavalkya has an immediate bearing on the conditions prevailing in the present-day civilization. The problem of modern man is increasing comfort and decreasing happiness. Man wants to find happiness through greater and greater comfort—but this is a frustrating path, for, comfort and happiness belong to two different dimensions of living. Maitreyī had no illusions in her mind, for, she said:

> What shall I do with that which does not make me immortal? Tell me, my lord, of that alone which you know to be the means of immortality.

Yājñavalkya, is naturally pleased with this inquiry of Maitreyī and says to her that he will teach her all that he knows about immortality—but she must listen intently and mentally dwell upon what is said. He speaks here of *Nididhyāsana*, which really means Meditation. She must meditate upon the teaching that Yājñavalkya is about to impart. Here follows a remarkable instruction by Yājñavalkya,. It says:

> Lo, verily, and not for the love of the husband is a husband dear, but for the love of the Self (**Ātman**) is the husband dear. Not for the love of the wife is wife dear, but for the love of the Self is the wife dear.
>
> Not for the love of sons are sons dear, but for the love of the Self are the sons dear.

> Not for the love of the wealth is wealth dear, but for the love of the Self is the wealth dear. Not for the love of the all is all dear, but for the love of the Self all is dear.
>
> The Self (Ātman), my dear Maitreyī should verily be realized —by hearing about, by reflecting upon It and by meditating on it.

The above statement of the husband or the wife or the sons being dear not for their sake, but for the sake of the Self has been variously interpreted. Some have said that we love others not for their sakes but for our own sake —others have interpreted it as meaning that in our loved ones we see ourselves and therefore, we love them. It seems, these interpretations are wide the mark—for, in the above statement, Self is described as Ātman Yājñavalkya says that it is for the sake of the Ātman that all things are dear. Now the Ātman is unborn and so the sage Yājñavalkya says that it is the intangible presence of the Unborn in all that is manifested which renders everything lovable. Why are things and beings loveable?—Not so much for what is expressed and manifested, but for what remains unexpressed and unmanifested. Love of the manifested is just a sentiment, an attraction, an infatuation—it does not endure, for the expressions change. If one sees only the changeful, then one would experience moments of pleasure and pain, of elation and depression. But if one communes with the Changeless, then all changes of expression and manifestation will appear intensely charming and lovable. Now the Changeless is the Self, the Ātman, the Unborn and the Unmanifest. The intimations of the Unborn are always subtle and intangible. It is these that open the doorway to the Unmanifest. He who grasps the tangible and clings to the manifest, misses this subtle and intangible intimation of the Unborn. Without communing with the Unborn, the diversities of expression and manifestation seem devoid of meaning. It is the Unborn which gives meaning and significance to that which is born. Yājñavalkya says, it is for the sake of the Unborn that all things become truly lovable. To commune with the Unborn is to transcend the realm of duality, it is to rise above the pairs of opposites—and when this happens, there is neither pleasure nor pain—there is only joy, eternal and indescribable. In love, when one experiences an element of "more" or "less", then surely one has not communed with the Unborn. Love knows neither "more" nor "less", for, with what shall the Unborn be measured? The Unborn is immeasurable. It is a communion with the Unborn which alone is love—such love knows no decay or diminution. It exists even when the continuing stream of time ceases to flow.

Yājñavalkya says—one must realize the Ātman, one must commune with the Unborn. But how? Here the teacher speaks of the three stages of spiritual quest, *Śravaṇa*, *Manana* and *Nididhyāsana*—the hearing, the reflecting and the meditating. The first stage is Śravaṇa or the hearing about Truth. One has to be a *Śrāvaka* first before he can proceed further. What is the significance of *Śravaṇa* or hearing? It is hearing that creates an interest. The order in which the senses developed says that the sense of hearing or *Śabda* was the first. To be a *Śrāvaka* is indeed to find out what one is truly interested in. It is indeed the process of *Pratyāhāra*, to use the terminology of Patañjali. Hearing enables a man to sort out his interests—to shift the essential from the non-essential. Ordinarily, our mind is in a confused state—in it good and bad are thoroughly mixed up. It is this which burdens the mind with all sorts of unnecessary things. The burden of the mind has to be lightened. This is the purpose of *Śravaṇa*—and this indeed is the function of a *Śrāvaka*. Hearing has to be not merely physical—it has to be psychological. This means that, not just the ears, but, the mind too must hear, when the mind really hears, then a beam of light is thrown into the dark corners of its abode. This beam of light reveals that so much junk is cluttered up with things that are good and precious. This hearing would naturally bring a man to *Manana* or Reflection. When the junk is thrown away, then the mind can dwell upon whatever good it may have collected. In reflection, mind is only looking at what it calls good or true or beautiful. From *Śrāvaka*, the spiritual aspirant becomes a *Manishī*—a thinker, one who reflects upon what he has gathered in the course of his life. It is here that man examines his ideals, his aspirations, his values—all that he regards as good and precious. This *Manana* is indeed *Dhāraṇā* in terms of the Yoga Sūtras of Patañjali. To reflect is to hold in the palm of the mind whatever needs to be examined. From *Śravaṇa* to *Manana*, the mind of man moves from one pole to the other. Having thrown away the non-essential in the stage of *Śrāvaka*, having determined what one's own interest is, having decided what discipline to follow, the mind must now reflect upon what it has retained, what it has declared to be good. The mind of man must dwell upon it, so as to examine it from all sides—to look at all the phases of what it calls good and true and beautiful. But that is not enough from *Śrāvaka* to *Manishī* and from *Manishī* to *Dhyānī*—such is indeed the path indicated by Yājñavalkya for communing with the Self or the Ātman, for experiencing the presence of the Unborn in that which is born. In meditation, one is concerned with emptying the image of the good, the true and the beautiful on which the mind has reflected. Into the Good, the True and the Beautiful to which the mind has arrived, it has put much of its own. The image is filled up with its own projections and so the good, the true and the beautiful of the mind have become opaque, unable to bring the intimations from beyond. It is in meditation that the opaque is made transparent—the image is divested of all its contents. When this happens, then the transparency of the image enables one to see beyond, it enables one to receive the intimation of the Unborn and the Unmanifest. To remove the opaqueness from all factors of human relationship, rendering it absolutely transparent, is to know, that, not for the sake of the wife is the wife dear but for the sake of the Self is the wife dear—not for the sake of the all is the all dear, but for the sake of the Self is the all dear. Yājñavalkya here speaks about the transparency of all relationships. He shows the way of transforming the opaque into something clear and transparent—and the way is

Śravaṇa *Manana* and *Nididhyāsana* —Hearing, Reflecting and Meditating. The Chinese philosopher, Chaung Tzu spoke of a transparency in human relationship when he wrote the following words:

> Suppose a boat is crossing a river and another boat, an empty one, is about to collide with it. Even an irritable man would not lose temper. But suppose there was some one in the second boat. Then the occupant of the first boat would shout to him to keep clear. And if he did not hear the first time, nor even when called to three times, bad language would inevitably follow. In the first case there was no anger, but in the second there was—because in the first case, the boat was empty and in the second, it was occupied.
>
> And so it is with man. If he could only pass empty through life, who would be able to injure him?

To pass empty—that is what is meant by transparency of the mind. It is the function of the mind to build images—but if the images are kept opaque with the contents projected by the mind, then the image would stand between the perceiver and the perceived. Then we see not the husband, the wife or the son—we see only their images, made opaque by the mind. But life cannot be imprisoned in image—the image must become an open window through which one can look at the Beyond. To love the window for the sake of the window is meaningless. To love the window for the vision of the Beyond which it gives—that indeed is true loving. When this happens, the whole world is transformed into a window, giving a vast vision of the Life beyond. But close the window and existence becomes monotonous and sterile. Even if the panels of the window are beautifully decorated, the boredom and the monotony are not gone. The relationship with the closed window becomes strained—for there is nothing fresh that it is able to show. This is exactly what happens in human relationship. We imprison the manifest and so the vital and refreshing touch of the Unmanifest is gone. In keeping the manifest imprisoned, we develop all types of resistances, lest the manifest be taken away or destroyed. We do not allow the person whom we love to move in the open spaces and enjoy the freedom of life. We create a framework and into that framework, the living individual must accommodate himself or herself. There is the vast Unborn and the Unmanifest which all the time speaks to us through our loved ones. We cannot hear this whisper of the soul because of the opaqueness with which we have filled the image. The opaque must be made transparent through hearing, reflection and meditation—this is what Yājñavalkya says to Maitreyī He explains further by saying:

> As one is not able to grasp by themselves the particular notes of a drum that is being beaten, but it is only by grasping the general note of drum or the general effect of particular strokes on it, that those notes are grasped.
>
> As one is not able to grasp by themselves the particular notes of a flute that its being played on, but it is only by grasping the general note of the flute, or the general effect of particular playings on it, that those notes are grasped.

The particular notes of a piece of music remain scattered, they do not have a unity. It is the steady note, supplied either by an instrument or by the human voice, that gives to the particular notes a unity, a cohesion. It is that which prevents music from becoming unmusical. The steady note is imperceptible. He who does not have a sensitivity of hearing may not know what the steady note is—and yet the whole superstructure of music rests on it. Any deviation from the steady note destroys all music. The steady note represents intimations of the Unborn music. Without it, the manifested music may fly off into something un-melodious, something disharmonious. As the above passages of the Upanishad say—the particular notes cannot be grasped—and if they are grasped, they remain merely notes, they do not constitute music. That which transforms notes into music is the steady note—for, it is this that imparts wholeness to music. If we can grasp the steady note of existence, then the whole music of life can be understood and enjoyed. The steady note is the quality of things—and the quality resides not in the Manifest, but in the Unmanifest. In the Manifest, one sees only the intimations of the quality. To know this quality is to commune with the Unborn and the Unmanifest. Love that arises from this communion is true love—all else is mere emotionalism. To grasp the steady note is to declare that, not for the sake of the husband is the husband dear, but for the sake of the Self is the husband dear, not for the sake of the wife is the wife dear, but for the sake of the Self is the wife dear—not for the sake of the friend is the friend dear, but for the sake of the Self is the friend dear. It is a magnificent vision that Yājñavalkya has given to Maitreyī.

The teacher says that the Unborn or the Unmanifest expresses itself in myriads of forms—but all these expressions are like the breath of Brahman. This simile is very apt, for, breathing is a very natural process—there is no effort involved in breathing. Such is, indeed, the case with the manifestations of the Unmanifest. The Limitless Reality gives birth to unlimited forms. Brahman or Ātman is undifferentiated, for there can be no differentiation in the Unborn. Although undifferentiated, it gives birth to countless differentiations. They emerge out of the Unborn and they merge into the Unborn. Yājñavalkya says:

> As the sea is the merging place of all waters, as the skin is the merging place of all kinds of touch, as the eye is the one merging place of all colours, as the ear is the one merging place of all sounds, as the mind is the one merging place of all deliberations, as the intellect is the one merging place of all knowledge—so is the Self the merging place of all differentiations.

Maitreyī had told Yājñavalkya, to tell her about the secret of Immortality. He explains to her about the Unborn and the Unmanifest—the root-base of all manifestation. He indicates that the fullness of existence resides in the Unborn—for the born is limited and partial. The Unborn is limitless and supplies a steady note, intangibly and imperceptibly, to the great music of life. The Unborn is the father of all manifestation—and the manifested forms emerge naturally and effortlessly like breathing, which is unconscious. But the point of emergence is also the point of dissolution. Creation and dissolution are like the breath of Brahman outgoing and incoming. All differentiation merge in the Ātman even as all knowledge merges in the intellect. But then what about Ātman itself?

Unless Yājñavalkya throws light on the question of Ātman, whether It too merges or it remains unmerged, Maitreyī's inquiry about Immortality would remain unanswered. Yājñavalkya takes up this inquiry in the following verse:

> As a lump of salt thrown into water dissolves in water, and none can pick it up, but from whichever part one tastes water, it tastes saltish, even so, my dear, this great endless infinite Reality is Pure Intelligence. On account of differentiation, the self stands out separately, and as soon as these are destroyed, its separate existence is also gone. In a formless state, it has no particular consciousness. In this lies the secret of Immortality.

Hearing this instruction from Yājñavalkya, Maitreyī said that he had confused her by talking of the Self having no consciousness after attaining isolation. Yājñavalkya, however, assured her that there was nothing confusing in what he had said. The above passage speaks of isolation—the word used in Sanskrit is *Pretya*. This would mean dis-embodied existence. It alludes to a Formless condition. The teacher here says that in the Formless state, the self has no particular consciousness. Once again, the word in Sanskrit is *Saṃjñā*. This word means a recognising gesture. It indicates doing something which is recognisable. This obviously refers to that which can be identified. Yājñavalkya says that in the Formless state, there is no recognisable or identifiable gesture of the Self. He does not say that the Self has no consciousness—he only says there is no particularized consciousness. What happens to the particularized consciousness? It is merged in the Universal consciousness. But then, is this not an annihilation of the Self?

Maitreyī is naturally confused because, if the Self is annihilated, then of what use is all talk about the Immortality of the Self? What indeed is the merging of the particularized consciousness in the Universal consciousness. Perhaps the illustration of the river and the ocean may explain this clearly. The river merges in the ocean and with this merging there is no particularized consciousness of the river—the river has no separate identity, just as the salt put into water has no separate identity. This is exactly what the river experiences. It loses its identity in the sea. Has the river been annihilated? It is true that the separate existence of a particularized consciousness is no more with the merging of the river in the sea. The river as river has ceased to be—there can be no Immortality for the particularized existence of the river. The Form of the river cannot be immortalized. But then does it exist? It has merged in the sea and exists as the sea. But surely this cannot be declared as the existence of the river—for it has lost its identity in the sea. But what is the sea? Is it different from the river? From whence did the river come? The river obviously came from the sea—in merging with the sea, the river therefore goes to its own home. Its true existence is the sea. It has not merged itself with something strange and foreign—it has merged with itself. The river was the manifestation of the sea—when it goes back to the sea, it has merged itself with the Unmanifest. The form of the river was the particularized consciousness. With the merging into the sea, this particularized consciousness is no more—the river has become the Universal consciousness. It is immortal as universal consciousness—and from this it will emerge out as many rivers, quiet or turbulent. These rivers will have a span of particularized consciousness—once again they will merge into the sea. Universal consciousness is the real home of the Self—surely one cannot call one's going to one's home as annihilation? A master musician may sing a beautiful melody and expand it in an extensive peirod of time. The melody ends—but is this an annihilation? No, for only the particularized form of the melody is over—it has merged in the universal consciousness of the musician. The form of the melody is no more—it has become formless. But out of the musician, it will again burst forth in a form similar or divergent. The melody lives not by being imprisoned in one form—but by expressing itself in myriads of forms. The great mystic-pôet of India, Rabindranath Tagore says:

> My mind must realize itself anew. Once I give form to my thought, I must free myself from it. For the time being, it seems to me that I want absolute freedom to create new forms for new

> ideas. I am sure physical death has the same meaning for us—the creative impulse of our soul must have new forms for its realization. Life must increasingly outgrow its dwelling place, otherwise, the form gets the upper hand and becomes a prison. Man is immortal—therefore, he must die endlessly.

To know one's immortality through constant deaths —this is indeed what Yājñavalkya is explaining to Maitreyī. When the prison is broken, man is not annihilated —man is indeed free in the breaking of that prison. It is only the prison that has been destroyed. Is immortality a continued existence in the prison? Most certainly not. But man believes that endless continuity in the prison-house is immortality. He is not seeking immortality—he is only demanding a continuous existence of the prison-house. A form is always a limitation to the creative impulse—it is only in outgrowing form after form and stepping out of the particularized forms, that man knows his immortality. The Formless cannot remain long in one form—it must move from form to form, and every stepping out of one form results in the breaking up of a particularized consciousness. It is existence without identity, which is the true home of the Self—from this home It emerges from time to time, assuming new identities—but every identity must needs be discarded, for, it is in such discarding that the Self asserts its Immortality.

Yājñavalkya says that "Self-knowledge is the means to Immortality." Without knowing the Self and its nature, how can one talk of the Immortality of the Self? How can the particular be ever immortal? The particular has no intrinsic existence—it has a derived existence. That which is derived is bound to disintegrate. Its existence depends upon That from which it is derived. It is like a shadow—how can the shadow be immortal? It can continue so long as the substance is there—but when the substance moves away, the particularized shadow disappears. To demand that the shadow must exist, even when the substance has moved away is to ask for the impossible. The substance must be free to cast new shadows —or to cast no shadow at all. To imprison the substance in the shadow is to demand something that is meaningless. To believe that when the particularized shadow is gone, the substance itself is annihilated, is to talk something which has no sense whatsoever. He who communes with the Formless rejoices in the ever-changing panorama of forms. He sees Immortality in constant death—and Immortality can be seen only in death and nowhere else.

But the question may arise here: From where do new forms come? Yājñavalkya poses this question in the assembly of King Janaka when he says, "If a tree is pulled out from its roots, it does not spring again. From which root does man sprout after he is cut down by death?" It is with this question that the Third Chapter of the Bṛhadāraṇyaka Upanishad is concerned. It seems once Janaka, the King of Videha, performed a sacrifice in which there was a profusion of gifts. Many learned Brahmins from different parts had assembled. Janaka wanted to know who was the most wise among the Brahmins who had gathered there. He had offered to give a thousand cows to the person declared to be most wise—and the horns of each cow were adorned with real gold. Janaka declared to the Brahmins: "Let him who is the greatest Vedic scholar, one who has realized Brahman, amongst you, drive these cows home." No one came forward—then Yājñavalkya rose and asked his pupil, Samasrava, to drive home all the cows. The pupil did as he was asked—but the assembled learned Brahmins became very angry. They said, "How can Yājñavalkya declare himself to be most wise amongst us?" One of the priests in the assembly of Janaka, by the name Aśvala, came forward and asked Yājñavalkya whether he was the greatest scholar in their midst. Yājñavalkya had a sense of humour and so he addressed Aśvala thus:

> I salute the greatest Vedic scholar, I only wish to have cows.

But this evoked a volley of questions from the assembled Brahmins and the first to ask was Aśvala himself. His question to Yājñavalkya was:

> Yājñavalkya, since all this is caught by death and overpowered

by it, through what does the sacrificer transcend the reach of death?

Yājñavalkya says that it is only by the process of liberation that man can transcend the reach of death. He says, "Liberation is transcendence". For transcendence, the word used is *Ati-mukti.* But how to bring this process of liberation into operation? It is interesting to note that this subject of death is developed in the subsequent passages by Aśvala in terms of the "reach of day and night", in terms of the "reach of the bright and the dark halves of the month" and in terms of the "reach of space which seems to exist without any support whatsoever". The reach of death, in above terms, is obviously Time and Space. How to transcend the reach of death?—that is the question of Aśvala. He wants to know—how can one go beyond time and space, for these are indeed the reaches of death?

The question of Aśvala is with reference to sacrifice. Now sacrifice is an act of worship. Can one transcend the reaches of death by acts of worship? The act of worship is an invocation to powers greater than what man possesses. It is an invocation to the transcendental forces. Yājñavalkya says that in this sacrifice, Agni or Fire must be the invoker, for, then alone can one transcend the reaches of death. The invoker must not be the sacrificer—but Fire itself. He says that Fire is the liberator. Fire is the energy that is enshrined in the Sun, in the Vāyu and in the Moon. This refers to the Solar, the Vital and the Lunar energies. It is only when these energies are released that man can know that which is beyond the reaches of death. What are the reaches of death? They are the *Annamaya*, the *Prāṇamaya* and the *Manomaya* vestures of man, for these are subjected to death. It is Sun which nourishes the physical body, it is the Vital force—the Prāṇa—which nourishes the Vital Body and it is Moon that nourishes the *Manomaya* kośa. How does Moon nourish the Manomaya Kośa? The passage of the Upanishad says that the "mind is looked upon as the Moon". The mind is the seat of kāma or desires and so it is mind which is greatly influenced by the Moon. The lunar energy is enshrined in the mind. The invocation by Fire really signifies the release of energy locked up in the physical, the vital and the mental vestures. It is that energy which alone can enable man to transcend the reaches of death. When man becomes the wielder of this three-fold energy, then does he liberate himself from the clutches of death —for the realm extends from the physical to the mental. He whose energy in these three vestures is not released is subject to death again and again. To release the energy from these three vestures is to make them the instruments of man—when the physical, the vital and the mental have become the instruments of man, then has death no sway over him.

Aśvala asks Yājñavalkya —"How many are the gods that the priest must invoke for the protection of the sacrifice against the ravages of death?" Yājñavalkya said, "Only one god has to be invoked." Aśvala asked: "Who is that one god by invoking whom full protection is assured?" Yājñavalkya said: "Mind alone—for mind verily is infinite—*Anantaṃ-vai-manaḥ*". All the gods are merely the products of the mind and so it is with the help of the mind that the sacrifice can be fully protected. Death establishes its sway through the instrument of time—but what is time? Is time itself not the product of mind? What can death do when the very instrument of time is taken away? Mind which creates time can also destroy time—and when time is destroyed, where is the sway of death?

Aśvala asked the last question to Yājñavalkya in which he inquired as to the kinds of hymns to be chanted so that the sacrifice may be protected? Yājñavalkya replied that there should be three kinds of hymns chanted—Preparatory, Oblational and Laudatory. On a further inquiry from Aśvala as to what would be the result of these three kinds of hymns, he said:

> Through Preparatory, the sacrificer wins the earth, through the oblational, he wins the sky and through the laudatory he gets the heaven.

Here again the reference is to the Physical, the Vital

and the Mental realms which are the reaches of death. He who conquers these three, goes beyond the reaches of death—this means that he whose physical, vital and mental energies are not entangled anywhere, but are free, has no fear of death.

The gathering at the palace of Janaka was indeed an assembly of the intellectuals. Among these was Yājñavalkya , a man of deep spiritual realization. He had to face an intense volley of intellectual questions, but he was able to hold forth most successfully, meeting intellect with even greater intellect. After Aśvala , came Ārtabhāga to place his questions before Yājñavalkya. He asked him: " Yājñavalkya , how many organs or *grahas* are there and how many objects or *ati-grahas* are there?" Yājñavalkya said both are eight in number. Here *graha* obviously means sense organs and the *ati-graha* means the functions of sense organs. Yājñavalkya, describes the five senses—the ear, the touch, the eye, the tongue and the nose—and also enumerates their functions. He adds to these the speech, the hands and the mind. The function of the hand is to work even as the function of speech is to pronounce names. He says that the function of the mind is to supply the impelling power of desire and aspiration. Here in this assembly, one of the subjects discussed is death and so Ārtabhāga askes Yājñavalkya : "Since these senses and their functions are food for death, who is the deity whose food is death?" Yājñavalkya replied saying "Fire consumes everything and so fire is death—but fire is the food of water and so death becomes the food of water." It is water that extinguishes fire and so water devours fire as food. But does water devour death too? The fear of death remains so long as there are unfulfilled desires. These burn as fire in the body and the mind. If the flames of unfulfilled desires are extinguished, then where is the fear of death? Desires by themselves do not devour a man—it is the unfulfilled desires that create fires in the body and the mind. Water signifies the elimination of unfulfilled desires—he who can do this goes above the reach of death. But Ārtabhāga has further inquiries. He asks

"Do the organs depart from man after his death or do they not?" And Yājñavalkya says that they do not, as they are dissolved along with the body. Ārtabhāga asks, "What is it then that man carries with him—that thing which does not leave him?" Yājñavalkya says, "The name does not leave him." The body of man is cremated and with it the organs of senses too are burnt—but the name of man remains, for he will be remembered by the name he has acquired—not the physical name, but the psychological name. This is called the *Akshara-deha*—this represents his glory or ignominy. The body is burnt, but the name remains. It is the name which is the connecting link between two incarnations. The name is the psychological memory—and what incarnates is the contents of the psychological memory. This is the psychic entity of man, the *skandha* of the Buddhists. But Ārtabhāga wants to know on what does the name rest? When everything is consumed by the flames, what indeed is that on which the name rests? At this stage, Yājñavalkya did not give any verbal reply. He said to Ārtabhāga :

> Give me your hand, gentle Ārtabhāga, we two only shall ascertain it. This topic of ours is not to be decided in an assembly.

The Upanishad says that they retired and discussed among themselves. It seems they discussed the secret of action—the mystery of Karma. But why did they not discuss the mystery of Karma in the open assembly? This is because Karma is such a great mystery that even great seers get confused about it. We do not know what secret of Karma, Yājñavalkya imparted to Ārtabhāga —but the latter became silent and had no further question to ask. Here in this section of the Upanishad, death is being discussed in two aspects—first, the conquest of death and the second, re-birth after death. The questioners ask questions as they like, dealing with the one or the other, so as to confuse Yājñavalkya. But Yājñavalkya had a keen intellect which was able to steer clear of all intellectual jugglery indulged in by the questioners. It is not necessary to relate all questions and counter-questions appearing in this section as some of them are merely to test the intellectual ability of Yājñavalkya and have no bearing on the mystical teaching of the Upanishad. There is however a question by Ushasta Cākrāyaṇa which is significant. He asked:

> Yājñavalkya, tell me precisely about Brahman that is immediate and direct—the Self that is within all.

Yājñavalkya said, "This your Self is the innermost core of everything." But Ushasta Cākrāyaṇa was not satisfied, for, he asked "What is it that is the innermost core of everything?" Yājñavalkya said:

> You cannot see the seer of sight, you cannot hear the hearer of hearing, you cannot think the thinker of thought, you cannot know the knower of knowledge. This is your Self that is within all. Everything besides this is perishable.

What could Ushasta Cākrāyaṇa say further—he naturally became quiet. But this question was carried further by Kahola, the son of Kushītaka, for, he asked of Yājñavalkya:

> Yājñavalkya, explain to me that Self which is innermost of all, which one sees as the immediate and direct Brahman.

Once again Yājñavalkya said: "This is your Self within everything". But the questioner persisted in his inquiry and said: "What is that Self which is within everything?" To this Yājñavalkya gave a profound reply saying:

> That which transcends hunger and thirst, sorrow and delusion, old age and death—knowing that Self, the spiritual man rises above the desire for progeny, wealth and worlds—and lives the life of a mendicant.
>
> The desire for progeny is the desire for wealth and the desire for wealth is the desire for the worlds—both are cravings. Therefore, a spiritual man, after completing his studies, should rely on the strength of his knowledge—transcending both strength and knowledge he should be a silent meditator—and transcending both meditation and non-meditation, he must truly become the knower of Brahman.

The above passage is indeed full of profound wisdom. It speaks of the three desires or impulses. It is interesting to see how ancient Indian psychology had understood certain factors of human consciousness to which modern psychological knowledge seems to be gradually coming. Here Yājñavalkya speaks of three *Eshaṇās* or impulses—these are the desire for children, the desire for wealth, and the desire for the worlds. In the first, we see the sex impulse of Freud. Of course, the sex has to be understood in its widest context, and not merely physical or biological expression for it. Then the teacher speaks of the desire for wealth. Wealth is a symbol of social recognition, of social significance. Here one sees the intimation of Adler's inferiority complex. The psychological inferiority always comes out with an over-compensation towards assumed superiority. The desire for wealth has indeed this element. It gives to man an instrument to show his social importance—to assert his superiority. Then comes the desire for the worlds. This refers to power, whether good or bad. It is not merely power in the material sense, but also in the so-called spiritual sense. The worlds refer to different layers of man's existence. Thus Progeny, Position and Power—these three, one sees as dominating factors in man's life. Jung declared that sex and superiority were not the only factors motivating man's actions —he referred to more than these but indicated that this must be a mixture of good and bad. The desire of man to make spiritual progress is also one of the *eshaṇās*—one of the desires. Yājñavalkya, declares all these to be cravings. He says that the truly spiritual man is free from all these and lives a life of a mendicant—one who is a wanderer, a person with no "home". There is no desire that pulls him—neither material nor so-called spiritual. He says that the spiritual man, after his studies, stands on the strength of his knowledge. Knowledge becomes his base—that is the strength on which he relies, not the strength which comes from outside—but the strength that arises from within due to knowledge. Yājñavalkya says even this he must transcend—both strength and knowledge, realizing how limited they are. But then where does he rest? He rests in silence. In the above passage, meditation does not give a correct rendering of the word used in the Sanskrit text. The word by the teacher is *maunam*

—silence. Yājñavalkya, however, speaks of a still further danger—and that is the attachment to silence that may grow in the spiritual man. And so he says that this spiritual man must transcend both silence and non-silence—both *mauna* and *amauna.* When he transcends even these, not merely desire, but strength and knowledge and also silence and non-silence—then does he come to the experience of Brahman. He has given a clear picture of the spiritual man—there is no wonder, Kahola became quiet, not desiring to ask any further question.

Then arose in the assembly a young woman by the name Gārgī, to ask questions of this great teacher. It is most significant to note that in such assemblies of intellectuals there were not merely men but also women. And these women actively participated in the discussions. They matched their intellects with men—and many a time to the discomfiture of the latter. This shows that in ancient India there was perfect equality of sexes—even in the spheres of intellect and spiritual inquiry, woman was equal of man. In that great assembly of Janaka, where large numbers of learned men had gathered, Gārgī did not feel awkward in rising and putting searching questions to Yājñavalkya. Neither did Gārgī feel awkward, nor did men feel anything unusual in a woman getting up in an assembly of intellectuals to ask serious questions. There must have been a perfect comradeship between man and woman in those ancient days. The examples of Maitreyī and Gārgī give us ample proof of the completely free society that must have existed in the days of the Upanishads.

Gārgī said: " Yājñavalkya, when all is pervaded by water, by what is water pervaded"? He said: "By air" —but Gārgī asked, "What pervades air?" and Yājñavalkya replied, "It is *ākāśa* or ether". Gārgī goes on asking question after question about that which pervaded the different layers of existence. At last she asked him—"What pervades the world of the Cosmic Being?" Here, Yājñavalkya pulled up Gārgī saying, " Gārgī do not go beyond the range where questions can be legitimately asked. You are now asking about something that cannot be known by reasoning—and that which transcends reason cannot be conveyed through reason". In the Upanishads, while the teachers have indicated something which lies beyond the intellect—they have not derided reason, they have not bypassed intellect. In fact, with the help of intellect they have pointed out how intellect is limited. There is a point beyond which the human intellect cannot go. The Upanishadic teachers brought their pupils to that point by unrelenting logic and with intellect as sharp as a razor. But nobody could take these teachers unawares. They knew where the intellect must stop and so they never replied, in terms of intellect, those questions that belonged to realms beyond the reasoning faculties of the mind. And so Gārgī, realizing that she had crossed the limit of legitimate questions, became silent.

Then arose Uddālaka Āruṇi asking Yājñavalkya whether he knew about *Sūtra*—the thread—by which this world, the next world and all beings are strung together—he also asked him about the Inner Controller— the Inner Ruler, who, dwelling within, governs this life, the next life and all beings. He also said:

> If you, Yājñavalkya, without knowing that Sūtra and that Inner Ruler remove the cows meant for the knowers of Brahman, your head shall fall off.

Yājñavalkya replied he knew about these—but again Uddālaka said: "Anybody indeed may say—I know, I know—tell me what you know". To him, Yājñavalkya replied saying:

> Vāyu verily is that sūtra. It is by the sutra, that is Vāyu, that this world, the next world and all beings are strung together. For this very reason, they say of a dead man that his limbs are loosened, because the limbs of the living man are strung together by the sutra that is Vāyu .

Yājñavalkya here speaks of a deep scientific truth He says it is energy or *Prāṇa* —that Vital force which binds all together. Modern science speaks of energy at various levels—the chemical energy and the atomic energy, the physical energy—the energy expressing itself in electro-magnetism and the energy or force known as gravitation.

The whole universe is just an expression of energy—science speaks of matter also in terms of energy. Yājña-valkya, speaks of this energy, the Vital Force, Vāyu, which is the thread stringing together the world of sentient and insentient beings. Today, modern science is engaged in mathematically measuring this energy—for, that is what is meant by the famous equation of Einstein. Uddālaka is naturally satisfied with this reply of Yājñavalkya. And so he says:

> It is indeed so, Yājñavalkya. Now tell us about the Inner Ruler—the *Antaryāmin*.

The reply to this question which Yājñavalkya gave, constitutes one of the most memorable passages of the entire Upanishadic lore. He said about the Inner Ruler Immortal, the *Antaryāmin* as follows:

> He who dwells in the darkness and within the darkness, whom the darkness does not know, whose body the darkness is, and who rules the darkness within, he is thy self, the Inner Ruler Immortal.
>
> He who dwells in the light and within the light, whom the light does not know, whose body the light is, and who rules the light within, he is thy self, the Inner Ruler Immortal.
>
> He who dwells in all beings, and within all beings, whom all beings do not know, whose body all beings are and who rules all beings within, he is thy self, the Inner Ruler Immortal.
>
> Unseen but seeing, unheard but hearing, unperceived but perceiving, unknown but knowing. There is no other seer but He, there is no other hearer but He, there is no other perceiver but He, there is no other knower but He. This is thy self, the Inner Ruler Immortal. All else but him is perishable.

It would be presumptuous to comment upon this magnificent explanation of the Inner Ruler Immortal, the *Antaryāmin*. Who can comment upon this? To meditate in silence over these words of wisdom would bring to man greater enlightenment than indulging in any further explanation. Unseen but seeing, Unknown but knowing—how can one explain this? It is indeed a matter of deep experience—and he who can know this by direct perception has verily become the Rock of Ages—nothing can shake him. He has come to the Imperishable state—as the above passage says—all else but This is perishable. This is Immortality—all else is mere verbiage.

But the assembly of Janaka was not over. The deep and penetrating replies of Yājñavalkya whetted the sense of inquiry of his listeners. The learned and distinguished members of the assembly must have realized that in Yājñavalkya they had met not merely a *Śrotriya* but a real *Brahmanishṭha* —not merely a man of learning but of deep wisdom. And so, the irrepressible Gārgī once again rose to ask further questions to Yājñavalkya. But before addressing Yājñavalkya she spoke to the learned members of the assembly. She said:

> Venerable sirs, with your permission, I shall ask Yājñavalkya two questions. If he will answer these, then none of you can ever defeat him in expounding Brahman.

The entire assembly gave its consent, for, the learned Brahmins, one and all, said "Gārgī, ask your questions." But Gārgī wanted to warn Yājñavalkya in advance of the difficult nature of her questions. She addressed Yājñavalkya thus:

> Yājñavalkya, I shall ask you two questions. As a resident of Kāśī or the king of Videha, son of a heroic line, strings his unstrung bow, takes in hand two bamboo-pointed arrows that extremely hurt the enemy, and approaches close by, even so do I approach you with two questions. Answer those two questions of mine.

Gārgī seems to indicate that her questions are such that he may not be able to answer and would be forced to accept defeat. Perhaps Yājñavalkya must have smiled on hearing these words of a "cheeky" young lady—but he was ready to meet any challenge of intellect, and so he told her—"Ask, Gārgī , whatever your questions may be". Gārgī's first question was:

> Yājñavalkya, what pervades that, which they say, is above heaven and below the earth, which is heaven and earth as well as between them, and which was, is and will be?

In short, Gārgī wants to know what pervades the whole universe—heaven and earth and the interspaces and also what pervades the entire region of time. In this question, she has covered the whole problem of Time and Space. She wants to know what is it that pervades the vast field of Time and Space. Yājñavalkya, replies:

> Gārgī, the unmanifested ether pervades that, which they say, is above heaven and below the earth, which is heaven and earth as well as between them, and which was, is and will be.

The Unmanifested ether is obviously Pure Space—Space without an object. The visible Space is pervaded by that Pure Space which has no object in it. Gārgī repeated the same question—probably to confuse Yājñavalkya, but the latter also repeated his reply in the same terms —then it was that Gārgī asked him: " Yājñavalkya, tell me what pervades the Unmanifested ether"? This was a very clever question. Gārgī must have thought that either Yājñavalkya will fail to answer the question—or he will be guilty of answering in terms of intellect something that transcends the whole range of intellect. Gārgī wanted to catch Yājñavalkya —but he was more than a match for the intellectual challenges of Gārgī He replied:

> O Gārgi, the knowers of Brahman declare it as the Absolute. It is neither tangible nor subtle, neither short nor long, neither shadow nor darkness, neither air nor ether. It is not a measure, and is devoid of interior or exterior.

Here, it is interesting to note that Yājñavalkya does not say that he declares the Absolute as the pervading spirit of the Unmanifest ether—he says "the knowers of Brahman" declare this to be so. He brings the testimony of the wise men of the world—those who have come to the realization of Brahman. This Absolute cannot be described in any relative terms—its only description can be the negation of the relative, and therefore, the Absolute is stated to be neither subtle nor tangible, neither short nor long, neither interior nor exterior. One can only say IT IS—but if some one were to ask—What is meant by IT IS? —even then no further description could be given. Needless to say, in description it is the language of the relative world that is employed. But how can the relative explain the Absolute?

It is interesting to note how Yājñavalkya, stresses the imperative need to know the Absolute—for without knowing IT, all activities, however noble they may be, are of no avail. He says:

> Whoever, O Gārgi, without knowing the Absolute, makes fire-offerings, performs sacrifices and practises penances, finds all that of no avail even though he may indulge in these for many thousands of years.

All religious practices without communing with the Absolute are utterly fruitless. One must enter the kingdom of God first—and then everything else will be added unto him. Without an experience of mysticism, for that is what is meant by a communion with the Absolute, all religious, moral and so-called spiritual disciplines are of no avail. And when a communion with the Absolute is established, then all disciplines and practices become natural and spontaneous. A maxim of spiritual life says, "Thou can'st not travel on the Path unless thou hast become one with it." Without a communion with the Absolute, all treading on the Path would be with motives. All actions that are rooted in motives, however noble these motives may be, bind the individual. But a motiveless action arises only in the Ground of the Absolute. Yājñavalkya says:

> Whoever, O Gārgi, leaves this world without knowing the Absolute is pitiable. But he who leaves this world after communing with the Absolute is a knower of Brahman.

It is significant to note that the word for Absolute used in the Sanskrit text is *Akshara* or the Imperishable. Why does Yājñavalkya lay emphasis on knowing the Absolute before leaving this world? The significance of this statement is that man must know death while alive. In order to know the Absolute, one has to die to the relative. It is in the complete negation of the relative that the Absolute is known. He who knows this goes beyond the reaches of death. He comes to the experience of Immortality. He who does not know death while alive has to die again and again and thus remain under the sway of Death.

About the Absolute, he says:

> Verily, this Absolute, O Gārgi, is never seen, but is the Seer; It is never heard, but is the Hearer; It is never thought about, but is the Thinker; It is never known but is the Knower. There is no other Seer than It, there is no other hearer than It, there is no other Thinker than It, there is no other knower than It.
>
> This very Absolute, O Gārgi, pervades the Unmanifested ether.

But if this pervades the Unmanifested ether, then how can it be called as Pure Space. That which pervades must exist in that Space—and the existence of it makes it into a space with objects—and not a Space without objects. The Absolute pervades and yet, It has no existence and so occupies no space. How can this be, asks the mind of man? But the mind of man cannot understand it. And when the mind of man gives up all efforts to understand it by its own cogitation, then does Absolute reveal itself to man and convey to him Its great secret.

So completely satisfied is Gārgī with these replies of Yājñavalkya that she addresses the Brahmins thus:

> O Venerable Brahmins, you should consider it enough if you can get off from Yājñavalkya with a salutation. Certainly none of you can ever defeat him in expounding Brahman.

When Yājñavalkya had dealt with all the questions and had satisfied the learned assembly with his replies, he rose and said:

> Venerable Brahmins, any one amongst you who wishes may question me, or all of you may do so. Or I may question you on such matters as we have been discussing here.

The Upanishad says—No one dared to get up and ask any further question to Yājñavalkya. And so Yājñavalkya put a question to the distinguished gathering of learned Brahmins. His question was:

> If they pull a tree out of its roots, it does not spring again. From what root does man sprout after he is cut down by death?

Not one single Brahmin was able to answer, and so, Yājñavalkya himself gave a reply in the following words:

> If you think he is born for ever, then I say—No, he is born again. Now who should again produce him? It is Brahman which is Absolute Bliss and Intelligence—the ultimate resort of all.

Yājñavalkya says that the reply to the above question is not to be found in postulating an endless continuity of that which is born. It is not in continuity that the answer to that riddle can be found. The teacher says that the man is born again—which implies that he dies and comes to rebirth. Immortality is not endless continuity. Death cannot be isolated from life. Death is involved in the very act of living. It is he, who does not know how to live, that is afraid of death. He who dies constantly, he alone knows, how to live fully. Such a man is beyond compulsions. He lives, dies and takes birth again in the ground of complete Freedom. Yājñavalkya says he is born by the act of the Absolute. The act of the Absolute is the act of perfect freedom. A man who knows how to die takes his birth in conditions of absolute freedom, because his roots are cut away. The cutting away of the roots is a complete break from the past. In an earlier verse, Yājñavalkya says that "when a tree is felled, it sprouts again from its roots in a newer form". The condition of most people is like this. For them death is just the felling of a tree—but the roots are undisturbed. They are born again and again on the same roots. The bodies are different but the psychological entity is the same. But when man is completely free from his past—then how does he take birth? What is the source of his rebirth? Surely, it is the state of complete freedom. He is new in every birth, for, he is free from the compulsions of birth and death. The compulsions are indeed the roots of man. To be completely uprooted is indeed to die in the psychological and the spiritual sense. In this state man is reborn again and again—he seeks not continuity, and so is ever new, from moment to moment. This newness is imparted by the touch of the Absolute. Yājñavalkya rightly indicates that man is Immortal and therefore he must die constantly. Such a man takes root in the fertile soil of the Absolute, and, so is ever new.

Yājñavalkya seems to have been a teacher of great repute and eminence during the Upanishadic period, for, even a king like Janaka was eager to learn from him and sought instruction from him on life's deeper problems. Once when King Janaka was seated in his court, Yājñavalkya came there. Janaka asked him as to why he had come to the court—was it to get some cows or was it to instruct him. Yājñavalkya told him that he had gone there for both these purposes. Then did Yājñavalkya give to Janaka instructions on profound subjects. His main theme was the Body of Brahman and the support and sustenance which the Body received. Speech and Prāṇa, Eye and the Ear, the Mind and the Heart were declared as the body of Brahman —the instruments of manifestation. But from where did these instruments of manifestation receive their support and sustenance? Yājñavalkya said, "From Ākāśa or the Undifferentiated". The Undifferentiated is described here as Ākāśa or Space. The Pure Space—Space in which there is no flutter—it is this which sustains the entire manifestation. Space is the father-mother of all creation, Yājñavalkya said that Brahman in manifestation stood only on one foot. As the *Bhagavad Gītā* says: "It is with one fragment of Himself" that the supreme remains in manifestation. But the one fragment in creation receives all its sustenance from the Unmanifest or the Unborn. He says that the Unmanifest sends its intimations through the manifest. It is through these intimations that the Unmanifest can be contacted. This needs reflection and meditation on those aspects of the manifest where the intimations of the Unmanifest can be most easily discovered. He says through Intelligence and Affection, through Truth and Infinity, through Bliss and Stability can one hear the intimations of the Unmanifest in the manifest. It is interesting to note that these three groups of elements, through which intimations of the Unmanifest can come, each contain a positive, and a negative aspect. Without the positive and the negative, the circuit of energy is not complete. They indicate movement and stillness. Intelligence, Truth and Stability signify stillness even as Affection, Infinity and Bliss symbolise movement. It is in the co-existence of the positive and the negative that the intimation of the Unmanifest comes to the realm of manifestation. Yājñavalkya says that it is the Unmanifest which is indeed the support and sustenance of the manifest—and the sustenance comes through the intimations which the Unmanifest sends for the support of the Manifest.

Yājñavalkya tells Janaka that the self in Its true nature is the Unmanifest and can be described only as *Neti, Neti*—Not this, Not this. The Unmanifest is:

Imperceptible, for It is not perceived, It is unshrinking for It does not shrink, It is unattached, for It is not attached; It is untrammelled for it does not suffer nor does It perish.

The Sanskrit words used for these four epithets are: *Agṛhyo, Aśīryo, Asango* and *Asito* which are respectively Imperceptible, Unshrinking, Unattached and Untrammelled. It is significant that all the four epithets are couched in negative terms—for nothing positive can be spoken about the Unmanifest and the Unborn. *Neti, Neti* is indeed the language of the Upanishads in describing the Ultimate Reality. Janaka asked Yājñavalkya a question of deep import. His question was, "What serves as Light for man?" The answer which Yājñavalkya gave represents one of the inspiring passages of the Upanishads. The conversation between the Sage and the King has been narrated in the Upanishad as follows:

What is the Light of Man?, asked the King—The Sun, O King, for alone with the help of Sun-light does man exist.

But the King was not content and so inquired again asking: When sun is set, Yājñavalkya, what then is the light of man? The sage replied: "When the sun is set, then the Moon, O, King, is the light of man, for with the help of her beams alone man lives."

But again the King asked: "When the sun and the moon are both set, what is the light of man then? Yājñavalkya, replied: "When the sun and moon both are set then fire remains the light of man". But the king asked: "What happens when the Fire is extinguished?" And the sage replied: "O King, when the sun and the moon are set, when the fire is gone out, and all those external sources of the world's light have failed and the world itself is wrapped about in darkness, then alone does the light of the soul shine forth—the True, Unextinguishable and Eternal Light of Man.

It is only when man realizes the inefficacy of external light that the light of the Self shines forth. And the Light of the Self never goes out—for the Self never sets. It is ever radiant, self-effulgent. Its light never fails. The external light is only "darkness made visible". The light from outside only brings one to the realization that it only makes one aware of darkness. But it is only when man becomes aware of darkness, when darkness is made visible, that man turns to the Light Ineffable, the Light, such as was never on earth or in the heavens.

But naturally Janaka asks what is this Self? The question of self occurs again and again in the Upanishads, for, it is so intangible. It eludes the perception of man and so the inquirer turns to it frequently in order to grasp a little more clearly that which lies beyond the range of Mind and Intellect. To this question of Janaka, Yājñavalkya replies thus:

> Of the Unmanifest self, nothing can be said. But in manifestation this self takes the form of knowledge among the senses, the light within the heart, in intellect it is both the state of Waking and Dreaming—it is that which remains in contemplation and movement.

The self in manifestation is knowledge among the senses, and light within the heart and it is the two poles of duality of the intellect—the poles of movement and contemplation, of waking and dreaming. It has to be noted that in Waking and Dream, the mind of man is caught in a duality. The self in manifestation is engaged in a Play of the Opposites. But the Play of the Opposites becomes a conflict of opposites when the mind of man is confused and loses touch with the Unmanifest due to its own projections. Yājñavalkya says that the state of Deep Sleep, which is neither the Waking condition nor the Dream condition, constitutes the region of self-illumination. It is Deep Sleep which brings the intimation of the Unmanifest. The Transcendent speaks to the Immanent only in the state of Deep Sleep. The Waking and the Dream conditions are full of modifications—but the deep sleep is a condition of Non-modification. Yājñavalkya says:

> The state of Deep Sleep is the condition of self in which there is no desire, no taint of virtue or vice.

He says that in Deep Sleep, there is as it were, the close embrace of the Manifest and the Unmanifest. In the embrace of love, there is no awareness of anything, not even of duality. Yājñavalkya says that if in this state the self does not see, it is not because it has lost the sight of seeing. It does not see because there is no other to see.

It is a non-dual state. In Deep Sleep there is non-duality and so the Manifest and the Unmanifest draw closer to each other—they are in closest embrace where there is no awareness of the other. When, from this, man returns to the Dream and the Waking conditions, he goes with an ecstasy of deep union with the Unborn and the Uncreate. Yājñavalkya says that the condition of non-duality, of Deep Sleep, is such that in that state:

> A father is no more a father, a mother no more a mother, worlds are no more worlds, the gods, no more gods, the Vedas, no more Vedas—a thief is no more a thief, a murderer, no more murderer, a monk, no more a monk, a recluse, no more a recluse. This state is unaffected by good actions as also by bad actions. —for here the self is beyond all afflictions of the heart.

In Deep Sleep, the undifferentiated can be known only in negative terms. What the undifferentiated is in its positive aspect, none can tell. It has to be realized by direct perception. In the Deep Sleep, the Undifferentiated gives intimations about Itself—and these intimations are couched in negative terms. Beyond *Neti, Neti* nought can be said of the Unmanifest. In Deep Sleep there is the Bliss of Non-Duality. Of this Non-Dual state, the Sage says:

> Where there is a different thing, as it were, there one can see another, one can smell another, one can taste another, one can speak to another, one can hear another, one can think of another, one can touch another, one can know another.

But when there is no "another"—how can one describe this condition? This experience of the non-dual is the Highest Bliss—and Yājñavalkya says that the world of duality lives only on a particle of this Bliss. The joys of the Waking and the Dream conditions are nothing more than a particle of that Bliss which is experienced in the State of Deep Sleep. Yājñavalkya says:

> A spiritual man must engage himself in an enquiry about this state—but for this, he should not think of many words, for it is sheer weariness of speech.

The teacher says "one should not think of many words" —thinking of words is indeed mind's verbalizations. This verbalization brings nothing but weariness—it prevents one from coming to the experience of that state. Deep

Sleep is a direct experience—and it indicates the non-existence of a duality—the duality of the experiencer and the experienced. When mind engages itself in verbalization, then the duality comes into existence. Where verbalization of the mind is, there the possibility of direct experience vanishes. But wherever there is direct experience—even though for a moment, there, because mind's verbalization has ceased, there is joy indescribable arising out of the close embrace of the Manifest and the Unmanifest.

So pleased was Janaka with Yājñavalkya that he told the teacher: "To your venerable self, I bestow the whole Videha country, together with myself." This is the supreme act of dedication—but it is spontaneous, born in the moment of joy, for, Yājñavalkya had transported him to the regions that lie beyond the riches of earth and heaven.

Here the Upanishad relates a story of Prajāpati who had three sons, undergoing training under him. The name of the Prajāpati is *Virāj*, meaning the shining intelligence. The three sons, under training, were the Demons, the Men and the Gods. These sons, on the completion of their training, asked their father, Virāj, for a message. The father said to the gods—my message is just one syllable—DA. The gods naturally approached him the first, for they had completed their training before the other two sons. The father asked the gods "Have you understood the meaning of this syllable DA?" They said that they had, for the meaning of DA was *Dāmyata* —Restrain yourself. The father was pleased and said to them: "Yes, you have indeed understood the meaning of the syllable". Then came men asking for the final teaching. To them also he said "My teaching is DA". He inquired of them whether they had understood its meaning—and the men said that they had, for, the meaning of DA was *Datta*—Be charitable. And then came the demons also asking for the farewell message. The father said: "To you also my final teaching is DA". He asked the demons whether they had understood the meaning of it. They said they had, for the meaning of DA was *Dayadhvam* —Be sensitive. What is the meaning of this story? It is Intelligence that speaks to its three aspects. Be it remembered that Intelligence is not intellect. Intelligence is that which transcends intellect. Its three sons are the three attributes of the mind. Intelligence says to the mind that you will understand the meaning of my intimation only if you know what DA signifies. The three attributes of the mind are *Sattva*, *Rajas* and *Tamas*—Harmony, Activity and Inertia. Intelligence gives a word of instruction to each of the attributes—and the word is the same DA, but each attribute must translate it in terms of its own true and proper functioning. To the attribute of *Sattva*, DA means Humility, Modesty—a sense of hesitancy. When *Sattva*, does not function in terms of modesty and humility, then it becomes proud of its own achievements. It becomes conscious of its virtues and attainments. To this, *Virāj* or Intelligence says—restrain yourself, be gentle, be modest, be humble—move in life not with an air of over-confidence but with hesitancy. If it does so, then *Sattva*, will become an instrument for the intelligence to function—and not a factor of limitation.

To the attribute of *Rajas*, represented by men, the word of instruction given by Intelligence is the same, namely DA. But to *Rajas* it must mean Charity—a sense of generosity. Charity has not to be understood in the sense of giving alms or distributing gifts. By charity is meant a charitable disposition, to look upon everything with a charitable outlook. It is this alone which will take all frustration out of *rajas* or activity. In the whole process of activity, the process of becoming, man gets frustrated. Why? Because he is unable to take a charitable view of things. He never sees the silver lining—his attention is fixed only on the dark clouds. The mind that is unable to take a charitable view of the weaknesses of others gets more and more frustrated—its activity results in defeat and depression. Such a man gets tired and exhausted. To men, in their realm of activity, Intelligence gives the message of Charity, for, that alone will render all activity fruitful. The *rajas* will become an instrument of Intelligence and no longer a limitation. What greater charity can there be than being charitable to the views of others? The demons too came to *Virāj* for final instruction. They represent *tamas* or inertia of the mind. Inertia too has its place—for it gives stability. Stability, Activity and Harmony are indeed the three functions of the mind. But these functions become limitations, and, when this happens, then Intelligence cannot shine forth to illumine the mind of man. To demons representing *tamas* or inertia, Intelligence gives the same message of DA—but to them it must mean *Dayadhvam* —sensitivity or sympathy. While *tamas* gives stability—a mere stability would mean death if there is no sensitivity in it. Out of *tamas* must arise activity—but this can happen only when the attribute of *tamas* shows forth a responsiveness. There must be mobility of consciousness in the midst of the stability of structure. When this happens, then *tamas* becomes an instrument of Intelligence and no longer a limitation. Humility, Charity and Sensitivity—this is the instruction of *Virāj* or Intelligence to the functioning attributes of the mind. For, thus alone mind can be illumined by *Buddhi* or Intelligence. And it is Intelligence that perceives the intimations of the Unmanifest in the Manifest. Intelligence is indeed the bridge that leads from Immanence to Transcendence, from the Manifest to the Unmanifest.

The Upanishad says that Nature speaks to man through thunder and lightning this message of DA-DA-DA. It is the Intelligence in Nature speaking to the Intelligence in man. The Upanishad says:

> The principle of Intelligence is verily Brahman. Like the gossamer web which spins out of the spider's body or like the sparks that spring and fly from the Flame, it is Intelligence which conveys to man the great tidings of Brahman.

Intelligence alone brings to man the intimations of the Unmanifest, it conveys to him the Voice of the Silence, it communicates to him the Call of the Unborn. The man to whom such intimations have come is a spiritually illumined person—he is the one with a Divine Afflatus in him—he speaks the language, not of words, but of the Spirit for, he is an inspired being.

XI

THE ONE—AND THE ONLY ONE

The Śvetāśvatara Upanishad is not included among the Ten Major or Principal Upanishads. And yet such is the beauty and profundity of its teachings that most persons who have commented on the Upanishads have regarded this Upanishad, as if it were one of the major Upanishads. This Upanishad derives its name from the teacher by the name Śvetāśvatara. It begins with an informal discussion among themselves by students, desirous of knowing the eternal verities of life. The subject matter of their discussion is indicated in the opening verse of the Upanishad. It says:

> What is the Cause? Is it Brahman? Whence are we born? What sustains us? Whither are we going? Who distributes pleasures and pain in the differing conditions of life?

These *brahmavādins*—the students engaged in deep inquiry—want to know the Cause of the Universe. Usually there are mainly two causes for the creation of anything. These two causes are the *Upādāna* and *Nimitta*—the material and the efficient. The material cause deals with the materials constituting an object of creation and the efficient cause deals with the instrument or the subject that brings the creation into existence—these are the objective and the subjective causes. For example, for the creation of an earthen pot, clay is the *upādāna* or the material cause —but the potter is the *nimitta* or the efficient cause. In order to go into the question of causation, one must inquire into both these causes. In discussing among themselves, these students of the Divine wisdom asked, "Is time the cause? Or is the very nature of things that has caused this universe? Or has the universe come into existence by some mysterious working of destiny? Or has the universe been brought into existence by the coming together of the Elements? Or is it that the combination of all these causes is the cause of the universe?" Having examined each cause separately and conjointly, they came to the conclusion that none of the above factors could have been the cause of the universe—they may have contributed to the material cause, having supplied the material—but they could not have been the efficient or the instrumental cause. The earthen pot cannot come into existence just because there is a lump of clay lying about. There has to be a potter to use the clay for the creation of the pot. They found the absence of the potter in all the above factors. And so they said that even a combination of all these material factors could not have created the universe. Then surely, the Soul must be the cause of the universe. But they ruled out even the Soul saying it is *Anīśa* —powerless—for it too is affected by pleasure and pain. If the soul cannot free itself from the effects of pain and pleasure, how could it be the cause of the universe?

It is interesting to note that this is the only Upanishad among the major ones to introduce Soul in its discussions. This Soul is obviously not the Spirit or the Ātman which the Upanishads have declared as Brahman. In fact, the main theme of the Upanishads has been that the nature of Brahman resides in the Ātman.. If this be the case, how can it be powerless? And yet, this Upanishad describes Ātman as *anīśa* or powerless, subject to the influence of pleasure and pain. It is quite evident that the Ātman of this Upanishad is not the same Ātman about which all the Upanishads have declared in such glorious terms. With the introduction of this new term, we have to postulate three entities: Brahman, the Ātman or the Self and the Soul. The Soul—that entity which is *anīśa* or powerless because of being affected by pleasure and pain—is obviously the Ego. The Ego, the Spirit and Brahman—this is the triplicity which arrests our attention as we turn to the teachings of this Upanishad.

What is this Ego or the Soul? It is a compound, an accumulation born out of the process of time. Why is it affected by pleasure and pain? Because, it is a product of a duality. In its very make-up there is a resistance to pain and the acceptance of pleasure. To be affected by pleasure and pain shows that there are centres of indulgence and denial in its very constitution. It nourishes what it considers as pleasant and it builds up a resistance against what it calls unpleasant or evil. In the Vedāntic classification this Ego has its abode in what is known as the *Kāraṇa Śarīra* —the Causal Body. It is causal only in the sense in which it supplies the material cause. *Upādāna* does not merely mean the physical material—it also means the psychological material. And this is supplied by the psychic entity known as the Ego. The causal body is the storehouse of psychological tendencies—the psychological memory which supplies the psychic material for the creation of mental, emotional and physical manifestations. The Ego is born of duality—it is the product of time. It is the accumulated and the acquired nature of man. How can this be the cause of the universe? It is subjected to the factors that constitute the universe. The students of divine Wisdom have rightly proclaimed this Ego or the Soul as helpless. But then what is the cause of the Universe? After quiet reflection and meditation, they came to the conclusion that:

> It is the Power belonging to the Absolute, hidden within it that must be the cause of the Universe—the Absolute is the one that presides over all those factors, beginning with Time and ending with the Soul.

They argued that the Universe must have come out of the Absolute—for it alone is without limitation. It is affected neither by Time nor by Necessity—nor by other material or psychic elements. The Absolute or the Supreme Being is the Cause—all else is but the effect. The cause is present in the effect—but, so intangibly and imperceptibly, that one misses the cause and regards the effect itself as the cause. If the Cause is in the effect, then can one find it by dissecting the effect? How can the Intangible be found by breaking up the tangible? When cause is not found by dissecting the effect, then does man say there is no cause—that the universe is just a product of chance or accident. Not finding the cause, man begins to modify the effects—and in this process, that which is earlier in time is regarded as the cause of that which comes later. He thus creates a time interval between cause and effect. He seeks the cause in the process of time. He is thus caught up in the false stream where cause and effect are separated by the interval of time. But the real cause of the Universe is not away from the effect. In the universe, there is a mysterious phenomenon of Cause-Effect, not cause and effect. He who knows this mysterious phenomenon, the secret of the co-existence of Cause and Effect, he alone is freed from all bondage. The Upanishad clearly states this idea in the following verse:

> In this infinite wheel of the supreme Being, in which everything lives and has its being, the swan, or the individual soul, is being tossed about, imagining itself and the promulgator as different.

When cause and effect are considered as separate, one from the other, then is there this tossing about in the whirl-pools of existence. The soul which is the acquired nature regards itself as different from the cause, which is Brahman. The soul or the Ego has a walled existence—it shuts itself behind the walls which it has created. Its one urge is to continue, and for this it builds all types of defence-mechanisms. It gives to these defence mechanisms noble and uplifting names—it calls them by ideals, aspirations, purpose, goal and many other similar epithets. The urge behind all this is its desire for continuity. It throws a veil of its own continuity on the entire phenomenal world. It assumes the lordship of all that forms part of the manifested world. But it is indeed the pretender to the throne—not the real ruler. It wants to usurp the powers of the ruler—but this it wants to do by isolating itself from the scheme of manifestation. It believes that it can continue with the assumed powers only if it shuts itself up in an ivory tower—if it mixes with others, then it would soon be found out. Thus is created a duality of the Higher and the Lower—the Ego regarding itself as the Higher. It must remain free from the unpleasant magnetism of the Lower! The ego must rule over its kingdom by fiats and ordinances—by what it calls the exercise of its will. There ensues an endless conflict between the Higher and the Lower—and man vows to maintain a ceaseless struggle against the lower nature. And the struggle remains endless—there is no end to it—there can never be any end to it. For, the Pretender is inherently weak and so is unable to bring about an integration in his realm.

All this struggle resulting in endless sorrow and suffering would cease, if only man could see the cause in the effect, the Intangible in the tangible, Brahman in the Universe—the Creator in the creation itself. But how can this be done? This is the main subject of all the Upanishads—but to it, the Śvetāśvatara Upanishad brings a fresh and vital understanding. The Upanishad says that it is only when the separate identity built up by the Ego or the soul is broken up, that there comes a realization that Ātman and Brahman are one. In this realization lies bliss eternal for man. Here the Upanishad states the triad of Ātman, Soul and the Manifested world. It says:

> The supreme Brahman is the imperishable and firm substratum of all—the knowers of Brahman, seeing the distinction in the triad, devote themselves to the Supreme Brahman, merge in it and are liberated from all bondage.

What is meant by seeing the distinction in the triad? This is indicated by the ego or the soul intervening and thereby creating a distance between the Ātman and the Manifested world. It is this intervention of the ego which prevents one from seeing the intangible presence of the Ātman in the universe. The above verse says that seeing this distinction, the knowers of Brahman devote themselves to the supreme Brahman. But how?

It may not be out of place to mention here that Śvetāśvatara Upanishad, being a later one, gives indications of those philosophical ideas which made their appearance in the course of religious development in India. One can see here the influence of the Sāṅkhya philosophy with its emphasis on duality. But inspite of this, the main theme of the Śvetāśvatara Upanishad remains Non-dual, in tune with the other Upanishadic thought. There is one difference, however, in this Upanishad, which needs to be mentioned and that is the Name given to the Absolute. While the other Upanishads have refrained from giving any name to Brahman or the Absolute, this Upanishad has described this Ultimate Reality as Śiva. But this does not cause any deviation from the main theme of Non-Duality. The mention of Śiva is not with reference to the Hindu Trinity, for, nowhere do we find any mention in this Upanishad about the two other aspects of the Trinity. This Upanishad has chosen to give a name to the Ultimate Reality—and that name is Śiva. This does not make it a theistic Upanishad as some commentators have suggested. The Absolute with Name that is the distinguishing feature of this Upanishad.

The question is: How does this Upanishad approach the subject of the realisation of the Supreme Being? It is evident from the foregoing discussion that it is the Ego or the Soul with its urge towards continuity, which is the greatest impediment in the search for the Real. The Upanishad says in one of its verses that Brahman has to be realized in immanence and not outside it. But this is possible only when one resolves the middle term in the triad constituted by self, soul and the world. When man discovers the undistorted self in the world, then does he know Brahman, the Ultimate and the Unmanifest. The Upanishad says:

> What is perishable is primary matter. What is immortal and imperishable is the Self. Over both the perishable and the Self it is Brahman that presides. But meditating upon Him, by union with Him, and by entering into his Being more and more is there cessation from all illusion.

It is interesting to note that while other Upanishads have described Brahman by the pronoun IT, this Upanishad speaks of Brahman as He. This is because of the name given to Brahman as Śiva. In the above verse it is stated that matter, Prakṛti, is perishable, but the self is imperishable. But in between comes Soul, the Ego, which identifies itself with Prakṛti, and thereby becomes the enjoyer.

It is this soul which deprives Prakṛti, of the living and intangible touch of the Self. Because the soul projects itself in the world, the reflection of the Self is not seen. The Ego creates agitations in matter for the sake of its own continuity. It is but natural that the reflection of the Self would be broken up when the surface of the lake of matter is agitated. The above verse speaks of meditation or reflection, union and finally the entry into the being of Brahman as the surest way of breaking the knots of all bondage. But before reflection, one has to be aware of the projections of the Ego. Here the Upanishad has indeed given four aspects of liberation— *Sālokya*, *Sāmīpya*, *Sārūpya* and *Sāyujya*—dwelling in the same realm, drawing near to Brahman in His realm, growing into the image of Brahman and finally entering into His Being. It is awareness which enables a man to step out of the world of the Ego. This awareness creates a dissociation from the activities of the ego. With this dissociation man begins to live in the Higher world. By reflection he draws near to Reality. It is this reflection or meditation which creates a miracle, where the son grows into the image of the father—and when finally even the image drops away and man becomes one with Brahman, the Ultimate Reality. Awareness, Meditation, Identification and Unification—these are the steps indicated in the above verse for the realisation of Brahman. The Upanishad says:

> Like oil in sesamum, like butter in curds, like water in river-springs, like fire in wood, the self is realized within oneself by him who perceives IT through Truth and Penance.

Here the Upanishad clearly speaks of the intangible presence of Brahman in all that is tangible. But how is the intangible to be perceived? The above verse speaks of *Satya* and *Tapa*—of Truth and Penance. Once again we see here the co-existence of the positive and the negative. Truth, undoubtedly is something positive—but Penance or *tapa* implies a process of negation. It is only when human consciousness is able to come to the point of the co-existence of the positive and the negative, that there comes the realization of the intangible in the tangible itself. How is butter extracted from the butter-milk? Surely by churning. In churning, it is the churner that moves, but the butter-milk remains steady. It is the movement of the churner in the butter-milk that enables one to extract butter. This is the positive and the negative to which the above verse makes reference by mentioning *Satya* and *Tapa*—Truth and Penance. Elaborating this idea, the Upanishad says:

> Just as an image covered up with mud, shines forth brightly when cleaned, even so realizing the truth of self, the individual becomes the One self. When with his own real self as with a lamp, he sees in concentration the truth of Brahman, he understands the Lord, unborn and unmoving.

Tapa or Penance to which reference had been made in the previous verse implies the process of cleaning up the image so that the mud that is gathered is removed. Then the image shines forth brightly. This is indeed the process of *Tapa* and *Satya*, Penance and Truth. *Tapa* is negating what has accumulated. The Ego or the soul is an accumulation—it is an accretion. And with this there comes into existence an acquired nature. *Tapa* or Penance is the negating of all that has been accumulated and in this process the ego is dissolved, and when this happens there is the clear vision of the self. In the perception of the Self is the discovery of Brahman, the Ultimate Reality. The Upanishad speaks of this as Brahman, the Unborn. Speaking about Brahman, the Upanishad in the next verse says that "Brahman is the born and yet to be born". Born and yet Unborn—that is the mystery of Brahman—but this mystery is unravelled in the discovery of the Self. Such discovery demands the breaking up of the ego, the elimination of the false and the acquired nature.

The Śvetāśvatara Upanishad describes creation as the casting of a net by the creator. This net of creation is the *Māyā*. *Māyā* is regarded as *Śakti*, power, by which Brahman creates the universe and maintains it. The subject of Māyā has been much misunderstood. The approach of Vedānta is not that of solipsism—it does not say that the world is unreal. There is the famous statement of Advaita which says *Brahma satyaṃ jaganmithyā* —Brahman is real, the world is false. But here the falseness of the world is not be construed as the unreality of the world. The *mithyā* indicates the absence of intrinsic existence. The existence of Brahman is intrinsic—it does not depend upon anything else. But *jagat* or the world is *mithyā* — meaning thereby, that it has no intrinsic existence—its existence is derived. It is dependent upon something else. To say that the image in the mirror is false is to make an incorrect statement. The image in the mirror exists—but its existence is derived and not intrinsic. The *Māyā* of the Advaita philosophy does not imply non-existence—it only indicates non-intrinsic existence—or a derived existence. That which is derived does not exist by itself—this is indeed the nature of the world. The thought-image of the mind does not exist by itself—it exists because it is held by the thinker. When the thinker does not hold the image, then it vanishes—it is dissolved. That indeed is the relationship between Brahman and the World. This relationship shows that Brahman is aloof and yet intimate. The Upanishads have declared the Ātman to be identical with Brahman—for IT is the Spark of the same Flame. And so what applies to Brahman applies to Ātman as well. Even though it is a Spark, it contains the Fullness of the Flame. The Ātman projects Its own world—and is reflected in that world like an image in the mirror. If the Ātman or the Self is the Person—the *Purusha*, and if the world is the image, then the question is: In what is this image cast? What is the medium in which the image is reflected? It is in the mirror of consciousness that the image is reflected. So long as the mirror is clean, the image is clear. When the mirror is spotlessly clean, then the intangible can be seen in the tangible, for the image is undistorted. But when the mirror is unclean, then begins the confusion, for the perception of the intangible is lost. The distortions of the image then do not seem as distortions at all—they appear to be real. This is indeed the process of being caught in *Māyā* or illusion. The distortions are the modifications of the image. The modifications seem real, and so man begins to give to the Real the attributes of modifications. Consciousness is indeed the mirror—but it is ego that makes the mirror unclean. This ego comes into existence by the dust that gathers on the mirror. Unless the mirror is cleaned, from moment to moment, there is no hope of man discovering the true nature of Ātman—and without the discovery of the Ātman, Brahman cannot be known. It is the cleaning of the mirror which is indicated in *tapas* or penance, when this is done then the Truth is revealed—and the Truth is the real nature of the Ātman—the Spark which contains the Fullness of the Flame.

When *Sat* or Truth is perceived, then its reflection in the clear mirror is experienced as Joy or *Ānanda*. The world is the expression of *Ānanda* or Joy. But for this experience, between the Ātman and the world, there must exist a mirror of Pure consciousness. Consciousness is the medium—*Sat* expresses itself as *Ānanda* only through *Cit* or Pure consciousness. The world does not seem to us as full of joy or *Ānanda* because the image of the Self gets distorted due to the unclean medium through which it passes. It is the impurity of *Cit* which renders *Sat*, not as *Ānanda* but as full of misery and woe. The living touch of the intangible is shut off—and so the image is rendered utterly lifeless. The image becomes dead and static—the symbol is divorced from a living touch with the substance. Man searches in vain for the Real in the image—he must look to the distorting medium—he must clean up the mirror—for unless this is done, *Sat* cannot be reflected as *Ānanda*.

It is most significant that the Śvetāśvatara Upanishad describes Śiva as the symbol of the Ultimate. In other Upanishads the Sacred word, OM has been stated as the symbol of Brahman. Here Śiva is equated with Brahman. Now Śiva is indeed the expression of *Ānanda*. In this Upanishad we see almost a devotional outburst to Śiva in his aspect as *Ānanda*. The verse in the Upanishad says:

> O Rudra, O Giriśanta, may you bestow upon us your grace, you who are the incarnation of the Good, the Fearless, the Self-effulgent and the Blissful.

The epithet *Rudra* is very apt for it means the destroyer of all that is false. Śiva has two aspects—the *Raudra* and *Saumya*—the Fierce and the Good. They are not contradictory—for, Śiva is Good because he is Fierce. He is Fierce—for, He destroys all that is false. How can there be goodness so long as the false projects itself in one's life? In the destruction of the false, Good comes naturally and spontaneously. This Upanishad speaks of Śiva as *Rudra* because its teaching lays emphasis on the destruction of the false—the wiping away of the assumed name, the elimination of the ego which struts about with its acquired nature. In the above verse, Śiva is described as *Rudra* and also *Giriśanta*—these signify that he is the dweller of the burning ghat, but he is also the dweller of the mountains. The burning ghat symbolises death—but the mountains are the receivers of the first rays of the morning sun. Śiva, the destroyer is also Śiva the resurrecter. Śiva presides over the realms of discontinuity where the manifest merges into the unmanifest and from where the manifest emerges once again. The Śvetāśvatara Upanishad sings in praise of Śiva, the Supreme Being. The verse of the Upanishad says:

> By knowing Him alone does one cross over Death—there is no other path to go.

One conquers death only by knowing Śiva—for to know Him is to probe the very depths of Dis-continuity. To know Him is to know the secret of manifestation and also the mystery of the Unmanifest. Śiva is the presiding deity of that Interval between two manifestations. He is not the Unmanifest as Brahmā is—he is not the Manifest as Vishṇu is—he presides over the Interval where the Manifest has merged into the Unmanifest and where the Unmanifest has not yet emerged into new Manifestation. The Upanishad rightly says that there is no other path to go to for understanding the meaning and the secret of Death. The Upanishad remarks:

> There is nothing beyond or better, nothing bigger or smaller than He.

Here is the description of Brahman—Beyond and Above—That which is the Cause of everything but that, which for ever remains causeless. Of this Brahman, known as *Rudra* in this Upanishad, one of the knowers of Brahman says:

> I know Him, the Mighty man
> Radiant like the Sun, beyond the darkness,
> Him and Him only knowing I cross over death
> No other path at all is there to go.

To say that there is no other path at all to go may seem narrow and dogmatic. But it is not in the sense of a dogma that this statement is made. Without knowing *Rudra* how can death be known? And without knowing death, how can one know Brahman, the Great Beyond? The burning ghat is indeed the pathway to the kingdom of death. Here the burning ghat is not to be understood in its physical sense—it is a place of cremation where all the possessions and accumulations of the mind are left behind. It is said in the Christian scripture that it is possible that from the eye of a needle a camel may pass but not a rich man. Here the rich man is one who has many possessions of the mind. To leave all possessions behind—that is the only path along which one can walk into the realms of death and return totally renewed and resurrected. To signify this, Śiva is described as one who has space as His garment. Clad in nothingness, He presides over that narrow path which leads through death to Immortality. The Upanishad says:

> That which is beyond this world
> Is without form and without ill,
> They who know that become immortal,
> Others go only to sorrow.

The two words used to describe this Ultimate Reality are *Arūpa* and *Anāmaya*. Arūpa is Formless but what does *anāmaya* mean? Literally it means free from all disease. It obviously means that which is incorruptible. It is the form that gets corrupted—the Formless is for ever uncorrupt and incorruptible. He who is subject to corruption can never know what immortality is. But to know a state beyond corruption, there is no other path except through a communion with the Formless. In another verse, Brahman is described as *avyaya* meaning One in whom there is no fluctuation. The Upanishad says that this Brahman, not bigger than the size of the thumb and residing in the heart of man, can be comprehended only through a totality of mind, a sensitivity of intellect and a firmness of faith. It is not a distracted mind, running hither and thither, that can know this Brahman. Nor can It be known by an intellect that is dull. The verse of the Upanishad says that man must have an unshakable faith. When can such faith be born? When there is a totality of attention. But what happens in this totality of attention so as to generate faith? The totality of attention brings a sensitivity of consciousness. And this sensitive consciousness is able to perceive the subtle and the intangible. He who can see the intangible in the tangible has a faith that can never be shaken. The perception of the intangible calls out that awe and wonder before which one can only stand in utter faith. One can see the support and the sustenance of the tangible—but by what is the Intangible supported—from what does it derive its sustenance? Apparently from Nothing. To see that the Intangible is rooted in Nothing is to stand speechless. It is the mystery of the Nothing which generates an unshakable faith. The verse of the Upanishad says that having pervaded the universe, It stands above that universe. In this, it is clearly indicated that Brahman, that is infinite cannot be contained by the finite. The universe is finite; how can it contain the Infinite? How can a form, however great it may be, contain the Formless?

We said in the earlier part of this chapter that the Śvetāśvatara Upanishad has sometimes been described as an Upanishad which advocates the *Sāṅkhya* philosophy as distinguished from the Non-Dual or the *Advaita*. But this is not correct, for it stands unequivocally for the Non-Dual approach which constitutes the main theme of the whole

Upanishadic philosophy. Any doubt on this point is completely cleared by the following verse:

> Brahman alone is—there is none other in the realm of time or beyond Time. The whole manifested world exists because of Him.

He alone exists—what greater indication of the Absolute philosophy can ever be given? In this Upanishad the Ultimate Reality is described as having a thousand heads and a thousand eyes and a thousand feet. This is to suggest that It pervades everything. How can one imagine Brahman as pervading everything unless we speak of Him as having a *Virāṭ Rūpa*, having a Body with vast extensions? But while the Upanishad speaks of a thousand feet and a thousand hands, it says something utterly strange in the following verse:

> Without hands It grasps every one, without feet It runs everywhere, without eyes It sees everything, without ears It hears everything—It knows everything—but nobody knows IT.

How utterly paradoxical it is—that Brahman who has a thousand hands and a thousand feet—has at the same time no hands and no feet! What is one to understand? Has Brahman hands and feet—or has It no hands and feet? Both are true. But if both are true, then it is something that the mind of man cannot understand. Intellect reels before such a statement. The intellect of man must for ever return from this effort—for it cannot find Brahman. How can it explain the following verse which appears in this Upanishad?

> Unborn and Timeless—and yet existing everywhere
> He is unborn and yet never ceases to exist.

Surely, that which exists must be born. How can that which is unborn exist at the same time? It is like saying that Existence and Non-existence are present at the same time. This is utterly meaningless to the mind of man. Even the subtlest intellect cannot grasp it. Unborn and yet existing everywhere—Timeless and yet present at every moment of time.

The entire Śvetāśvatara Upanishad is a hymn of adoration in praise of the Supreme, the *Maheśvara*. It is because of this that it is known as the Upanishad surcharged with a feeling of devotion. It has not gone into philosophical questions—nor has it dealt with the doubts of the students. It has sung hymns in adoration of the Great Being, the Infinite *Purusha*—who is both existent and non-existent. The Upanishad says:

> He who Himself is without any colour, imparts colours to all things with a purpose known by none—He is the One who is both the end and the beginning of all the worlds.

The *brahmavādins* —the students of the Divine Wisdom say—"May He bestow upon us a clear intellect." Why this prayer for the bestowal of a clear intellect? Will man be able to know the Supreme Being with a clear intellect? No, he cannot—but a clear intellect is one which enables a man to know what intellect is unable to give. There is no clearer intellect than the one which knows its own limitations. So long as the intellect does not know its limitations, so long does it engage itself in ceaseless efforts. All these efforts are fruitless—but it does not give up its efforts, for, it feels that it has limitless powers. Wisdom dawns upon the consciousness of man only when the effort of the intellect ceases. But the effort of the mind cannot be ended by a conscious effort—the cessation of effort itself has to be effortless. This happens when the mind becomes aware of its own limitations—when it realises that its efforts can lead nowhere.

In the above verse Brahman is described as One in whom both the beginning and the end find their abode. Here one is reminded of what the *Bhagavad Gītā* says, where it speaks of the beginning and the end being the Unmanifest and only the middle state representing the Manifest. It is the Unmanifest which is the fundamental nature of all things—the Manifest is only a condition which arises between the two states of the Unmanifest. The grace and the charm of the manifest lie where the manifest does not cling to its existence—where it makes no effort to prolong its continuity. The expressed must come like the wink of the eye—like a flash of lightning. It is only as a flash that it becomes enchanting. Any effort to give a continuity to the expressed condition—to the manifest state—is devoid of grace and modesty. To give a continuity to any expression is to impart to it an exaggeration—and all exaggeration is vulgar. Poet Rabindranath Tagore says:

> Beauty knows to say, "enough"; barbarism clamours for still more.

Any effort to give a continuity to the expressed and the manifest is barbarism. The Manifest is only a passage from the Unmanifest to the Unmanifest. In the passage one must move on—one cannot settle down. As a Sufi Saint says—"Life is like a bridge, pass over it, do not build upon it". The beginning and the end reside in Brahman—the world is only the passing phase of the Manifest—such is the inspiring teaching of the Śvetāśvatara Upanishad. It is to this all-pervasive and yet ever elusive nature of Brahman that the following verse of the Upanishad refers:

> Thou woman dost become, and man and youth, and also tender maid, when old, Thy steps with staff dost thou support—Thou takest birth with face on every side.

Viśvatomukha —with face on every side, that is the description of Brahman in manifestation. There is no limit to Its expression, there is no restriction to the Form in which the Formless incarnates. The Manifest is impermanent—it moves on, it is ephemeral—like a flash it comes and goes. It is ever changeful—the Unmanifest alone is changeless. But the Changeless appears in myriads of changeful forms. He who does not hold on to any particular Form, sees the beauty of the Formless in form after form. He sees the Formless appearing in new forms from moment to moment. The Formless appearing in new forms is the great play or the *Līlā* shown by Śrī Kṛshṇa to the simple cow-herd maidens, the Gopīs. The Upanishad says:

> Of what use is the repeating of the sacred hymns of the Vedas, if one does not know the Imperishable source from where all the Vedas have emanated?

The Upanishad does not say—Do not adore the Perishable. It only says—of what use is this adoration if the

Imperishable, which is the source of all manifestation is not known? Of what use is the symbol if the substance is not known? The symbol has its place—but only after knowing the substance. The symbol is the Form even as the substance is the Formless. The form of anything derives its meaning and significance from the Formless. It is the Formless which gives life to the form. But men worship the Form without knowing the Formless—and so their worship and adoration tend to become a mere ceremonial, a routine, a dead monotony. And the drudgery of this monotony tires and exhausts such a person. He is bored by the sameness of life—for he has clung to the form and thus closed his doors of perception to that which alone can give newness to things. The Form is the *māyā* or the illusion, for, it has no intrinsic existence—it exists because of the Formless. The Formless is the *māyin*—the producer of illusion—and the Form is the *māyā*—illusion itself. The Upanishad says:

> The *Prakṛti* or Nature is the *Māyā*—illusion, and the *Maheśvara*—the Mighty Lord, is the *māyin* or the illusion-maker. The whole world is pervaded with beings that are parts of Him.

The whole manifested world consists only of the parts—the whole is the Unmanifest. The Whole is the creator—the creation consists only of the parts. The whole is in the parts and yet, the whole cannot be found by collecting the parts together. The mystery of the whole resides in the part—and yet this mystery cannot be unravelled by bringing the parts together. The whole resides as the quality of things and the quality cannot be understood by bringing the parts together. By no quantitative effort can the quality be comprehended. To comprehend the quality of things is to know the Ancient Wisdom—it is ancient not because it is old—it is ancient because it is ageless. The Ancient Wisdom resides everywhere—even in the tiniest speck of matter—for it is the quality of things. How can one find this quality of things? The Upanishad says:

> It is beyond all mentation—it is to be seen when there is neither day nor night—where there is neither cause nor effect.

The Śvetāśvatara Upanishad says that it is from this

condition that the Ancient Wisdom is born. It is born neither during day nor during night—it comes from a realm where there is neither cause nor effect. The Ancient Wisdom has its abode in the Non-Dual—for, cause and effect exist only in the realm of duality. The Upanishad says that it is Formless and so no form can contain it. Of what use is the construction of frame after frame—when It cannot be grasped in any frame? In one of the verses of the Upanishad, it is said that there is no picture—*Pratimā* available anywhere of this *Maheśvara* —the Supreme Lord, the creator of *māyā*.

When no picture is available, of what use is the creating of frames, however beautiful these frames may be? The Upanishad does not speak about the Picture without a frame—it speaks of Frame without a picture! Without knowing the Person—the *Maheśvara*, all our efforts are like putting up a frame in which there is no picture whatsoever. The frame without a picture is useless—and when *Maheśvara*, the Supreme Lord, is known, no frame becomes necessary.

But how is one to know the *Maheśvara* —one who cannot be put in any frame, however subtle it may be? The Upanishad says that the Supreme Being cannot be known by the senses nor by the mind. But then how? The Śvetāśvatara Upanishad says that he, whose intellect abides in the heart—he alone knows the nature of the Supreme Being. The intellect abiding in the heart—that is the strange condition which this Upanishad has prescribed for the realisation of Brahman, for the comprehension of the Nature of *Maheśvara*, the Supreme Being.

Intellect abiding in the heart—this obviously refers to the simultaneous existence of Impersonality and Intimacy. The intellect is impersonal and objective but the heart is always warm and intimate. It is said that mere intellect is as cold as snow—and mere heart is as fleeting as vapour. But when these two come together, then is there the arising of the living waters of life. Impersonal and yet intimate—that indeed is the approach which will enable man to unlock the secrets of life. He can be initiated into the mysteries of man and universe when there is complete fusion of the mind and the heart. It is the fusion of the positive and the receptive, for the intellect is positive and the heart is receptive. One of the forms of Śiva is *Ardha-nārīśvara* —it is a form in which the masculine and the feminine aspects co-exist—it is a state of intellect abiding in the heart. To know Śiva, the *Ardha-nārīśvara* —one must have a consciousness where the impersonality of the masculine co-exists with the intimacy of the feminine. To such a consciousness the Supreme Being reveals Himself in all his glory and majesty. Of this Supreme Being, the Upanishad says:

> In the unbounded Imperishable Being, the pair of knowledge and ignorance, *vidyā* and *avidyā*, are mysteriously co-existent. Ignorance is perishable, knowledge is immortal. He who controls both knowledge and ignorance is beyond the realm of both. This Supreme Being is neither male nor female.

The negative state of consciousness is that where the Positive and the Receptive co-exist. A consciousness that is only positive tends to become aggressive—but a consciousness that is only receptive tends to become inert and inactive. Active and yet not aggressive—receptive and yet not inert—that is what Śiva, the *Ardha-nārīśvara* is. It is only Śiva that can know Śiva—it is only when the consciousness of man shows forth the qualities of the *Ardha-nārīśvara* that he can comprehend the nature of the Supreme Being, the *Maheśvara*. But with this consciousness where is He to be found? Where is one to see? The Upanishad says He is *anīḍa* —He is one who has no abode. How can one find one who has no abode? The consciousness of man cannot find Him—He comes to the consciousness in which the quality of the *Ardha-nārīśvara* manifests itself. There He comes—He cannot be sought after. Existing nowhere, He comes from anywhere.

The knower of Brahman, the *brahmavādins*, the students of the Divine Wisdom, say of Him thus:

> We know Him, the Over-lord, Supreme of Lords,
> The God, Supreme of Gods,
> King of Kings, Supreme of the Supreme
> Lord of the Universe, the God of our adoration.

Nowhere in the entire range of Upanishads do we find such expression of deep devotion as we see in the Śvetāśvatara Upanishad. Knowledge must culminate in devotion—if it does not, then it is not true knowledge, it is mere verbiage—a collection of words and names. He who knows, becomes speechless—for in the moment of true knowledge he sees the Splendour of Splendid things. Even Śrī Śaṅkarācārya, the greatest exponent of the Non-Dual philosophy, the teacher of uncompromising Advaita, who emphasised knowledge above everything else, speaks of Him, the Imperishable, in words that are replete with deep and profound devotion. He says:

> Lord of Gaurī, as the swan loves the lotus-bed, the Cātaka bird, the dark, water-laden cloud, the Koka bird, the sun every-day and the Cakora bird, the moon—even so, O Lord of Beings, my mind desires your lotus feet, which, sought through the path of knowledge, bestow the happiness of salvation.

In various religious disciplines one speaks of the Three Paths—the Path of Knowledge, the Path of Devotion and the Path of Action. There are no three paths, distinct and separate one from the other. These three together form the whole spiritual life. Life consists of action—for without action no one can live, not even for one moment. But an action that does not spring from devotion is no action at all—it is a mere reaction. Action must emerge from the Fullness of Devotion, if it has to have a spiritual quality. Similarly, knowledge will remain dry as dust, if it does not find its fulfilment in devotion. Knowledge is like directing the course of many rivers—but where will these rivers go? They must merge in the sea. The merging of the separate rivers in the sea is indeed an experience of devotion. The Advaita, in terms of mind's knowledge, can speak only of Non-Duality—it cannot go further than that. But Advaita, in terms of Devotion, brings to man an experience of One-ness. The Non-dual is negative—the One-ness is positive. Into the negative state of the mind must flow the positive experience of devotion. Man cannot act from the point of negativity —he can act only from the Ground of Positivity. But the positive is outside the range of the mind. Knowledge can create the conditions of negativity—and that is the highest to which the mind of man can go. It is devotion which brings the positive content of experience. Devotion is indeed the meeting place both of knowledge and action. Śrī Śaṅkarācārya says, in the above verse, that after having sought the Supreme Being through knowledge, his one desire is to touch the lotus-feet of the Lord—for it is only thus that he can come to the happiness of salvation. It comes as a grace from on high—but the grace comes in the moment of the perfect negativity of the mind. It comes when the mind of man declares—*Neti, Neti*—Not this, Not this.

The Śvetāśvatara Upanishad is indeed the culminating point of the whole process of knowledge which the other Upanishads have indicated. The Upanishadic teachers were not engaged in dry, metaphysical speculations —they were sages who spoke the language of experience. They led their disciples through the path of negation to the positive experience of Brahman. They showed the path leading from the *Brahmavid* to the *Brahmanishṭha*. Along the path of knowledge, one becomes a *brahmavid*, but this is not enough—he must become a *Brahmanishṭha*—but this experience comes only in the moment of deep devotion. It is to this experience of devotion that the Śvetāśvatara Upanishad leads the students of the Divine Wisdom. Of the Supreme Being, the Upanishad says:

> He is the one Being, hidden in all creatures, pervading all, the inner self of all, the perceiver of all deeds, the presider of all beings, the witness, the knower, the only one, completely devoid of attributes.

He pervades all and yet at the same time is the witness of all that happens. He is immanent and yet at the same time, He is the witness to His own immanence. The Upanishad says that he who can see this Supreme Being within his own heart—he knows what Eternal Bliss is. But it is only as man becomes both the actor and the witness at the same time, that he can come to this comprehension. To be a witness in the midst of participation—

that is the secret which the Upanishad gives to the students of the Divine Wisdom. It says:

> Alone in this universe, He comes and goes,
> It is He who is the fire, the water He pervadeth,
> Him and Him only knowing, I cross over death,
> No other path at all there is to go.

There is no other path at all to go—so declares the Śvetāśvatara Upanishad in unmistakable terms. But which is this Path? It is the Path of knowing Him and Him alone. But He can be known only in the act of complete surrender. A surrender is indeed a total action—there can be no reservation in it. Wherever a man acts totally, without any reservation, there he comes to the experience of this Supreme Being—it does not matter what the field of total action is. This totality of action is verily death. Death does not permit of any reservations—death demands a totality of action. The Supreme Being whom this Upanishad has described as Śiva can be known only in the realm of death. Strangely enough, the experience of death is indeed the experience of love—for love too is a total action. In fact, Love and Death are not two different things—they are the two sides of a medallion. He who knows how to die, knows in that act of dying what supreme love is. Death is a negation—love is the positive experience. But the positive experience of love comes only in the moment of death. In the moment of death one is stripped of everything—one is divested even of oneself—and is this also not the moment of Love? Death is indeed a surrender—but it is only in surrender that the Gift of Love comes. The student of the Divine Wisdom declares:

> I surrender to Him, who is the bridge of Immortality, who is without parts, who is motionless, who is beyond corruption, who is above all attachment—who is like the Flaming Fire that emits no smoke.

The Fire that emits no smoke—this is the description of that Supreme Being to whom one surrenders in the moment of highest knowledge. The next verse in this Upanishad indicates that it is only as man regards space as his only covering that he will come to the realization of the

Supreme Being. To be covered by space alone—this is the condition of being divested of everything. To know Space as the only covering is to live under the canopy of heaven. To live in the open, seeking no shelter except the shelter of space—this is the path of spiritual wisdom. Indeed, there is no other path at all to go.

It is very significant that this Upanishad ends with an instruction by Sage Śvetāśvatara to his pupils in which he says that the Esoteric Wisdom of the Upanishad should not be imparted to one who is *Aśānta*, one who is *Aputra* and one who is *Aśishya*. It is not to be given to one who has a restless mind—a mind distracted hither and thither, for, it is a superficial mind feeding itself on sensations and excitements. To such a mind, it is utterly useless to give this Supreme Wisdom. It is like casting pearls before an indiscriminate being. But the Upanishad says that its teaching should not be given to one who is *Aputra*—one who has no son. This indicates a mind that is barren. It signifies a mind that is utterly dry, devoid of deep and passionate interest. Of what use is the teaching to a person who is devoid of feeling? The Upanishad further says that the teaching of the Divine Wisdom should not be given to one who is *aśishya* —One who is not teachable. *Aśishya* is one whose mind is closed—there is no space in it. Thus the Upanishad says that for the understanding of the great spiritual Wisdom, it is of the highest importance that one should possess a mind that is not fleeting, a mind that is not barren and a mind that is not closed. A fleeting mind is a dull mind, moving only when an external stimulus comes. A barren mind is a frustrated mind for, it is engaged in an effort that can never bear fruit. An unteachable mind is a closed mind—a mind in which there is no room whatsoever. The Wisdom of the Upanishad can be known only by a mind that is alert, a mind that is full of a deep passion and a mind that is completely open —a mind that is thoroughly vulnerable—for it has nothing to defend. It is only the defenceless mind that can know what total surrender is—its surrender has no reservations, it has nothing to keep back, nothing to hide or to protect.

But it is not the surrender of a dull or a barren mind. Alert and vibrant with life—and yet completely defenceless—that is the condition in which total and spontaneous surrender comes. The moment of surrender is indeed the moment of consecration. Having wandered far and wide, the individual has returned to his home—to the realm that belongs to him. Received and welcomed by the King of Kings, the Supreme of the Supreme, he comes to his true stature and dignity, the Prince of the Realm, over which presides the Supreme Lord of Lords—He from whom the universe comes, by Whom it is sustained and in Whom it is dissolved—He is indeed One without a second, the source of all Bliss, radiant like the sun, beyond all darkness—Him and Him only knowing one crosses over death—for no other path at all is there to go— *Nānyaḥ Panthāḥ Vidyate Ayanāya.*

ACKNOWLEDGEMENTS

1. *A Source Book in Indian Philosophy*—Radhakrishnan and Moore.
2. *The Indian Heritage*—V. Raghavan.
3. *The Wisdom of the Upanishads*—Annie Besant.
4. *The Upanishads*—T. M. P. Mahadevan.
5. *Upanishads—In Story and Dialogue*—R. R. Diwakar.
6. *Himalayas of the Soul*—J. Mascaro.
7. *Principal Upanishads*—Swami Sivananda.
8. *The Upanishads*—Swami Nikhilananda.
9. *The Brihadaranyaka Upanishad*—Ramakrishna Math, Madras.
10. *The Upanishads*—G. R. S. Mead and J. C. Chattopadhyaya.
11. *The Religious Mysticism of the Upanishads*—R. Gordon Milburn.
12. *Upanishads for the Lay Reader*—C. Rajagopalachari.
13. *The Foundations of Indian Culture*—Sri Aurobindo.
14. *The Perennial Philosophy*—Aldous Huxley.
15. *Vedanta for the Western World*—Edited by Christopher Isherwood.
16. *Vedanta for the Modern Man*—Edited by Christopher Isherwood.
17. *The Yoga of the Kathopanishad*—Sri Krishna Prem.
18. *The Upanishads*—Published by the Gita Press (In Hindi).
19. *Nine Upanishads*—Nalin Bhatt (in Gujarati).
20. *The Chandogya Upanishad*—Nalin Bhatt (in Gujarati).
21. *The Living Zen*—Robert Lissen.
22. *Sadhana*—Rabindra Nath Tagore.
23. *Mundaka Upanishad*—Swami Chinmayananda.
24. *The Divine Vision*—C. Jinarajadasa.
25. *Thoughts for Meditation*—N. Gangulee.
26. *The Twelve Principal Upanishads*—T. P. H. Madras.
27. *The Meaning of Personal Existence*—A. W. Osborn.
28. *Mysticism and Philosophy*—W. T. Stace.

INDEX

(The words *Brahman* and *Ātman* have not been indexed as they occur constantly in the text.)

Ācārya, 188
Action, Path of, 110
Acquired nature, 40, 142, 253
Adhvaryu, 122
Adler, 145, 151, 275
Advaita, 173, 299, 303, 310
Afflatus, Divine, 290
Agni, 41, 42, 44, 47, 212
Ajara, 112
Ajātaśatru, 255, 256, 257
Ākāśa, 247, 276
Akratu, 69
Akshara, 67, 118, 281
Alan Watts, 9
Alone, 2, 24, 115, 131
Alūksha, 190, 191
Amana, 132, 276
Amara, 112
Amṛta, 226
Anāmaya, 302
Ānanda, 300
Annamayakośa, 97, 270
Anantam, 194
Anavadyāni, 189
Anīḍa, 309
Anīśa, 292
Antaka, 60
Antaryāmin, 278
Apāna, 102, 213
Apara, 116, 117, 121, 122, 123, 129, 132, 133, 134, 139, 197, 223
Aparigraha, 20
Apīti, 166, 167, 168, 170
Āpti, 150, 154
Aputra, 313
Ardha-nārīśvara, 309
Aristocrat, Spiritual, 17
Arnold, Edwin, 258
Articulate, sound, 66, 67, 110, 111, 147, 148, 149, 225
Arūpa, 302
Aśānta, 313
Aśishya, 313
Asmitā, 236
Atharva Veda, 116, 146
Ati-mukti, 270
Atipraśna, 100
Ativādin, 249
Audible sound, 147, 148
Aurobindo, Sri, 7, 8
Austerity, 89, 90, 91
Avataras, Hindu, 205
Avyaya, 303
Avidyā, 236
Awakening, 39, 81
Ayana, 248
Āyatana, 210

Bala, 178, 179
Becoming, 14, 15, 16, 17, 43, 248, 253
Behaviour, 25, 26, 37, 53, 200
Being, 14, 16, 17, 20, 57, 237, 238, 239, 240, 252, 256
Belief, 25, 26, 51
Beloved, 49
Beyond, 60, 61, 62, 63, 65, 66, 67, 68, 69, 70, 79, 86, 263, 302
Bhagavad Gītā, 10, 15, 144, 181, 284, 305
Bhārgava Vaidarbhi, 97
Bhakti, 111
Bhṛgu, 201
Bhūmā, 249
Brahmā, 46
Brahmacarya, 90, 91, 92, 187, 188, 223, 229, 230
Brahmanishṭha, 130, 133, 229, 279, 233, 311
Brahmavādin, 291, 305, 309
Bṛhaspati, 197
Buddhi, 73, 74, 75, 76, 111
Buddhic plane, 94, 109, 112, 114

Causeless Cause, 132
Chaung Tzu, 263
Choicelessness, 157
Christian scriptures, 204
Clairaudience, 147
Clairvoyance, 119, 120
Communication, 63, 65, 72, 114, 115, 161, 178, 182, 183, 184, 226, 233
Communion, 21, 51, 52, 63, 64, 115, 158, 183, 233, 234, 265, 281
Conscious, 105, 152
Consciousness, Pure, 68, 70, 84, 150
Continuity, 27, 28, 29, 39, 46, 56, 57, 59, 61, 77, 79, 85, 86, 93, 95, 98,

103, 143, 156, 157, 158, 160, 161, 162, 163, 166, 169, 187, 188, 189, 193, 194, 198, 218, 235, 247, 268, 294, 305, 306
Convocation address, 184, 185, 187, 191, 192, 200
Cosmic Mind, 93
Cosmogonies, 204 ,206
Cosmography, 205
Creative Living, 9

DA-DA-DA, 290
Dāmyata, 288
Darwin, Charles 204
Datta, 288
Dayadhvam, 208, 290
Death, 26, 27, 28, 46, 50, 51, 54, 55, 56, 57, 58, 59, 60, 61, 62, 63, 72, 73, 77, 78, 81, 82, 83, 84, 85, 86, 281, 282, 301, 312
Deep Sleep, 105, 107, 108, 166, 167, 168, 170, 171, 172, 173, 174, 215, 252, 286, 287
Depth, dimension of, 9, 134
Destroyer, 46
Dhāraṇā, 262
Dharma, 185
Dhātu-prasāda, 69
Dhyānī, 262
Diagnosis technique of, 144
Discipline, 52
Discontinuity, 27, 28, 29, 46, 77, 85, 156, 157, 160, 166, 170, 187, 188, 199, 301
Dream, 105, 106, 107, 152, 153, 154, 155, 156, 252, 256, 286
Duality, 93, 94, 95, 96, 97, 98, 138, 143, 162, 168, 171, 182, 195, 214, 248, 254, 288, 295
Dzyan, Stanzas of, 206

Ecstasy, 39
Education, 175, 221
Egg-born, 209, 211
Ego, 292, 293, 294, 295, 296, 297
Einstein, 204, 278
Elixir of Life, 225, 226
Emptiness, 13, 22, 24, 45, 70, 71, 72, 242, 250, 253
Energy, 89, 91, 92, 223
Eshaṇās, 275
Esoteric, 134, 231, 313
Evolution, 204, 205, 216
Existence, 57, 80, 81, 83, 101
Experience, 25, 26, 221
Expression, 25, 26, 221

Faith, 89, 90, 91, 92, 122
Formless, 19, 114
Freud, Sigmund, 145, 151, 153, 275

Galelio, 204
Gandha, 177
Gārgī, 276, 277, 279, 280, 281, 282

Head-Learning, 130, 190
Hearer, Order of, 177
Homo-Sapiens, 211
Hotā, 122
How, Why and What, 30, 31
Humanities, 184, 222

Identity, 142, 143
Immanence, 27, 139, 140
Immanent, 19, 20, 28, 34, 35, 79, 112, 121, 254, 311
Immortality, 26, 27, 28, 59, 60, 72, 77, 86, 138, 215, 216, 255, 266, 267, 269, 278, 281, 282, 290, 302, 303
Imperishable, 67, 68, 81, 82, 86, 120, 130, 138, 140, 143, 147, 202, 278, 307, 310
Inarticulate Sound, 66, 67, 110, 111, 147, 148, 149, 225
Incomparable, 21
Inaudible Sound, 147, 148
Incorporeal, 18
Incorruptible, 18, 19, 79, 117, 234
Indra, 42, 44, 47, 123, 197, 250, 251, 252
Inner Ruler, 277, 278
Inquiry, curiosity and, 30
Intangible, 19, 35, 77, 78, 79, 80, 82, 83, 86, 101, 104, 171, 172, 183, 214, 215, 238, 257, 293, 297, 303
Intelligence, 73, 74, 75, 76, 108, 202, 219, 220, 289
Interval, 37, 39, 46, 47, 70, 170
Invulnerable, 18, 19

Jāgarit, 150, 152, 154, 155, 170, 215
James Jeans, 93
Janaka, 2, 269, 276, 279, 283, 284, 285, 286, 288
Jānaśruti, 226, 231
Jesus, 137, 142
Jinarajadasa, C., 257
Joad, C. E. M., 241
Jung, Carl, 145, 153, 275

Kabir, 174
Kahn, Dr., 241
Kāmaloka, 55, 56
Kant, Immanuel, 171
Kāraṇa Śarīra, 293
Kātyāyana, Kabandhī, 93, 97
Kātyāyanī, 258

Kausalya. 100, 101
Kavi, 21, 23, 24, 27
Knower, 37, 38, 68, 88, 143, 195
Known, 37, 38, 88, 143, 195
Kośa, 104

Learning, 116, 175, 176, 184, 190
Līlā, 306
Livingness, 32
Lokas, 207, 208, 223
Love, 22, 49, 96, 97, 121, 173, 203, 260, 261, 265, 312

Madhu-Vidyā, 226
Mahāvākya, 147, 215, 239
Maheśvara, 304, 308, 309
Mahidāsa Aitareya, 206
Mahimā, 107
Manana, 261, 262, 263
Manīshī, 21, 23, 24, 27, 262
Maitreyī, 258, 259, 260, 264, 265, 266, 268, 276
Maṇḍūka the teacher, 146
Manomayakośa, 101, 104, 105, 109, 112, 270
Mātrā, 110, 112, 178, 179
Max Muller, 87
Māyā, 11, 133, 298, 299, 307, 308
Meditation, 109, 110, 111, 136, 157, 158, 259, 274, 297
Middle Way, 76
Montessori, Madam Maria, 144
Motion, Infinite, 13, 14, 15, 73, 140, 239
Mutation, 255
Mysticism, 8, 12, 30, 53
Myths, 153, 154, 163, 168

Naciketā, 51, 52, 53, 54, 55, 56, 57, 58, 59, 60, 61, 62, 64, 65, 68, 69, 70, 72, 73, 74, 76, 77, 78, 79, 80, 82, 83, 85, 86, 259
Nāda-brahma, 148
Nāma, 113
Name, 43, 142, 143, 173, 225, 245, 296
Nameless, 173, 174, 237
Nārada, 221, 222, 223, 224, 245, 247, 249, 250
Negative State, 69, 129
Negative Way, 12, 13
Negativity, 70
Nescience, 115
Neti, Neti, 257, 258, 284, 285, 287, 311
Newton, 204
Nididhyāsana, 259, 261, 263
Night, Silent, 45
Nimitta, 291
Nivṛtti, 141

Non-Being, 57
Non-Distraction, 141
Non-Existence, 57
Nothing, 18, 45, 239
Nothingness, 12, 13, 46, 131, 224, 233, 240, 241, 245, 253

Occult, 57
OM, 65, 66, 67, 68, 109, 110, 111, 112, 147, 148, 225, 300
Omnipresence, 12, 78, 119
Original, 21, 22, 23, 24, 27, 68, 70, 236, 237

Padam, 65, 66, 67
Para, 116, 117, 120, 121, 128, 129, 132, 133, 134, 137, 141, 143, 223
Para-dharma, 17
Paradox, 12, 13, 18, 70, 81, 136, 147
Paribhū, 21, 22, 24, 27
Paroksha, 117
Perception, Right, 16
Personal Memory, 151, 152, 153, 154, 155, 157, 158, 159, 160, 161, 162, 163, 165, 166, 167
Personal Unconscious, 145
Pervader, 21
Philosophy, 144, 146
Pippalāda, 89, 90, 91, 94, 97, 99, 100, 102, 109, 114, 222, 223
Pitṛ, 99
Pleasant, 60
Plenum, 13, 70, 249, 250
Prajñāna 219
Prajāpati, 93, 94, 97, 197, 250, 251, 252, 288
Prājña, 170
Prakṛti, 296, 297, 307
Prāṇa, 80, 81, 93, 94, 98, 99, 100, 101, 102, 103, 106, 107, 109, 248, 270, 277
Prāṇamaya-kośa, 99, 101, 104, 270
Pratyāhāra, 26
Pratyaksha, 117
Pravṛtti, 141
Pretya, 266
Psychology, 144, 145, 146, 153, 159, 241
Psycho-analysis, 144
Psychiatrist, 145
Purity, 89, 90, 91

Quality, 10, 11, 14, 15, 16, 17, 18, 19, 20, 24, 29, 31, 32, 33, 34, 69, 307

Racial Memory, 153, 154, 155, 156, 157, 158, 159, 160, 161, 162, 163, 164, 165, 167, 168
Radhakrishnan, S., 4

Raikva, 226, 227, 228
Rajas, 43, 45, 289
Rasa, 177, 203
Rayi, 93, 94
Rest, Infinite, 13, 14, 15, 73, 140, 239
Robert Lissen, 235
Rudra, 301, 302
Rūpa, 113, 177

Sadhana, 13
Sāma, 178, 179
Samāna, 102
Saṃhitā, 179, 180
Sanatkumāra, 221, 222, 224, 245, 247, 248, 249, 250
Sanātana-dharma, 201
Sandhāna, 180, 181, 182, 183, 187, 193, 194, 195, 199
Sandhi, 180, 181, 182, 183, 187, 193, 199, 200
Sāṅkhya, 295, 303
Saṃsāra, 11, 124
Sattva, 43, 44, 45, 289
Satyam, 194
Satyakāma, 109, 112
Satyakāma Jābāla, 228, 229, 230, 231, 232, 233
Sannyāsa, 187, 188, 199, 200, 201
Śaunaka, 116, 118, 132, 134, 135
Sauryāyaṇī Gārgya, 103, 105
Science, 50, 87, 88, 94, 184, 204, 277
Self-luminous, 83
Senses, selectivity of, 87, 88
Śabda, 177
Śaṅkarācārya, 310, 311
Śakuntalā, 191
Śraddhā, 90, 91, 92, 223
Śravaṇa, 261, 262, 263
Śrāvaka, 177, 261, 262
Śrotriya, 133, 134, 197, 279
Śiva, 46, 47, 72, 296, 301, 302, 309, 312
Sorokin, Pitrim, 146
Soul-wisdom, 130
Space, Immensity of, 21, 22, 23, 24
Sparśa, 177
Spirit, 17, 18, 19, 20, 21, 23, 24, 28, 29, 30, 32, 33, 34, 35, 41, 45, 100, 101, 142, 207, 208, 209, 210, 211, 214, 215, 216, 217, 227, 239, 240, 243
Sthāṇu, 81, 82
Sub-conscious, 105, 107, 108, 145, 146, 151, 152, 153, 154, 155, 159, 163, 168, 169, 171
Sukeśa, 113
Sushupti, 166, 215
Svadharma, 17, 43
Svapiti, 256
Svara, 178, 179
Svapna, 152, 170, 215
Śvetāśvatara, teacher, 291
Śvetaketu, 235, 236, 237, 238, 239, 240, 242, 243, 244, 245, 250
Svayambhū, 21, 22, 23, 24, 207
Symbols, 153, 154, 163, 168

Tadvanam, 49
Tagore, Rabindra Nath, 13, 203, 267, 306
Taijasa, 153, 154, 155, 157, 170
Taittiri, 177, 178
Tamas, 42, 43, 44, 45, 47, 289, 290
Tapa, 90, 91, 92, 120, 121, 202, 223, 297, 298, 300
Tattvamasi, 239, 250
Thought-form, 95
Tillick, Paul, 9
Time and Space, 10, 12, 19, 39, 48, 119, 247, 279
Timeless, 12, 17, 28, 29, 39, 48, 49, 68, 72, 81, 112, 119, 128, 130, 148, 201, 304
Totality, 11
Transcendence, 27, 28, 139, 140, 290
Transcendent, 34, 35, 48, 112, 121, 254
Turīya, 172
Truth, 52, 89, 90, 92, 116, 130, 131, 141, 165, 172, 224
Tryambaka, 46

Ubhayatvam, 162, 168
Udāna, 102
Udgata, 122
Udgītha, 225
Umā, 42, 45, 46, 47
Unconscious, 105, 108, 145, 146, 153, 154, 155, 158, 159, 161, 162, 171
Unfamiliar, 92
Unique, 21, 22, 23, 24, 27
Universal Space, 206
Universal Unconscious, 145, 153
Unknown, 33, 46, 78, 88, 92, 216, 221, 223, 234
Unmanifest, 12, 28, 36, 46, 47, 67, 82, 86, 88, 101, 104, 148, 149, 159, 195, 214, 215, 228, 254, 256, 264, 265, 267, 284, 288, 290, 296, 301, 305, 306, 307
Unpredictable, 37, 50, 198
Upādāna, 291, 293
Upakosala, 232, 233
Upāsanā, 24, 236
Utkarsha, 154, 155, 157, 163, 168

Vājasravas, 52, 53, 54
Vaiśvānara, 150, 152, 153, 160, 170
Vajra, 44
Vāmadeva, 215, 216

Vānaprastha, 187, 188, 193, 194, 196, 199, 200, 201
Varṇa, 178
Varuṇa, 201
Vāyu, 41, 43, 44, 47, 212, 234, 270, 277
Vedānta, 87, 88, 105, 298
Vedas, 118, 122, 129, 130, 134, 139, 185, 189, 197, 198, 232, 233, 246, 247
Verbalization, 33, 173, 225, 235, 236, 237, 238, 246, 287, 288
Vigilence, Eternal, 129, 130
Vijñāna, 195, 196, 246
Vijñāna-ātma, 109
Vijñānamayakośa, 109, 112
Vipaścit, 68
Virāj, 288, 290
Virocana, 250, 251, 252
Vishṇu, 46, 237, 301
Viśvatomukha, 306
Viśvajit, 52
Vision of Life, 9
Vitality, 98, 99
Viveka-cūḍāmaṇi, 144
Vocation, 17, 113
Voice of the Silence, 233
Void, 224, 232, 233, 234, 235, 240, 241, 242, 244, 245, 247, 250, 253
Vyāna, 102

Waking, 105, 106, 150, 151, 152, 153, 156, 160, 163, 165, 166, 167, 168, 169, 170, 252, 286, 287
Whitehead, A.N., 241
Whole, 10, 11, 14, 19, 35, 36, 146, 238, 254
Wink of the Eye, 48

Yājñavalkya, 2, 258, 259, 260, 261, 262, 264, 265, 266, 268, 270, 271, 272, 273, 274, 275, 276, 277, 278, 279, 280, 281, 282, 283, 284, 285, 286, 287, 288
Yama, 51, 52, 54, 55, 56, 57, 58, 59, 60, 61, 62, 64, 65, 66, 67, 68, 69, 70, 72, 73, 74, 75, 76, 77, 78, 79, 80, 81, 82, 83, 84, 85, 86, 259
Yoga, 85, 101
Yoga Sūtras, 144, 236
Yoga Vāsishṭha, 144
Yuga Dharma, 201

Zen, Living, 235